100 WOMEN
architectsinpractice

First published in 2024 by RIBA Publishing, 66 Portland Place, London, W1B 1AD
This paperback edition first published by RIBA Publishing, 66 Portland Place, London, W1B 1AD

ISBN 9781915722706

British Library Cataloguing-in-Publication Data
A catalogue record for this book is available from the British Library.

Commissioning Editor: Ginny Mills
Assistant Editor: Clare Holloway
Production: Jane Rogers
Designed and typeset by Sara Miranda Icaza
Printed and bound by Short Run Press, Exeter
Cover image: Mariam Issoufou, Mariam Issoufou Architects. Dandaji Market, Niger, 2019. © Mariam Issoufou Architects.
Photo by Maurice Ascani

www.ribapublishing.com

MIX
Paper | Supporting
responsible forestry
FSC® C014540
www.fsc.org

Harriet Harriss | Naomi House | Monika Parrinder | Tom Ravenscroft

100 WOMEN
architectsinpractice

RIBA Publishing

CONTENTS

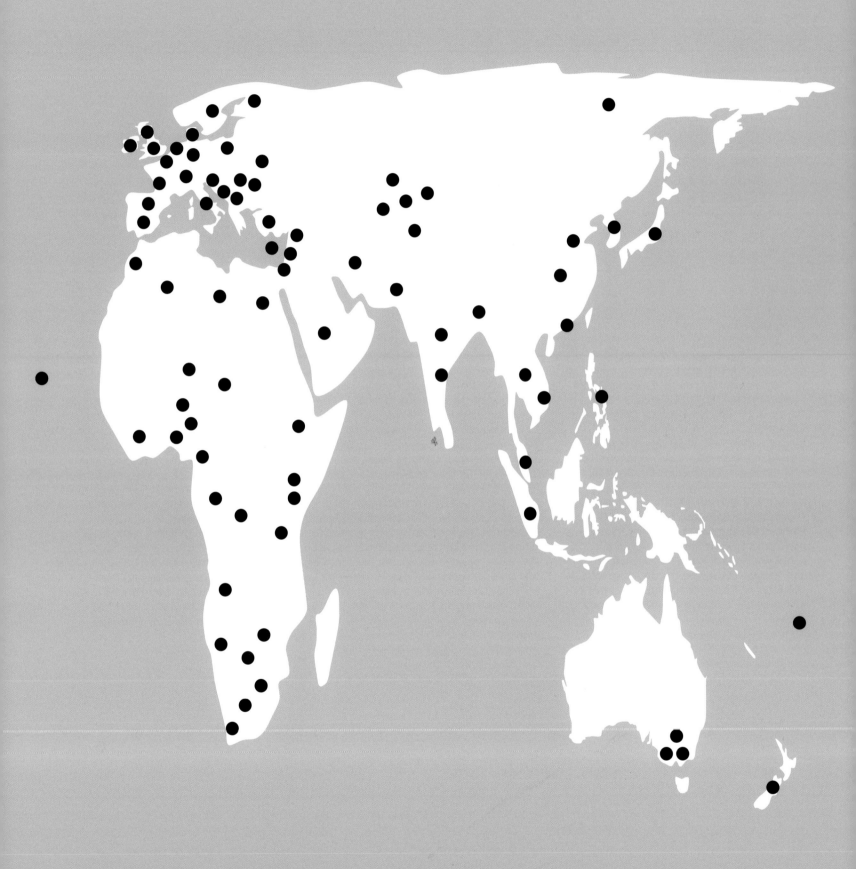

ACKNOWLEDGEMENTS

We wish to thank several architects and representatives of organisations for helping to research and recommend people for the book, including: Mia Roth-Čerina, Marina Tabassum, Philipp Meuser, Mike Oades, Justine Clark, Mark Raymond, Layton Reid, Elise Owusu, Hanne Van Reusel and Ashraf Salama. Thanks to Clare Holloway, Jane Rogers, Ginny Mills, Elizabeth Webster and the team at the RIBA for the time they have dedicated to the book, often mediating difficult conversations. Thanks to our colleague Barry Curtis for editorial support, and to former graduate assistants at Pratt Institute – Bhavini Kapur, Kay KoFong Hsia, Sonya Feinstein and Vineeta Mudunuri – for their help with the initial collection of materials. Thanks to Amina Amber for her spreadsheet wizardry. Thanks to Caroline Coon and Lucy Soutter for encouraging the overarching interview analysis, and to Alison Brooks for agreeing to write the foreword.

We are very grateful to our 100 architects for their commitment to the project, taking the time to be interviewed and helping us to gather all the materials for the profiles. In support of the call for change to working conditions and work-life balance, we acknowledge the profound challenges under which many of these tasks have been undertaken, by their teams and, for the most part, by the architects themselves. They have fitted this around massive project commitments, deadlines, travel and sometimes, wonderfully, to receive awards. It has included negotiating climate stresses like floods, heatwaves, earthquakes, power and amenity shortages and war, in which some of the architects' buildings have been razed or damaged. Personal challenges have come up, such as illness, operations, family emergencies and the need to be sensitive about the security of recorded formats in the face of death threats.

The project began in 2019 at the suggestion of Tom and, realising the potential and scale of the work, the rest of us were quickly invited on board to develop it. We have all been juggling more than full-time jobs, sometimes in difficult situations – and often with one, and sometimes two, authors down. The book nevertheless has progressed through an assault course of the Coronavirus pandemic and chronic sicknesses, family illness, bereavement, chemotherapy and the birth of two babies!
Finally, we wish to thank our families and friends, including non-human species, for inspiration, patience and making life good: Severn, Rudyard, Huxley and Tank; Paul, Holly, Martha, Bea, Maud and Sadie; Matt, Mia, Eve, Nina West and Suki; Margaret, Otto, Bear and Tiny Boy.

ABOUT THE AUTHORS

Harriet Harriss is an award-winning educator, writer, architect and professor at Pratt Institute, New York, where she served as the Dean of the School of Architecture for three years. Her research and scholarly specialisms confront the relationship between the built (and un-built) environment and questions of diversity, equity and inclusion, and propose climate crisis and social justice curricula and pedagogies. Harriet has spoken about these matters across a wide range of media channels including the BBC, Sky TV and Fox Nation, and was nominated by Dezeen as a champion for women in architecture and design in 2019. Her highly regarded past publications include *Radical Pedagogies; Architectural Education & the British Tradition* (2015), *A Gendered Profession* (2016), *Interior Futures* (2019), award-winning *Architects After Architecture* (2020), *Greta Magnusson Grossman: Modern Design From Sweden To California* (2021), *Working at the Intersection: Architecture After the Anthropocene* (2022) and *Architectural Pedagogies of the Global South* (2023).

Naomi House is a designer, educator and writer. Director of Research and Knowledge Exchange for the department of Design and Senior Lecturer in Interior Architecture and Design at Middlesex University, London, she is an experienced academic who also taught for many years in Critical and Historical Studies at the Royal College of Art, and previously at The Bartlett School of Architecture, UCL, London Metropolitan University and University of the Arts, London. Naomi's particular expertise is in the field of interiors, using forensic methods as a strategy for exploring and questioning how objects, environments and their interactions can be analysed, interpreted and animated. She has recently published Greta Magnusson Grossman: Modern Design From Sweden To California (2021) and Working at the Intersection: Architecture After the Anthropocene (2022). She is currently collaborating on various projects around themes of social justice and climate emergency, urban regeneration and practices of empathy and care, including Kilburn Lab (2022-23) and Endangered Domesticity (2023).

Monika Parrinder works at the intersection of design, research and education. Coming from a graphic design practice background, she has spent two decades in art schools, teaching contextual studies to designers, artists, curators and historians. She works at Central Saint Martins, with previous roles at the Royal College of Art and Goldsmiths, University of London, including external work in Europe, the USA and India. Her cross-disciplinary experience feeds into facilitation for interdisciplinary funding bids and impact research. She is often commissioned to write about emerging patterns of practice and future trajectories, through writing, public speaking and convening events. Publishing includes magazines and essays in books, including 'The Future of Publishing' (2012); 'Typography Today and Tomorrow' (2015) and 'Interior Futures' (2019). Her books include *Limited Language: Re-writing Design – Responding to a Feedback Culture* (2010).

Monika is a Trustee of the Arts Foundation, which provides funding for creatives, where a focus has been the long-running Materials Innovation awards, for which she convened The New Materialists event at the Design Museum.

Tom Ravenscroft is a multi-award-winning architectural journalist and writer. He is currently the editor of *Dezeen*, the world's most influential architecture and design website. He holds Masters degrees in architectural history from both the University of Edinburgh and The Bartlett School of Architecture, UCL. Tom's writing has been published in numerous architecture publications, including the *Architects' Journal*, *RIBA Journal*, *Icon*, *BD*, *City Metric*, *The Architectural Review* and *ArchDaily*. Videos on architecture featuring Tom have had over five million views on YouTube.

FOREWORD

by Alison Brooks

In this book you will find a global survey of 100 visionary, inventive, wise, enterprising and accomplished architects practicing around the world today. Each is on a mission to transform the way human beings understand, produce and experience architecture so that it is more equitable, meaningful and instrumental; each tailors their work to represent and honour a particular geography or social group. Each of these architects can be considered a creative genius. Through their diverse works, teachings and forms of practice they are transforming architectural culture itself.

Placing adjectives and superlatives before gender identity makes two points: first, that the skill and attributes of a great architectural practitioner are gender-free, and second, to remind readers that those emotive words: 'visionary', 'inventive', 'wise', 'enterprising' and 'creative genius' are rarely found in the descriptions of women, either in popular culture or in professional disciplines such as architecture. The content of this book goes a long way to correct that.

More important, the stories of these architects and their philosophies of practice outline, what I believe, is a fundamental shift in architectural epistemology. Their approaches, across a 40-year timespan, reflect a deep and accelerating shift: from the colonising impulses and ideologies of the western canon, from modernism's universalising scientific rationalism and from the heroics of post- and post post modernism to a pluralist, research-based and relational understanding of architecture. How does a place or space make you feel, and affect your relations with others? How can architecture translate both cultural memory and contemporary desires, meaningfully, to offer new, and somehow truthful, identities? What unique stories can architecture tell that help under-served communities feel valued, seen and heard? And last but not least, how can architecture evolve to support nature, as an act of reciprocity rather than extraction?

You will find the architects featured in this book and those outside it are protagonists in the momentous cultural shift of the past 40 years. I understand this movement as an opening of the architectural mind.

Each of the architects in this book have navigated a predominantly patriarchal, colonial architectural education and profession. They have forged a path of autonomy: of creative thinking, being and acting that continues to challenge the societal conventions or milieus that surround them. Their paths can be seen as a form of resistance against low expectations, stepping up to fill the void in female role models – in the built environment professions and elsewhere. I still find it astonishing that during my architectural studies I was never taught a design studio by a woman professor. My school of architecture's encyclopedic three-year cultural history course, covering the western canon in works of literature, art and film from the dawn of Mesopotamian civilization to the late 20th century lacked a single female author, artist, philosopher or critic. I didn't think anything of it at the time, indoctrinated as I was with modernist dogma and male dominance in the arts, sciences, politics and history. Instead these omissions motivated me to challenge this norm through my professional practice.

Reading this book, I recognise and share the same impulses to reject the 20th century's architectural ideologies and its entrenched biases, to seek the expressive potential of architectures founded in local geographies, social structures and ecologies; to stand our ground and persist.

Some of the architects in this book have returned to their 'home' countries to serve communities who would otherwise lack access to the transformative power of 'good' design, to unearth and reinterpret climate-friendly patterns of inhabitation and cultural tradition, in their processes and outcomes. These anthropologically inspired acts are critical responses not only to the climate crisis, but to the role architecture can play in socio-cultural healing.

As a Canadian, I can identify with the call for a global project of acknowledgement, reconciliation and repair. Until recently, few people born in Canada were aware of its 150-year old institution of church-run boarding schools where Indigenous children were forcibly placed. Nor that the country's name is an Iroquoian word: *kanata*, meaning 'settlement'; or that Toronto derives its name from the Mohawk word *tkaronto*, meaning 'where trees stand in the water'. These linguistic traditions reflect North America's Indigenous people's understanding of everything in nature as animate; beings with whom all humans should form reciprocal, fruitful relationships. In stark contrast, we know that Canada's settler colonisation involved ecological and cultural erasure at a scale we can hardly comprehend.

Globally, legacies of colonial governance and discrimation on grounds of race as well as gender are still embedded in our political and cultural constructs, limiting our collective ability to address social and climate injustice. Discrimination on grounds of race as well as gender debilitates architecture's ability to participate in the reconciliation/repatriation needed. But, the teachings of Indigenous peoples, ancient sub-cultures and pre-mass-consumption societies are beginning to transform and enrich the architect's understanding of place and time, meaning and environmental impact. The architects in this book are listening hard, and asking the questions: Whose place? Whose time? Whose knowledge? They are enacting change through their design imaginations, dogma-free and without fear.

There is no better time to acknowledge, honour and celebrate the empathy, intellect and worldview of the architects in this book: their work gives the art and service of architecture new life.

Alison Brooks, London, July 2023

PREFACE

Towards new spatial practices

This book begins with a simple statement of fact: that the 100 profiles featured herein offer a *sample*, and not an exhaustive *survey*, of some of the world's leading architects – who happen to be women.

To identify and recognise this sample as innovative, interesting and intriguing is not intended to diminish or disregard the efforts of other architects – whether they are women or identify differently. It is a snapshot of innovative architectural practice from across the globe at this point in time and includes a great many women architects who are missing from architecture's authoritative list of key figures, its design studios and history seminars, the construction industry press and its architectural awards systems. There are several reasons why this is a decolonisation and not a diversity project.[i] Diversification often assumes that sprinkling a few mistresses into the canon of architecture's majority of masters is sufficient – a kind of sanitisation rinse on its biased infrastructure. Decolonisation, on the other hand, contests the design of the canon by transforming the selection metrics and mechanisms beyond the major commission and the monograph, to include 'other' kinds of spatial practices and ways of working.

Sisterhood semantics, suffixes and prefixes

Full disclosure: this book had many near-miss titles: *100 Women Architects, 100 Architects: Women in Practice*... There were some intense discussions – with our publishers, practitioners, students and colleagues – and yet none of the titles felt quite right, including the one that ended up on the cover. The title sits uneasily, as if trying to decide whether it is a clinical statement of fact or a provocation. Perhaps it's both. Perhaps it needs to be both; if it fuels contention then all that tells us is that there is work still to do. And since there is no discomfort in resolution, this unease simply affirms that the book,

regrettably, remains necessary, and that any problems with the prefix are a matter of prejudice not prose.

This publication is not a product of the authors and contributors' politics or personal identities. It is a product of an unequal profession and all four authors eagerly await the day when this publication is rendered obsolete, because when it is, it will mean that the perennial problem of gender-prejudice is placed firmly in the past.

Selecting and approaching the women featured in this book was not straightforward either. We were expecting more of the women we approached to decline to be involved with a gendered book, but only one of them did. We were also cautious of the need to contend with what constitutes a brilliant 'woman architect' when the metrics that determine profile and presence, as much as project integrity, have long been biased against women, and specifically women in the so-called Global South and who are not Caucasian. We acknowledge that the metrics are also biased towards spatial production that sits in homage to the pre-eminence of an 'International Style'. This is, in itself, derived from the 'orders' of the Graeco-Roman Empire – which thinly conceals the perpetuation of imperialist, hegemonic aesthetics and an act of cultural colonisation by another name. And yet, while we recognise the inevitable Western biases that ensue, going back over the last decade, Vietnam and Turkey are the only countries where women architects form the majority of the profession, with Norway, Sweden, Spain and Germany achieving (or close to) 50/50 representation.[ii] It is shameful and ironic that Vietnam – a former French colony – at the time of writing, has more women architects than France,[iii] a country whose GDP is eight times higher than that of Vietnam.[iv] Surveys showing the state of working practices for women architects are, of course, hard to find. Working with material available, we see that Japan, the world's third-largest economy,

has been considered the worst place to be a women architect with, at the time of the survey, nine male architects to every female architect, as well as an unforgiving system of parental leave entitlement.[v] Since the survey date of 2013, fathers have been granted paternity leave, although in 2022 it was noted that few take it.[vi]

So while architects-who-identify-as-women quite rightly want their work to be judged on its architectural integrity and not its author's identity, this is not (yet) how the work itself is being judged, whether by contractors, clients, employers, educators, students, the mainstream architecture media and by awards committees. Becoming an architect remains a privilege irrespective of where you are from, and all of the women we interviewed for this book acknowledge the privilege of their education. It is ironic, then, that while it is often tougher to be a female architect than a male architect, when women succeed by mainstream metrics it is often used as proof that prejudice is 'no longer a problem', rather than proof of exceptional talent and an excess of hard work.

The scale of contribution within its regional context

The women architects in this book should all be household names. And while most of us can name more household products than we can women architects, this book also features women from countries and regions where most of us can't name a male architect, either. We are usually blind to the fact that the prescriptions, protectionisms and validation processes of the architectural profession have the power to affirm Western pre-eminence.

As for the feminist, but not all-female, authors – we are journalists, writers, academics, practitioners and parents, located within two of the world's largest and most affluent post-imperial countries – the UK and USA. Our context offers testimony to the advantages of privileging subordination and appropriation, and the enduring damages that disproportionate power can enact on regions, peoples and the planet for decades. Our self-critique recognises that it is not enough to be non-sexist but necessary to be anti-sexist as well – in the same way that it is not enough to be non-racist, but actively anti-racist.[vii]

And while we, the authors, are privileged across regional contexts, we are insecure *within* our immediate contexts, given that higher education is now considered the most precarious workforce,[viii] and the media and journalism workforce faces similar corrosions.[ix] When combined, these issues make it even harder for both sectors to confront perennial, internal inequalities and support the cost to decolonise the discipline and profession of architecture that was ignited by the first wave of the #Blacklivesmatter movement in 2013 and the Rhodes Must Fall campaign in 2015. The 2018 Shitty Men in Architecture list[x] offered an industry-specific rendering of the #Metoo movement, that followed in the wake of the Harvey Weinstein scandal.[xi] Yet women architects' inequitable pay and prospects differentials have remained largely unaltered and the urgent need for gender equality remains at the centre of a worldwide agenda.

On failing to represent all regions

The authors' methodological approach in pursuit of creating a global book was to present the work of all the women – independent of region, nation or identity – as unequivocally equitable. We wanted to ensure that colonial biases were not perpetuated by this publication; instead, we hope that readers will find a more profound connection to innovative architecture beyond their context, culture and curricula.

To do this we created a regional selection framework based on the United Nations Geoscheme: a system that places the countries of the world into regional and subregional groups that are intended to be devoid of political or other affiliation of countries or territories.[xii] In doing this, we tried to avoid Western and Global North biases that prevail in many other books on women in architecture, and yet we are mindful that this means we could only present a sample, rather than a more exhaustive survey. The UN Geoscheme divides the world into five regions: Americas, Europe, Africa, Asia and Oceania, with each region further broken into subregions. This created 18 subregions – due to its low population, we chose to treat Oceana differently, allocating the same number of women as a subregion – that form the chapters of this book. We interviewed between four and six architects in every subregion with an aim to gain perspectives from architects in numerous countries, although in some subregions – most notably Central America – one country is certainly better represented. This was a combination of start-of-book enthusiasm, an abundance of quality in some countries and the limited nature of English-language internet research. In the main we believe we have achieved an equitable representation from each region and the book contains interviews with women from, or based, in almost 80 countries.

Almost invisible but not dead yet

What was clear from the outset is that women are still hugely underrepresented in the industry. In 2017 only three of the world's 100 biggest architecture firms were headed by women and only two had management teams that are more than 50% female.[xiii] Have things got better? Well, the results will vary region to region but let's just say that, in the UK alone, the gender pay gap has got worse in the year up to writing.[xiv] Add to this the lack of promotion prospects and the routine reports of sexism in the workplace, of which our interviews with the 100 women architects for this book provided ample accounts. It is little wonder that young women leave the profession at a far greater rate than men.[xv]

Yet, with solid data to support the idea that women directors and diverse boards are more strongly correlated with successful firms,[xvi] what's at stake here isn't just gender equity in the architecture profession, but the survival of the profession at all.[xvii] This also led us to turn our attention to the present day. Rather than focusing on historical figures, we took the view that a publication offering a snapshot of the most exciting women architects practising now could well serve to support these women and their careers in real-time. While Despina Stratigakos' 2016 publication asked *Where Are the Women Architects?* We intend to say *Here are the Women Architects*.

Beyond the primacy of the individual

In her book, *Architecture: The Story of Practice* (1991), Dana Cuff rejected the way in which schools of architecture obligated students to work in isolation in the design studio, pointing to the fact that the reality of professional practice is profoundly social. Yet despite this, the architectural media and, to some extent, individual architects themselves, have perpetuated this myth. In doing so, the contribution of women within the design team is routinely obscured.

This prompted us to get beyond our industry's inclination towards promoting individualism and to invite the women we have selected to describe the social production of space and their role within it. Conversations about what collectivism can do to address social and political inequality are part of the wider social justice movement that is now characterising the context in which this book is produced. A benefit of placing the emphasis on collectivism – defined as cohesiveness among individuals and the prioritisation of the group over the self, with the group identifying and working towards common values, objectives and goals[xviii] – is that it allows the reader a fresh evaluation of the integrity of the work that these women are producing. It also helps the reader engage with the process of making architecture, and not just the end product. Collectivists differ from collaborators because the former unite around a single purpose and agree on the best process to achieve that purpose. Collaborators, on the other hand, tend to use different or varying approaches towards the same purpose, which is where hierarchies concerning expertise, power, pay, role and status can easily set in.

Collectivism in architecture is not new and, indeed, continues to prove successful as an organising principle – from the Rochdale Co-ops of 1844 to the work of Matrix, MUF and Assemble (to cite a few British examples), collective endeavours illustrate the scope of working with others.[xix] However, as Mimi Zeiger highlights, there is an 'ongoing skirmish' between the 'glossy pictures' at the end of the process and what we would choose to characterise as the everyday office mess, late nights, compromised parenting, low pay, scrappy invoices and exploited interns that practising architecture *truthfully* involves.

In this book we wanted to avoid the disconnect between women and images of women, between completed buildings and the making of buildings, between an architect and images of architecture, between an architect and the many acts of discreet collectivism that serve to perpetuate what being an architect actually involves.

Privileging processes over outcomes

Providing a more accurate and honest account of what *being an architect actually involves* is central to the intentions of this book. It is alleged that architecture's forebears – the cultish freemasons – insisted upon keeping their methods and processes a secret. They were conferred through oral instruction and apprenticeship-based demonstration as a means to protect what we would now describe as 'intellectual property'.

In doing this, architecture processes were shrouded in a value-adding mystique that the academisation of the Beaux-Arts in Paris sought to leverage rather than change. Fast forward to today's contemporary practice culture, and it is evident from the criteria for almost all of the available architectural awards that the product and not the process is what matters. Coupled with a climate crisis, the unease increases. We are no longer in a position to assume that architecture's fetishisation of the object can continue when we are all faced with calls to consume less, make less, reuse more and abandon the illusion that growth means progress rather than accelerated destruction.

No more 'manels'

We hope that this book will provide a key role in ending the spectre of architecture 'manels': the male-exclusive and/or male-dominated panels that prevail in all areas of architectural advancement, including school-based design juries, architecture project competitions and commissions selection panels, professional and academic headhunters and hiring committees, promotions and tenure committees, awards and accolades juries.

Further, this book hopes to provide increasingly frustrated architecture students with the means to contest the canon and avoid having to recapitulate the achievements of the same five Caucasian men that schools of architecture have insisted that they write about in their essays and reference within their design work in order to progress within the field.

This book is also for the professors who instruct them to do this; and those who can't find citations or sources that enable them to write about or reference women whose contribution is missing from the library, magazines and journals. This book is for the professional and academic headhunters who claim that 'women never apply' (while soliciting applications from men) and for the clients who say they can't find these women and require architects or university deans who are 'established names' and 'highly experienced'. This book is a coffee-table trojan horse, formatted and presented to prove aestheticism can no longer resist activism. And, finally it is a book intended to support everyone – whether identifying as a woman, non-binary or a male ally – because, independent of who we are and how we choose to identify, we all need mistresses as much as masters, heroines as much as heroes. We also need relatable roadmaps for anyone determined to evolve architecture beyond its many obsolete paradigms and who, quite instinctively, knows that architecture should focus on the urgent needs of the planet and all its life forms and not on perpetuating prejudices among peoples.

Interviews with the 100 women for this book revealed an overarching agenda of transformation and empowerment. In the Introduction to this book, we look across the individual profiles to find patterns of practice and identify key approaches that point a way forward.

INTRODUCTION

Re-envisioning and empowerment

Patterns and repetitions in the words and work of the 100 architects featured within this book reveal an overarching agenda of transformation and empowerment. Socially engaged, future-building and sustainable agendas aren't new. Yet often they have involved top-down building projects for the benefit of the few, or with little attention to real and systemic impact, obscuring the reality that one group's comfort or convenience becomes another's housing or waste problem. Taken together, the architects in this book show a different way forward, re-envisioning how architecture relates to people and land with approaches that are reality-based, authentically democratic and, at their most radical, supportive of systemic change. For Indigenous Canadian architect Eladia Smoke, an important part of this work is 'revisioning' the destructive transformational agendas of the past.

The urgency is social justice and climate collapse, but what the research for this book makes clear is that architecture is part of the problem. The architects profiled are universally responding to a profound disconnect between architecture and the people and landscape it serves. Bringing architecture into a more reciprocal relationship with the world is, arguably, *the* common agenda for transformation. Through this process, many of the ways that people can be (dis)empowered by architecture are highlighted. Taking care of our environments by reconnecting with them is critical – human bonds require strengthening, the relationships to place and landscape need to be meaningful and, for all this to happen, social and climate justice must be served.

Throughout our conversations with the architects profiled here is a marked, and indeed exciting, sense of potential. Within this context, the evolution and efficacy of architecture as a discipline and practice is inextricable from technological innovation, fluctuations in the global economy and, of course climate collapse. In these times of uncertainty and fast-paced change, architects and their approaches are necessarily *adaptive* – foregrounding pragmatism over ideology, need over desire and, where possible, reuse over newness. US architect Liz Diller reminds us that while conventional architecture tends to be 'slow, geo-fixed, heavy and expensive', architects should embrace 'lightness, suppleness and responsiveness to programme change, economic change and population increases'. They need this level of adaptability if they are to remain relevant or be ready for as-yet unimagined scenarios.

Advocacy is a big part of an architect's work. With many of the women stepping into high-profile roles, they are showing the value of architecture to those who have been hitherto excluded, where trust has been broken, or where profit-seeking has prioritised developers over architects – and, of course, advocating for women architects and diversity in the field. Some also influence policymaking. For instance, with the benefit of experience, Thai community housing architect Patama Roonrakwit shows how lobbying government can effect the greatest change.

Many of the architects interviewed amplify their reach through writing, curating exhibitions and public talks. Activist intervention is increasing too, like the 'flash mobs' organised by Takhmina Turdialieva's Shaharsozlik To'lqini organisation, dedicated to 'raising the voice of young architects' in Uzbekistan. If architecture has the potential to change behaviour, these forms of communication architecture have the potential to alter mindsets and imaginaries. For all, there is a recognition that public and political engagement are key to effective change.

Across the 100 profiles – the different worlds, different forms of architecture and the place-sensitive approaches – we identified areas of common focus that seem to point a way forward: practice innovation; care and connection; unpredictable participation; future place-making; equity; and what we call *women's work*.

Practice innovation

What the architects featured here collectively evidence is that many of the established preconceptions about architecture are no longer tenable, be they universally applicable approaches or world views, ideas of the lone, genius architect, stand-alone buildings or contexts, or of architecture as a bounded discipline. These preconceptions remain at the root of Western architecture and, when left unchallenged, stand in the way of progress. The didactic perception of the architect imposing values on others has been stripped away. Instead, the architects we interviewed aim for a more collective and democratic relationship with others – as part of a feedback loop. Featured projects are often client-centred or community-led with architects actively learning from other specialists and craftspeople. This demands alternative and reciprocal models of leadership, such as Romanian architect Oana Bogdan's 'follow me, I'm right behind you' approach.

The cultural unit is no longer the single, iconic building. Instead, a building is understood as a component within a broader set of processes, including urban challenges, social issues and ecological systems. This obviously broadens the question of what architecture is. As Algerian architect Samia Henni argues, 'Architecture is not only about form and building, it can also be about walls, camps, barbed wire and borders... and giving voice to those from whom we should learn.'

The bedrock of architectural thinking – problem solving, which often tackles single issues – has been blown apart. Increasingly supplemented by research and impact studies, architects take into account a multitude of (often competing) needs at a range of scales: human, systems-based and ecological. As USA architect Katherine Darnstadt explains, thinking systemically is *not* about the impact of a design on a building, but the building in a wider context, so as to understand who and what is impacted. This, she says, 'often creates questions that are definitely larger than the project brief'. The benefit of siloed disciplines has been dismantled. While the core of the work featured here drives change through the architectural profession as an established and highly regulated entity, much of it nevertheless pushes at what Cabo Verde architect Patti Anahory describes as its 'fugitive edge'. Indigenous practices in particular refuse the binary between architecture and landscape, with experimental practitioners looking for tactics, tools and means of expression through art, performance, anthropology and more. Simple, linear ideas of innovation as 'progress', often characterised by tech-fetishisms, are superceded by hybrid approaches to innovation, which retrieve past/suppressed knowledge and local/to-hand materials, combining them with new technologies. Filipino architect Cathy Saldaña, who specialises in sustainable development, stresses the importance of combining ancient, traditional strategies with cutting-edge technologies. Belgian architect Veronique Tavernier warns other practitioners to 'not let aspects of their work unknowingly slip to automation, and risk losing the core skills needed in good architecture practice'. Overall, the interviews in this volume challenge the dominance of a single world view, with the need for variations in practice models to become more prevalent. Every architect featured in this book testifies to this fact and, without exception, they are mindful that a plurality of worlds, with their traditions and knowledge-bases, co-exist. They aim beyond diversity. They are not simply adding more perspectives and visual languages to expand the existing framework (which, too often, still preserves the hierarchy of dominant values and aesthetic judgements). Instead, they are often working across several contexts, navigating how different world views can better relate to each other. It is this up-ending of hierarchies that so disrupts the status quo.

Care and connection

Visions of transformation and empowerment throughout the book are framed by a culture of care, consciously or not. This offers an alternative role and responsibility for the architect – as carers of a broken planet. The emphasis is always holistic – understanding how social, environmental and economic sustainability are interconnected. It demands new kinds of professional empathy – for the context, for the people and for the environment. And alternatives for how we conceive architecture too. Brazilian architect Carla Juaçaba envisions using 'a design process that emerges from rigorous historical-ecological investigation', while Mexican architect Rozana Montiel believes architecture should work with nature as 'ecological infrastructure'.

Reconnection is often about community-building and creating places that engender a sense of belonging. Many of the architects featured are working in post-colonial contexts, with the legacy of an environment explicitly created for exploitation, only furthered by rampant one-size-fits-all 'modernising' development. As Syrian architect Marwa Al-Sabouni reminds us, architecture has been used as part of the colonial agenda to 'unravel the social fabric by dismantling the urban fabric' and she, like many architects in this book, works to reverse this process, to 'bring back a sense of neighbourliness and a nurturing built environment'. In the case of Indigenous groups, coloniality has deliberately broken community ties and destroyed ways of living. Sarah Lynn Rees, of the Palawa people of Tasmania, argues that 'architecture has the power to give identity and health back that architectures of the past have taken away'. A culture of care and connection is regenerative in the sense that it aims to give back more than it takes. Perhaps if architects are not doing this, then they shouldn't build at all.

Unpredictable participation

'Architecture is a social-human thing', according to Mexican architect Tatiana Bilbao. 'At university, everybody spoke about proportions, beauty, light and different geometries. It's hard to think about structural somersaults when there is a complete disconnect from human needs.' Bilbao voices a sensibility that the majority of the architects featured here identify with. From client-centred and/or community-led projects that embrace local experience and knowledge, to the role of mentoring emerging practitioners, the shift is towards an alternative understanding of 'good design' that *strengthens relationships*.

Against an architectural culture that is 'too fragmented and adversarial', British-Nigerian architect Yẹmí Aládérun argues that the need for 'greater collaboration between client, constructor, consultant team and end user to achieve better project outcomes' has never been clearer. Between client and community, the crux is facilitating *authentic* dialogue – what Indian architect Takbir Fatima calls a 'design construction feedback loop'.

The reasons for participation are myriad, but in Libya, as architect Nada Elfeituri explains, community involvement is key to mentally reclaiming public spaces that became 'places of fear' – as locations for executions and crushed protest – during the Gaddafi regime. There is always a danger that 'participation' can be used for processes that do no more than add user-centred perspectives without any real stake in the outcome. Co-design tools are used by a number of the practitioners here as a means to give communities *real* agency in the process of conceiving, designing and sometimes making the buildings they will inhabit. Many of the usual tools of the architects' process are reimagined for shared use, often in workshop settings. Diagrams, visualisation techniques and even rudimentary model-making become a means for collective envisioning. Dedicated collaborative design tools help articulate individual and shared goals and – mentioned more than once by interviewees – 'mutual benefit'. Participatory practices are now being used for advocacy and 'urban activism', for instance Asel Yeszhanova's Urban Forum Kazakhstan. Participation and the practice of mutual benefit demand alternative models of design leadership. As Australian architect Kerstin Thompson says, 'True design leadership is to accommodate with intent.' Many of the architects make it clear that the *enjoyment* of participation comes from the process – evolutionary, unpredictable, with varied and often unforeseen aesthetic outcomes.

Future place-making

One emphasis of the book is towards meaningful, context-appropriate architecture. Across the interviews, a noticeable way into this mode of working has involved addressing the disconnect between a globalised education and the buildings that the majority of people in the world are living in. This led many architects to return 'home' after graduating – albeit a story of global flow – with some locating their practices in two or more places, as well as in unfamiliar regional contexts. When relocating, some architects recall the realisation that their learned global strategies don't always work locally– for instance, in contexts of economic and political upheaval, where infrastructures like water and electricity and high-tech skill sets aren't in place, or where funding is scarce or must be applied for as part of the project, often in stages.

These moves have led many of the architects to build their architectural practice and tools anew. This typically involves historical and urban research followed by acts of translation to bring elements together into spatial form. Many of the architects talk about extracting the 'essence' of a site, helped by collaboration with landscape designers, local builders and craftspeople whose specific knowledge offers essential insight into contexts and conditions. Kazakhstan architect Togzhan Aubakirova describes a common trope when she says, 'My role in the process is to be able to see and distinguish these factors, translate them and bind together a place and programme for a future building.' Indian architect Anupama Kundoo is not alone in approaching architecture as bricolage, 'assembling the various material components from what is locally available'.

What emerges, rather than a sense of fragmentation, is a coherent philosophy and approach. Niger architect Mariam Issoufou characterises this clearly: 'I want to create a universal way of working that produces completely different results depending on where you are. It is attention to the local conditions – what is available locally, what the local skills are and what the local history is – then having this process that can happen everywhere.'

Where and how people live has a profound effect on how they self-identify and envision their future. Thus, an outcome of place-based architecture is the way it builds identity. As New Zealand-based, Māori architect Elisapeta Heta explains, projects that 'intrinsically weave through the stories of place' result in a deeper connection to site. In fact, thinking about place-making in terms of storytelling is a notable trait in the book. This often highlights people's experiences and world views. South African architect Sumayya Vally points out that of particular importance is telling 'other narratives', especially when expression is needed 'for hybrid identities and territory'. Her example references African and Islamic contexts, both rooted and diasporic, but this would hold true almost everywhere. Context-sensitive architecture also supports nation building. Against the bland, internationalising impulse of modern architecture, an overwhelming number of architects in the book describe the latent potential of the cities they practise in and different ways to develop what South African architect Sarah Calburn describes as cities that are 'geared to their own characteristics and eccentricities'.

Place-based approaches are future-facing. The process encompasses both zooming-in on the specificity of local conditions and, at the same time, looking outward. By establishing an architectural heritage that is specific to place, like many have done, it becomes possible to foresee the emergence of an architecture that is both authentic to place and equipped to address global concerns.

Equity

At the core of architectural practice for the women we interviewed sits a profound concern for equity across the built – and unbuilt – environment. Often this is more broadly framed as making architecture more accessible. Saija Hollmén, Jenni Reuter and Helena Sandman, a collaborative architecture practice based in Finland, reveal that 'among emerging architects and students there is a positive thirst towards a well-crafted, equal and socially sustainable future in architecture'.

US architect Deanna Van Buren reminds us that 'the built environment foments, anchors, and amplifies the beliefs of the elite and the powerful. Therefore, it does damage to those that aren't valued.' Thus, as with the broken bonds of care and community, a different approach to architecture can repair this process, and be a means by which equity can be achieved.

Architecture's compliance with capitalist (and divisive) processes such as gentrification is challenged by a number of the architects featured. They often reframe the transformation of urban space through regenerative practices that are sensitive to time, place and people.

The power of architecture to facilitate equity is most visible in regions of the so-called Global South, which are impacted disproportionately by the climate emergency. In Bangladesh for example, Suhailey Farzana's practice voices the needs of the local community – women in particular – enabling them to work towards the renewal of their shared environment. For her, this is what architecture can do. Mexican architect Fernanda Canales offers a vision for the role of women: 'I am interested in a future where we can see cities designed by women and we can lessen the oppositions between the public and the private realms, between owners and dispossessed, the rural and the urban, and resources and waste.'

Other architects featured speak of knowledge equity where the vernacular, and its associated skills and practices, is retrieved or reimagined in new contemporary guises. Chad-based architect Hayatte Ndiaye argues for the benefits of an 'inclusive urbanisation', highlighting the loss of a '1,000-year-old bioclimatic constructive tradition', while the importation of high-cost building materials limits access to 'basic amenities such as housing'. There is also the widespread call for greater recognition of the way that ecological practices have always been integrated into Indigenous knowledge, and thus of the role that Indigenous architecture and knowledge plays in the search for climate justice.

Equity also applies to the profile of the workplace. As we discuss in the Preface to this book, architecture is a profession profoundly marked by gender inequality as well as geopolitics. After the Balkans War in Europe, Bosnia-Herzegovinan architect Vedina Babahmetović says, 'The challenges were incredible, and the disorientation in the new economic conditions even greater. I was in my 40s and had a family and an architectural practice.' Many architects are using their positions to push the agenda for change in working environments, from liveable wages and work-life balance to family-friendly practices. Where an earlier focus has been to get women into architecture, increasingly the issue is how to keep them there.

Women's work

'Upon telling someone in Botswana that I am an architect, I am often met with a look of disbelief or, at best, a polite, dismissive smile,' says Sithabile Mathe. The problematic relationship between architecture and gender is explored more fully in the Preface to this book, but it is also keenly felt by the architects we interviewed.

Cameroon architect Caroline Barla says that the 'daily challenge' of being a female architect means that 'psychology, patience, pedagogy' must be an integral part of her profession. And, while Danish architect Dorte Mandrup describes the profession as a 'men's club' that is difficult to access, she states unequivocally that, 'we need to create networks. Not because we are women but because they are the only networks we have.' Throughout our conversations, what is clear for almost all the architects is how hard their architectural journey has been in a paternalistic profession: being the only woman in the room; the first woman in a top role; the perennial problem of 'manels' (male-dominated architecture review and judging panels); the 'macho' culture of the building site; balancing professional and mothering responsibilities; the lack of childcare at key architecture community events and the list goes on. It's not surprising then that a huge proportion of the women we interviewed push an agenda for change in working practice as well. A good number of the architects we interviewed have found productive ways to navigate these circumstances through advocacy and activism. There is a need for action on multiple fronts – including fighting for visibility, agency and justice – emphasises Nigeria-born, UK-educated architect Yẹmí Aládérun. She is hopeful: 'Architects can tackle any injustice by turning our attention to reimagining existing systems and economies that prioritise profit for the few at the expense of people and climate.'

The need for activism is also, in part, a response to the lack experienced in their architectural training. There has been a distinct absence of alternative approaches and relatable role models at the centre of architectural education across the globe. Many of the architects interviewed look to circle the critical agenda and tools of their practice back into teaching and mentoring – for some, passing on knowledge is understood to be part of their responsibility in a gift economy.

To tackle social and climate injustice, a complete re-envisioning of relations between the built environment, people and land is more urgent than ever. To return to the words of Indigenous Canadian architect Eladia Smoke, 'Now is a critical time to seek out every opportunity to transmit this knowledge to future generations.'

AFRI

"My goal is to see women participate in the built environment actively, with a clear understanding of what they think is acceptable for their future and what isn't."

TATU
GATERE

Fig. 1 Design for Equality, 2020. Workshop.

Kenyan architect Tatu Gatere is on a mission 'to see more women working in every area of the built environment'. For the past four years, she has been running Nairobi-based social enterprise company Buildher, an organisation she founded with British architect James Mitchell. Buildher aims to equip disadvantaged young women in Kenya with accredited construction skills. 'We were both very passionate about women being involved in the built environment, women getting a say on how their cities look and how their cities function in years to come. That's what drove us to start Buildher,' she tells us.

A chance encounter with an architecture magazine led Gatere to abandon her dream of becoming a chef, enrolling instead to study architecture at Nairobi Institute of Technology. Later she moved to the USA to study at the University of DC and then at the University of Arkansas. Gatere quickly became aware of a disconnect between her education in the USA and the buildings that the majority of people in Nairobi were living in. 'I was having a crisis, not really understanding how my Western education applied to my culture. I was starting to have the feeling that, if I went home, I wouldn't know what to build.'

After graduating, Gatere worked at a couple of studios in North America and Johannesburg before finding her way back to Nairobi, where she co-founded Buildher. But at both the commercial studios where she has worked, and in her own practice, Gatere has struggled to find ways to impact the wider city through architecture. Rarely designing buildings anymore, she focuses instead on using Buildher to enact change. Through its training and advocacy programmes, hundreds of women have gained professional accreditation, giving them greater financial prosperity.

Fig. 2 Design for Social Change, 2021. Classroom and office design fit-out.

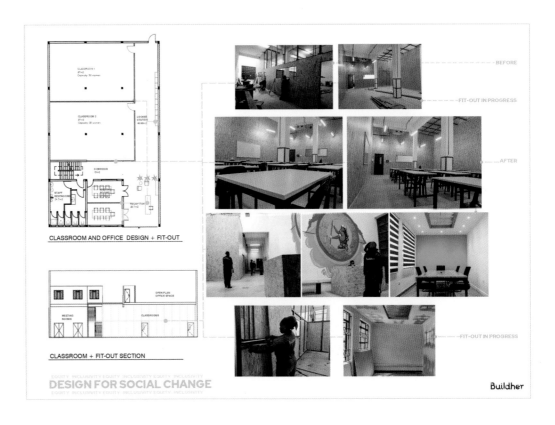

The organisation's data shows that women who complete a four-month course have a five-times greater earning power.

Along with the technical skills training that it offers, Buildher also aims to promote equality within the construction industry, empowering its trainees to challenge gender stereotypes. 'Our programme is split into technical and holistic life skills – 70% is focused on hands-on training, theory and technical drawing,' Gatere explains. 'The other 30%, which is the core of the programme, asks "Why are you here?" "What do you want to accomplish?" "What obstacles have you been facing?"

And "How are you going to take responsibility for them, to focus on this opportunity and create a life and career that supports your goals?"' She believes that having women co-create their streets, buildings and communities will contribute to the establishment of safe, accessible and inclusive environments. ''If you can't practise for the 60% of women, then you can't practise. The end goal is to see women participate in the built environment actively, passionately, in an informed way and with a clear understanding of what they think is acceptable for their future and what isn't.'

Such ambitions illustrate the power of architecture to improve the quality of our urban environments and, looking ahead, Gatere hopes that women artisans from Buildher will become instrumental in enacting permanent change within the construction industry, across the city and beyond. 'If we can design more for our culture, and respect and celebrate our culture, we will have healthier, more dynamic spaces in Nairobi,' Gatere tells us. For her, architecture is less about building and more about enabling others to build.

Fig. 3 Design for Economic Empowerment, 2021. Mwihaki furniture collection by Buildher.

"Architecture is about what you do for your community, to improve the lives of other people."

VICTORIA MARWA HEILMAN

Fig. 1 Pongwe Primary School, Tanga, Tanzania, 2018. A school for children with special educational needs. A project for NGO Tanzania Women Architects for Humanity.

Dar es Salaam-based Victoria Marwa Heilman is a Tanzanian architect who runs her own studio. Over the past 12 years she has led Tanzania Women Architects for Humanity (TAWAH), a non-governmental organisation that she co-founded in 2010. TAWAH's aim is to 'enhance social justice by mobilising women to spearhead building adequate shelter for marginalised communities in Tanzania'.

'Architecture is about people,' Heilman tells us, 'and by people I mean the communities that are really struggling to make ends meet day-by-day.'

Heilman runs a successful practice, Alama Architecture (formerly VK Green Architects), but it is projects initiated through TAWAH, alongside mentorship and teaching, that absorb most of her time. TAWAH includes a team of volunteer women architects, engineers and quantity surveyors who design the shelter structures and also fundraise to bring projects to completion. 'The way I see architecture is working with communities who don't have anything, then finding the resources from those who have plenty, and connecting the two in order to improve the local community's infrastructure. So, I work as a bridge.'

With a focus on education, among the complete projects is a three-classroom block for a school in Tanga, built to replace a cracked and leaking structure dating from 1949. The TAWAH architects worked with the students themselves, or 'clients' as Heilman calls them, to conceptualise a design.

Fig. 2 Pongwe Primary School, Tanga, Tanzania, 2018. Interior view of one of the new classrooms.

The collaboration continued through the building phase when students from Ardhi University, where Heilman taught, together with girls from a local high school, joined other volunteers on site to build the classroom block. 'The goal is to get a more sustainable, environmentally compatible space that is friendly for the kids and involve them in the design. When we finished, the pupils decorated the classroom walls with murals, making them feel that the new structure is truly their own.'

Heilman did not grow up wanting to be an architect. In fact, she was not aware that architecture was a profession until she finished high school, lacking the grades to attend medical school. Heilman recalls, 'I just assumed that all buildings were designed and constructed by engineers.'
Heilman was one of four women in her graduating class of 2001 – the highest gender ratio up to that time – at the University College of Lands and Architectural Studies (now Ardhi University). Through TAWAH she

mentors women studying architecture, helping them to complete their degrees, introducing them to industry and helping to expand their ideas of architecture. 'The aim is to be a role model for the younger generation,' Heilman explains. 'I'm demonstrating that architecture is not just an elitist career to gain a reputation and accumulate wealth. It's about what you do for your community, to improve the lives of other people.'

Fig. 3 Pongwe Primary School, Tanga, Tanzania, 2018. Volunteer students participating in the construction of classrooms.

IRENE
MASIYANISE

"My rise to presidency brought
a lot of interest in breaking barriers."

Fig. 1 Events Venue, Borrowdale, Harare, Zimbabwe, 2019. The building was designed to integrate
with the environment.

With a strong belief in the innate marketing value of built works, over the past 20 years architect Irene Masiyanise has built a reputation as one of Zimbabwe's leading architects. After 11 years studying in Portsmouth and working in the UK, Japan and Taiwan, she returned to Zimbabwe and established Masiyanise TI Architect (MTI Architect) in 2004. In 2014 she became the first female president of the Institute of Architects of Zimbabwe.

Masiyanise has designed everything from private residential homes, schools, churches and housing estates, through development estates for large mining companies and banking institutions, along with commercial buildings for offices and retail. 'I wanted to have exposure to international architecture and build up my vocabulary, but ultimately I wanted to come back and have involvement with our community because I knew that the landscape in Zimbabwe would allow me more opportunities.'

Through her work abroad, Masiyanise developed a minimalist aesthetic design approach; however, working in Zimbabwe, she has found the need to 'translate' the demands and needs of her clients. 'I got exposed to more organic forms,' she explains. 'As my minimal style was not really selling, I realised that ultimately I am not the end user, so I try to blend what they want with my aesthetics.'

Although Masiyanise is willing to negotiate on aesthetics, the spatial arrangement of her architectural designs, along with a desire to take advantage of the country's favourable climate, are non-negotiable. 'My absolute control is in the floor layouts,' she asserts.

Fig. 2 Events Venue, Borrowdale, Harare, Zimbabwe, 2019. This multipurpose events venue can accommodate approximately 500 people.

'I really do try to influence clients on how the space works and the circulation within the space. In Zimbabwe we have a subtropical climate where we have to take advantage of the abundant natural light and ventilation. In my works glazing is strategically placed to allow indoor/outdoor transitional spaces.' This philosophy extends to community buildings like the Events Venue designed for a Harare suburb.

Beyond her own work, Masiyanise is an advocate for architecture in a country where there is widespread misunderstanding about the role of the architect. As president of the Institute of Architects of Zimbabwe she aimed to encourage participation in the institute and promote the role of positive architecture in the country. 'I became president at a time of turmoil when it was faltering and brought back interest in participation in the institute. I brought in new ideas and we started conferences, which had just been talked about in the previous years.' The series of conferences brought interest not just from architects but also from the public, giving exposure to the institute.

Masiyanise's term as president also had historic significance in a country where there are, at the time of writing, still fewer than 20 qualified female architects. 'Before me it was just men,' says Masiyanise, whose presidency has sharpened understanding of how to overcome the complex barriers women face in the industry. 'I've had young women saying that they've looked up to me as a role model, so hopefully it made it a little easier for them to see that they can go into architecture.'

Fig. 3 Cluster Housing Development, Borrowdale, Harare, Zimbabwe, 2014. The design of this upmarket development of cluster houses used the concept of the falcon for the roof to create a distinct profile on the skyline.

EMMA
MILOYO

"Be the change you want to see."

Fig. 1 JCAM Africama House, Nairobi, Kenya, 2019. Administration centre for clients for the Jesuits of Africa and Madagascar.

Co-founder of Nairobi-based architecture studio Design Source, Emma Miloyo aims to create a 'more liveable, sustainable city, one building at a time'. With the distinction of being the first female president of the Architectural Association of Kenya (AAK), she is also keen to use architecture to contribute to wider, fundamental change across the country. 'Be the change you want to see,' she tells us. 'I wanted to influence the built environment, so I needed to be in an organisation that could talk to the government.'

Miloyo is acutely aware of the importance of visible role models, citing her maths teacher, her mother and a woman architect who visited her high school, as helping to shape her interest in the male-dominated profession. Although she did not set out to become president of the AAK, key roles on a series of committees and working groups led to a realisation that she could break down barriers by taking on the leadership of an organisation that has a 90% male membership. 'Being the first female president of AAK had an added responsibility – I knew I had to make it work so that people would see that women are able to lead.' In 2019 the AKK elected Mugure Njendu as their second female president.

Miloyo studied at Jomo Kenyatta University of Agriculture and Technology near Nairobi. Her early memories of architectural practice are of being the only woman on a building site, often with over 100 men, and in board rooms with clients she was 'always conscious of the fact that [she was] the only woman in the room'. Miloyo believes that the increasing number of women working in architecture and construction will ultimately benefit Nairobi as a place to live. 'Not to speak too much of traditional roles, but we are primary caregivers', she says when discussing the important contributions women can make to the design of the built environment. 'We see everything in terms of design, even the layout of a city... And they say, a city that's safe for children is safe for everybody.'

With Design Source, Miloyo's architectural practice encompasses a broad range of typologies including university campuses, schools, housing blocks, hotels and churches – including a headquarters building for the Jesuit church. The Moi Educational Centre (MEC) in Nairobi exemplifies the scale of project that the studio is experienced in tackling. Educating around 1,400 students, the series of buildings that comprise the MEC are designed to be both energy efficient and low maintenance. JCAM Africama House – also in Nairobi – is similarly sensitive to the environment. Reflecting the values of its Jesuit clients, the architecture is welcoming, encompassing a sequence of domestic-scale interiors that offer comfort and privacy. Miloyo aims to create architecture that directly responds to a client's needs: 'The interesting thing about architecture is that it is a human science. You don't know it when you go into it, but with years of practice you realise it's very little to do with drawing and a lot more about human relationships – you're putting someone's vision down onto paper ... Most of the time [a client] know[s] what they want and you translate that into built form.'

Fig. 2 Moi Education Centre, Nairobi, Kenya, 2019. Aerial view.

RAHEL SHAWL

Fig. 1 Embassy of Ireland, Addis Ababa, Ethiopia, 2011. The building tries to separate itself from its dense neighbourhood context. This provides the necessary security measures of an embassy building while meeting tight space and budgetary requirements as well as aesthetic and green building solutions.

Over the past 30 years, Ethiopian architect Rahel Shawl has designed buildings from private homes to hospitals and from shopping malls to breweries all across Ethiopia. Her work also includes numerous embassies and institutions for European and African countries in Addis Ababa.

Shawl graduated from the Ethiopian Institute of Architecture and Building Construction (EIABC) in 1991 at a time when Ethiopia was experiencing great change following the end of 17 years of communist dictatorship. While many of her family and friends had to relocate to other countries, Shawl chose to stay and work in Ethiopia. In 1994 she co-founded a small studio named Abba Architects and, a decade later in 2004, she established her own studio, RAAS Architects. 'I felt very connected to my country,' she explains. 'Where else in the world would a young Ethiopian architect, fresh from college, be able to have such a first-hand experience? So, I stayed and started working through the small opportunities created within the chaos of change. In a weird way, and against advice of my family, here I was, a young, energetic girl simply in the right place, at the right time.' As the country opened, and the economy started to grow, the construction industry was the first to show the positive change. Both local and international clients started investing in property and Shawl began winning major commissions including as architect of record for the Royal Netherlands Embassy which, in 2007, received the prestigious Aga Khan Award. Her work and knowledge of architecture in context of Ethiopia grew as she continued to design, both by herself and in collaboration with international architects.

Fig. 2 The Royal Netherlands Embassy, Addis Ababa, Ethiopia, 2004. The building blends the metaphorical landscape of the Netherlands and the rock-hewn churches of Lalibella, with the chancery building and ambassador residence standing as representative monuments of the two cultures.

Projects like the Fistula Hospital, the Embassy of Ireland, the British Council, the South African Embassy, Cure Hospital, Heineken Breweries and SKA Apartments are a few examples that demonstrate Shawl's commitment to making contemporary forms using Ethiopian building materials and local knowledge. 'I'm what the project needs me to be,' she explains. 'My buildings have simple volumes; I don't like exaggerated lines and chaos. I like contemporary as a style because it allows me to bring in elements like light and air, texture and materiality in a very simple yet attractive way.'

Although varying vastly in scale and programme, all of Shawl's buildings share a dedication to creating spaces that respond both to the environment of Ethiopia and how they will be used. 'They're very simple projects when you see them, but they're also very detailed in every sense – in the facade, internally or in the landscape – you'll see there has been a lot of effort behind this, and that's why the architecture tends to stand out.'
Shawl believes that her buildings are often more than the sum of their parts, something

that she attributes to the fact that she truly cares about how each of her buildings will be experienced and the process by which they are created. 'I care', she says, 'not only about the building, but also about the process and how the people around me work.' And she will ask herself, 'How can I get the people on the ground inspired by my vision?' As part of this desire to inspire, Shawl runs the mentorship programme abRen through RAAS, designed for young professionals in the industry, especially focused on female architects.

Fig. 3 SKA Apartments, Addis Ababa, Ethiopia, 2019. The design uses interlocking boxes, where intruding-extruding forms define unique spaces. The openings and terraces create shading, light and panoramic views.

"I was determined to become an architect, despite being told 'It's not a job for girls'."

CAROLINE
BARLA

Fig. 1 Lycée Dominique Savio, Douala, Cameroon, 2020. This community workshop aimed to restructure one of Douala's neighbourhoods.

Cameroonian architect Caroline Barla believes that an architect's 'primary mission is to guide the art of living'. She studied at the École Spéciale d'Architecture in Paris, returning to Cameroon to work as an architect before establishing her own studio in 1987. 'Our parents raised us to return to Africa and work in our country and, in my case, build it,' she tells us. 'Once I finished my studies I felt invested with a mission that I have aimed to fulfil throughout my life: to allow people to live well in relation to their environment with ethics and probity.'

Architecture is in Barla's family. Her father was the founder of the Ordre National des Architectes du Cameroun – the country's national architecture institute – and her son is also an architect. He joined the studio in 2016, leading to it being renamed Barla Barla Architectes. Barla herself knew she wanted to be an architect from the age of seven, enticed by the idea of 'being able to draw for the rest of my life'. This ambition persisted, despite some resistance, with Barla becoming one of the first women registered as an architect in the country.

Since establishing her Douala-based studio, Barla has created numerous homes, apartments, schools, villas and hotels across the city. Her architecture aims to consider its context and sustainability, but it is people's needs that are Barla's primary concern. 'Since I have been practising, I always try to care about users and the spaces I am asked to create for them,' she explains. 'Who are they, how do they live, what do they live on, what do they need, is the project within their reach? What are they dreaming of? Will it contribute to their development and their well-being?'

Fig. 2 Render of Lycée Dominique Savio, Douala, Cameroon, 2020. Design for a new permanent science centre for the French high school.

At Lycée Dominique Savio, a French high school, her studio created a temporary science centre in containers, designing the permanent building to replace it with 'a sense of belonging to its context'. Her studio also leads multiple community projects including the recent AIRA workshop, which aimed to restructure one of Douala's neighbourhoods. 'We can contribute to the improvement of the living conditions through small fundamental gestures in precarious neighbourhoods,' Barla observes. It is 'an approach that should be systematic and reproduced on a larger scale'.

Aesthetically, Barla Barla Architectes' work combines contemporary and traditional African motifs, aiming to build upon Cameroon's architectural heritage. 'We have an extraordinary architectural heritage, including local methods of construction and locally sourced materials,' she says. 'The qualities of these vernacular architectures, including those of colonial architecture, are not sufficiently analysed or exploited in new constructions. We must move forward based on a past that acts as a foundation for the future.'

Reflecting back on her journey into architecture, Barla says, 'I was determined to become an architect, despite being told, "It's not a job for girls."' Although she has seen the number of women in the profession growing over her almost 40-year career, she believes that being a woman architect in Cameroon is still difficult. 'The clichés persist,' she says. 'More and more women are deciding to become architects, but still to this day, being a female architect remains a daily challenge: psychology, patience, pedagogy must be an integral part of her profession.'

Fig. 3 Atelier AIRA, Douala, Cameroon, 2016. Here a bench is constructed using recovered plastic bottles.

"An African aesthetic in art and architecture takes its roots in the materiality used."

VALÉRIE MAVOUNGOU

One of a handful of women architects in Republic of the Congo, Valérie Mavoungou is the founder of the Pointe-Noire-based studio Atelier Tropical.

With projects in four countries in Africa, Mavoungou describes herself as a 'Pan-African architect'. She studied at the Belleville National School of Architecture in Paris, as well as in Tokyo, Cambodia and South Korea, but always 'had a dream of coming back to Congo and having a practice back home'. She established Atelier Tropical in 2016 with the aim of creating architecture with a 'modern African aesthetic' embedded in the 'climate, culture and history' of central Africa. 'In Asia I saw an expression of understanding of culture that was very integrated in the landscape, and it made me think that there was something that could be done back home,' she explains. 'We have a background of colonial architecture, but there was no

Fig. 2 Ecolodge Kunda, Kouilou, Republic of the Congo, 2016. Mavoungou designed three differently scaled cabins to be delicately inserted in their natural landscape.

expression of what we are. What is Congolese architecture? How can we push that question? These questions made me decide to go back home.'

Mavoungou aims to discover and create architecture that has its roots in Congo and central Africa but is modern and appropriate for a rapidly urbanising country. 'I tried to discover a Congolese architecture,' she says. 'We cannot go back to what is traditional, we are all living in big cities, we are globalised. But we cannot design a place in the same way we'd design in Europe. We have to design in response to the place.'

In order to create modern Congolese architecture Mavoungou has spent time researching the country's architectural heritage. A key element of this is creating architecture that is responsive to the climate in central Africa, a climate which gave her studio its name. She has visited the countryside to see how traditional buildings are made and spoken to numerous craftsmen working directly with local materials. 'The idea is to meld traditional crafts with a contemporary design aesthetic. We had a deep physical sense of the materiality we use and, somehow, we lost it in the course of modernisation. I try to match traditional culture with modern contemporary design.' Mavoungou is one of a growing number of African architects who left the continent for education but returned to establish her studio. However, to truly change how buildings are created in Congo, along with people's perceptions of the role of an architect, Mavoungou believes that the country needs a school where people can complete a full architectural education.'

This is not a gender issue, it's really a general one. We have a lot of challenges; the first thing is that we don't have a school of architecture,' she says. 'I see African countries where they have invested in a school, at least one, and every year you can see that there is a movement, there is more knowledge and more understanding.'

Fig. 3 Ecolodge Kunda, Kouilou, Republic of the Congo, 2016. With generous views of the ocean, the aim was for each cabin to have the feeling of being outdoors yet protected from heat and heavy tropical rain.

"I see the industry becoming more complex and inclusive, more geared towards cross-disciplinary collaborations."

PAULA NASCIMENTO

Fig. 1 Angola Pavilion, Expo Milano, 2015. A collaboration with architects Daniel Toso and Masterplan Studio for a temporary pavilion whose facade was inspired by Angolan textiles.

Paula Nascimento is an architect and independent curator based in Luanda, Angola. She was co-founder of Beyond Entropy Africa (2010–16) with Stefano Pansera, a research studio that worked in architecture, visual arts and geopolitics. Nascimento's practice encompasses several artistic and curatorial projects including 'Luanda, Encyclopaedic City', the award-winning Angolan Pavilion at the Venice Architecture Biennale in 2013, as well as collaborating in the design of the Angolan Pavilion at Expo Milano 2015 and Expo Dubai 2020.

Having studied in London at the Architectural Association and South Bank University, Nascimento began her architectural career as a trainee at Alvaro Siza's office in Porto, Portugal. After also working for two London-based architectural firms she returned to Angola to establish her practice. Nascimento soon realised, she tells us, 'My education and early industry experience offered "the necessary tools" for building buildings, but those tools were not enough to understand and intervene in the complex spatial reality I live in.' She continues 'Whilst I think that architectural education is fantastic, there is a big gap between education and being part of an industry that operates in a very specific way. I started working when I was still at university. This experience was helpful as an introduction to the sector; however, going back to Angola, and because of the nature

Fig. 2 Angola Pavilion, Expo Milano 2015. The temporary pavilion included exhibits of architecture and scenography.

of my work, I still consider myself a bit of an outsider.'

Nascimento's approach to architecture is largely collaborative, working with a range of professionals from artists, designers, writers and filmmakers to other architects and engineers, as well as clients and institutions. She was a member of Colectivo Pés Descalços between 2012 and 2020, a multidisciplinary collective in Luanda, which focused on developing a range of projects across the broad spectrum of Angolan culture. Her curation, as part of 'Beyond Entropy Angola', of the Angolan Pavilion at the Venice Architecture Biennale in 2012. entitled 'Luanda, Encyclopaedic City', featured the photography of Edson Chagas, winning the Golden Lion Award for Best National Participation that year. She has also curated the African Galleries at Arco Lisbon 2019, 2020 and 2021.

Regarding her architectural practice, Nascimento suggests, 'I don't know if I have a signature project, but I would say that my practice is transdisciplinary and research based. It involves not just the design of buildings, but mostly research on spatial practice and forms of intervention in the context of the contemporary African city.' The starting point for each project is always contextual research in order to then delineate the approach, tools and professionals needed. Outcomes may vary, however, from project to project – not always a building or something built. For Nascimento, process has always taken precedent, and the temporality and ephemerality of an intervention is an integral part of this.

Fig. 3 'Luanda Encyclopaedic City', Venice Architecture Biennale 2013. The project, co-curated with Stefano Rabolli Pansera, explored how the knowledge of a city can be organised through the taxonomy of its spaces.

"The advantage of being an architect in an emerging country is this vast experimental field that is offered to us – a space for creation and exploration that allows great freedom of imagination."

HAYATTE NDIAYE

Fig. 1 Mother and Child Hospital (HME), N'Djamena, Chad, 2011. Presentation of the hospital logo to the Head of State. Here the logo design can be seen as part of the gates.

Hayatte Ndiaye is a history-making architect. Not only was she the first woman architect in Chad, but in 2019 she became the first female president of the country's architecture institute, the National Order of Architects of Chad (ONAT). 'As the first woman architect in my country, and because I was only 37 at the time, my accession to the head of ONAT was the fruit of a long struggle,' she tells us.

After studying in France and Belgium at the Institut Supérieur d'Architecture Intercommunal Victor Horta, Ndiaye worked at Architecturestudio in Paris. She returned to N'Djamena, Chad in 2007 to establish her own practice, Hayatt Architecture. Ndiaye believes that architecture has the power to improve people's quality of life and over the past decade has designed public parks, social housing and city sanitation networks that aim to address many of the challenges facing the country. Ndiaye observes, 'The social, economic and environmental impact of inclusive urbanisation, taking into account the most vulnerable segments of the population, is a constant in my work.'

Ndiaye aims to create, and encourage others to make, 'responsible architecture' that is appropriate to Chad's hot climate by adapting traditional building techniques and rejecting 'imported models of construction'. She notes, 'With globalisation and the massive introduction of cement in recent years the country is unfortunately losing its 1,000-year-old bioclimatic constructive tradition. At the same time, the cost of imported materials is beyond the reach of a large part of the population and limits its financial accessibility to basic amenities such as housing.'

Fig. 2 Proposal for Assass social housing project, N'Djamena, Chad, 2017. The preliminary studies phase for this low-cost housing project.

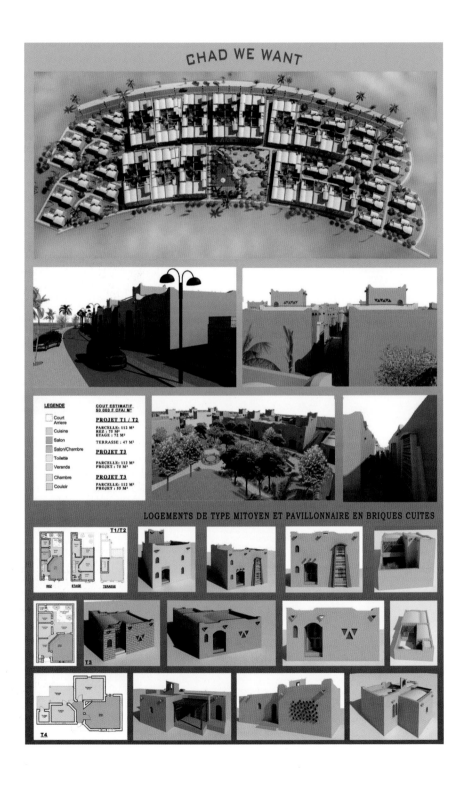

Ndiaye acknowledges the important role architects can play in creating more sustainable futures. 'As professionals in the architectural sector, we have a responsibility to reclaim traditional construction techniques that have already proven themselves for millennia and modernise them to fulfill their contemporary missions.' The Assass social housing project, which will be made up of homes that combine modern design with traditional techniques and motifs, exemplifies this approach. 'Sensitive to the improvement of the living environment in the city as well as the problem of access to decent housing for all, this project offers new standards of sustainable and low-cost social housing, integrating traditional construction techniques and local materials, in order to allow as many people as possible equal access to the city', she explains.

As president of ONAT, Ndiaye aims to 'reposition Chadian architecture', arranging a series of conferences in N'Djamena to debate the future of African cities. However, she believes that the greatest change can be achieved by influencing people's understanding and awareness of what architecture can offer. 'The most important local project is popularising the architectural profession among the population and defining an architecture that responds to context with a guarantee of inclusive development.' By establishing an architectural heritage that is specific to Chad, Ndiaye foresees the emergence of an architecture that is equipped to address both the local and the global.

Fig. 3 Assass social housing project, N'Djamena, Chad, 2019. On-site.

"Architecture, for me,
is the art of co-creating the world."

CAROLINE
PINDI NORAH

Fig. 1 Conversations with women on the importance of financial autonomy in the fight against domestic violence, hosted in the multipurpose hall of the parish of Our Lady of Fatima, Kinshasa, Democratic Republic of the Congo, 2022.

One of only around 100 women architects working in the Democratic Republic of the Congo, Caroline Pindi Norah believes that 'equality is a right and a necessity for a balanced and fulfilled society'. As the current president of the Association of Women Architects of Congo (AFARC), she aims to both encourage more women into the profession and provide additional training to the small number of women currently working as architects. 'We are training more women architects because the more of us there are, the more the myth that women architects are unusual will be erased,' Norah tells us. 'People are afraid to work with female architects in Congo because of stereotypes. They feel that women are not competent. They are wrong and we are working to overcome this.'

The group also aims to change people's perceptions of women through campaigns to demonstrate the accomplishments of women architects with exhibitions, conferences, workshops and seminars.

'Consciences are awakening to the need to entrust your building to an architect and we women architects are beginning to find our place,' says Norah. 'It is progressing little by little and our association is fighting so that women architects become more competitive to snatch their place in the emerging architecture market.'

Pindi Norah studied architecture at the National Institute of Building and Public Works (INBTP) in Kinshasa and, in her own work, she designs buildings that are 'modern and, above all, tropical'. She has designed numerous apartment blocks and single family villas in the country's capital and across the Democratic Republic of the Congo – most of which are renovations to existing buildings. In her residential work (which often features signature stairs), she aims to create homes that people want to live in. She emphasises a co-creative role between architect and client: 'We grow buildings with multiple functions from the ground, while adding an artistic touch. Above all it's a question of

comfort – more than the appearance of the building, it is essential for me that the occupants of the building feel good there.' Beyond her own architecture, Norah dedicates much of her time to advocacy. Along with AFARC, she is the president of the Association Mille et Un Espoir, which aims to fight against gender-based violence with a particular focus on marital and domestic violence. She was also the initiator of the pan-African event WANAWAKE WA AFRIKA – a forum aimed at highlighting the African heroines who have written, and who still write today, the history of the African continent. 'I have often been the victim of sexual harassment and injustice in my life since I was little,' Norah tells us. 'I was fired from a position because I was pregnant. I almost lost a member of my family because she was beaten by her partner. In short, in the face of all these injustices, I feel challenged and invested with the mission of doing my part to restore the balance of things.'

Fig. 2 Conference on female architecture at the Higher Institute of Architecture and Town Planning, Kinshasa, Democratic Republic of the Congo, 2021.

NADA ELFEITURI

"The built environment is a collective project."

Libyan architect Nada Elfeituri believes that community involvement is key to creating a 'renewed sense of public life' in the country – something that she is putting into practice reconstructing a series of plazas in her hometown of Benghazi. Born in Libya, Elfeituri grew up in Canada before returning to Benghazi as a teenager. She went on to study architecture and urban planning at Benghazi University. Her studies were interrupted, however, when the Libyan revolution began in 2011. This life-changing event was a 'moment of awakening' and she joined a group of youth collectives creating social space projects. 'In my second year of architecture suddenly everything changed,' Elfeituri tells us. 'My generation was out marching in the streets and, for the first time in our lives, the air was filled with a sense of euphoria and opportunity. We were young and inexperienced – didn't know what we were doing – but all of us in Libya were learning how to build a country.'

Despite this initial sense of opportunity, as the war continued, and she was repeatedly displaced, 'life turned into a waiting game'.

In 2016, Elfeituri left Libya to work on reconstruction projects around the world, including in Tunisia and Nigeria. 'With half the city under armed conflict and the other half fleeing, it was the worst time to be an architect,' she says. 'Many of the projects I worked on before the war were destroyed and it created this sense of hopelessness. Being an architect in a war zone is a Sisyphean task – constructing, seeing the destruction and then reconstructing.'

Unable to 'disconnect from Libya', Elfeituri continued working on projects in the country,

Fig. 2 Western view of Silphium Plaza, Benghazi, Libya. Site before reconstruction work begins, projected to start in late 2024.

mentoring other designers and running the architecture-focused website Brave New Libya. After five years abroad she returned to the country to work on the reconstruction of several public spaces including the historic Silphium Plaza in downtown Benghazi.

'For the first time since the war, the city isn't just trying to recover, but looking beyond,' she explains. 'There are large-scale projects happening, urban development plans being discussed and a lot of conversations about the future of the city. I wanted to return so I could take part in this new chapter and have a say in what the future of Benghazi looks like.'

Elfeituri is working with numerous organisations including UNESCO, World Monuments Fund and Architecture Sans Frontières. She believes that community involvement is key to mentally reclaiming public spaces in Libya that became 'places of fear' – as locations for executions and violently shut down protests – during the Gaddafi regime.

As she says, this can be a 'messy process'. 'I don't want to create tensions,' she tells us, 'but my inner rabble-rouser has led me to challenge the status quo of architecture in Benghazi. Libyans are already being vocal about the changes they see in their city.' Integrating a participatory approach to projects allows Elfeituri to emphasise the importance of the process as much as the end result.

Fig. 3 Northern view of the historic Silphium Plaza, Benghazi, Libya. Site before work begins (ongoing).

SHAHIRA
FAHMY

"What if an architectural output could be freed from its history and the burden of its expectations?"

Fig. 1 Site plan, Ahmed Bahaa El Din Culture Centre, Assyuit, Egypt, 1999–2013.

Cairo-based Shahira Fahmy is an architect, urbanist and researcher. She works between teaching and practice, taking a strong theoretical approach. In 2005 she founded and became principal of Shahira Fahmy Architects (SFA). Since then, her projects have encompassed both product design and master planning and have included everything from a single bench to a cultural centre, as well as all the spaces in between.

After graduating in 1997 from the Department of Architecture at Cairo University of Engineering, Fahmy took a job as surveyor at an NGO in order to stay in touch with the process of 'tracing, mapping and documenting' her urban surroundings.

This process has become a conscious method for 'describing cities, their histories, futures and present'. She observes that this is a 'committed search for a language discovered rather than designed. A language that serves territories and identities, and that navigates the in between, the disjuncture of the real and the represented.'

Figs. 2 and 3 Ahmed Bahaa El Din Culture Centre, Assyuit, Egypt, 2013.

'Growing up in a hybrid context you get entangled in many identities,' Fahmy tells us, 'Muslim, Coptic, Pharoah, Egyptian, Arab or North African?' For her, this complexity is also evident in Cairo's built fabric – an assemblage of colonial past with an ever-shifting present, where 'buildings appear and disappear, memory is relative and histories can be rewritten'.

Fahmy's main interest is in the gaps between lived experience and the abstractions of space that are represented in drawings and maps. In her work, both building and terrain are conceived as spaces of potential, where new activities arise from unforeseen encounters. It is within these contested spaces of the city that Fahmy positions her work. 'This field has all the ingredients that allow for experimentation as well as more obvious architectural gestures.'

Reflecting back on her journey as an architect, Fahmy recalls the challenges she faced in pursuing a career in architecture, a decision largely contrary to society's expectations. 'In the 1990s Cairo had no architectural scene per se, no magazines, no platforms, no networks or groups and hence no dialogue. This made it harder to explore or share languages of expression,' she tells us. 'In the beginning it wasn't easy to find clients who were willing to take a risk.'

And yet, in Fahmy's first project we can already witness both her resilience and her approach to collaboration. The Ahmed Bahaa El Din Culture Centre is a public project for an NGO that is located in a small village, remotely situated at the edge of Assyuit Governorate in Egypt. It was designed and built over the span of 13 years (1999–2013) in collaboration with technical firm Dar El Handasah. Throughout the course of the project, money had to be raised in order to fund the build.

The lengthy process of making the Ahmed Bahaa El Din Culture Centre nevertheless resulted in an outcome that represents the power of architecture to facilitate dialogue within communities and encourage the coming together of different agencies to improve the public realm.

Today, in Egypt, investment is still not forthcoming except in commercial projects and so Fahmy has turned her attention to Saudi Arabia, with a private residence in the old town of AlUla and a competition win for 'The Architects in Residence – 100 Architects for 100 Houses' in 2022. She responded to the brief with a proposal for nomadic living, extending her explorations of lived experience, human nature and the desire to make a place home, even if only for a while.

Fig. 4 100 Architects for 100 Houses, Winner. An International Competition for AlUla, Saudi Arabia, 2022. The proposal, Carpet of the Wind, took inspiration from the way that a carpet laid on the desert floor, to mark a stop in a journey, starts to craft a relation between human and earth.

"Architecture is not only about form and building, it can also be about walls, camps, barbed wire and borders."

SAMIA HENNI

Fig. 1 The first iteration of 'Discreet Violence: Architecture and the French War in Algeria', gta Exhibitions, ETH Zurich, Switzerland, 2017. Propaganda on the French 'civilising' project is juxtaposed with documents of evidence.

Algerian-born Samia Henni began her architectural studies at the École Polytechnique d'Architecture et d'Urbanisme in Algiers during the 1990s civil war and completed her studies at the Academia de Architettura in Mendrisio. This violent context to her studies and early career has informed her concern with the lived experience of architecture. For Henni this encompasses 'built, destroyed and imagined environments'.

Subsequently, her training broadened to take in humanities subjects and curatorial knowledge as she moved from Algeria to Switzerland, the Netherlands, England, Scotland and then the USA, where she teaches history and the theory of architecture and urbanism, after having gained her PhD at the ETH Zurich. These experiences have fused to inform an approach that is transdisciplinary and experimental in nature – taking in work as a historian, theorist, educator and exhibition maker.

She reminds us that architecture is not only about form and building. 'It can also be about walls, camps, barbed wire and borders – interventions in the landscape,' she tells us. 'For me, it's really about the histories of these spatial interventions, their possibilities and limitations – and giving voice to those from whom we should learn.'

This long history of violence has now become the subject of her writing. She is the author of the award-winning 2019 book *Architecture of Counterrevolution: The French Army in Northern Algeria* and the editor of *Deserts Are Not Empty* (2022) and *War Zones* (2018). Henni also explores the way that exhibitions provide an accessible way of communicating untold stories to a wider audience. A good example is her exhibition *Discreet Violence: Architecture and the French War in Algeria*, which toured Europe, the USA and Africa from 2017 to 2021. This revealed the histories of French military camps that were used to forcibly relocate thousands of people during the 1954–62 Algerian Revolution. The curatorial treatment foregrounds conflicting visions and sources. Audiovisual

Fig. 2 The first iteration of 'Discreet Violence: Architecture and the French War in Algeria', gta Exhibitions, ETH Zurich, Switzerland, 2017. Mirrors reflect documents of evidence on top of photos.

materials, used to peddle propaganda on the French 'civilising' project, were juxtaposed with materials that reveal what was going on, on the ground – officer communications, reports and journalism. Henni used mirrors to compound the effect so that photographic documents were overlaid with the reflections of contesting accounts on the walls.

'Welcoming all these layers in the display was extremely important,' she explains.

In colonial architecture, naming objects and spaces is important, Henni tells us. Thus, the show emphasises the differing interpretations of imposed spaces. For instance, military camps, called *centres de regroupement* ('regrouping centres') by the French army and colonial authorities, were renamed 'camps' by progressive journalists.

In Henni's practice, architecture extends to include both the content and practice of exhibition-making. She is interested in how a touring exhibition can change in response to a new space, elements of display and new socio-political context prompting new interpretations.

'What is really interesting is the deterritorialisation of an exhibition,' she tells us. 'Not only the displacement of it, but all the other layers that make it more resonant to the audience.'

Henni's contribution has been to help us understand the relationship between architecture, urbanism, colonial practices and military measures. Moving forward her challenge is to continue to open up this discussion, exploring the role of nuclear weapons and their impact on the Anthropocene – 'the human-made environmental destruction that we call climate change'.

Fig. 3 Cover of *Architecture of Counterrevolution: The French Army in Northern Algeria*, designed by Philippe Monthon, gta Verlag, Zurich, Switzerland, 2017.

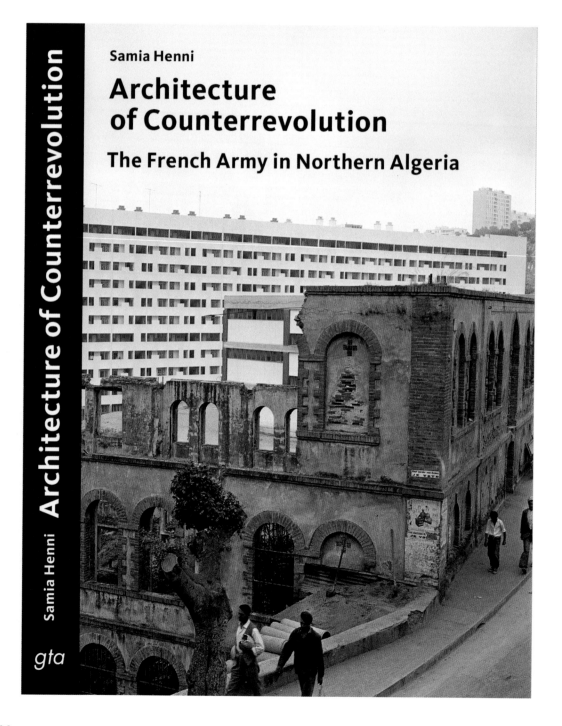

SALIMA NAJI

"Low tech is the way of the future."

Fig. 1 Restoration of Adkhss n'Arfalen granary, Tata Province, Morocco, 2018–19. Image shows the gradual stages of rescue, from the crown to the heart of the construction.

Over the past 20 years, Moroccan architect and anthropologist Salima Naji has been working to rehabilitate and transform dilapidated traditional *igoudars* (citadel grain stores) and *ksours* (fortified villages) in southern Morocco. She has also built numerous contemporary structures that make use of traditional techniques including the stone Ait Ouabelli cultural centre. Her work has been shortlisted for the Aga Khan Award for Architecture in 2013 and 2022 for the Issy Valley Improvement.

Practising what she terms 'research-action', her work brings together her experience as an architecture graduate of the École d'Architecture de Paris-La-Villette and her PhD in Anthropology from the École des Hautes Études en Sciences Sociales in Paris. She works with local craftspeople to redevelop structures to best suit their communities. 'My architecture is terrestrial, anchored in a site, history, heritage and vital connections,' she tells us. 'Every individual action has collective repercussions and the choice to favour certain materials, in certain places, for certain uses, automatically impacts all environmental, territorial and social balances.'

Naji takes a participatory approach to preservation. She has developed a model for 'common sense conservation' routed in local communities, which is outlined in her book *Architectures of the Common Good: For an Ethic of Preservation* (2022). She has collaborated with numerous local masons and craftspeople to rejuvenate historical, stone structures into spaces fit for contemporary, community use across the Anti-Atlas Mountain range. This includes sacred and collective architectures of the oases the Amtoudi granaries, the fortified villages of Assa and Agadir Ouzrou and the minaret of Akka. 'My approach is focused on sustainable architecture that meets the needs of often isolated populations with low incomes at a lower cost,' she says. 'Craftspeople using local materials are at the heart of all these issues. Indeed, the so-called ancestral know-how is the result of a long transmission of experiences carried out in a context of scarcity.'

In her work, low-tech materials and modalities are privileged alongside 'paleo-inspiration'. She explains, 'It is a question of going beyond the heritage dimension as a simple image of a mythologised past to inscribe it, rather, in a rethinking of the inherited techniques as a resource and a modality of action in a specific context that can address contemporary concerns: climatic reheating, scarcity of resources and the desire for well-being.' Although Naji employs materials and techniques that have been understood for centuries, she argues that this is a contemporary approach to architecture. 'It is based on hygrometric and climatic

Fig. 2 Restoration of Agadir n'Aguellouy granary, Amtoudi, Oued Noun-Guelmim Province, Morocco, 2007–15.

comfort. What could be less modern than expensive and, ultimately, very vain, unsuitable architecture? What I'm building is contemporary.' Indeed, today, the big questions are about vulnerability and respect for others.

Naji hopes that through numerous, often small-scale interventions, she can 'present a real alternative' to the redevelopment of Morocco's historic sites. 'There is a current trend towards the concretisation and destruction of the historical witnesses of a very rich past. This loss is tragic because it deprives people of their reference points in their daily lives.

'At a time when a post-colonial history is being written, it would be appropriate to emancipate ourselves from preconceived categories based on transnational standards and allow local logics to flourish.' She continues, 'Historical logics remain and can be reactivated. It is not a question of opposing modernity and tradition in a binary way but, rather, of reflecting on the necessary diversity of public places developed and used by and for a community.'

Fig. 3 Dar Sania, House of the Craftsmen, Oum Gardane, Tata Province, Morocco, 2016–19.

"My motto is 'Never give the client what they want' – get your creative spatial intelligence into gear and surprise the hell out of them, while listening closely."

SARAH CALBURN

Fig. 1 (top and below) Sea House, Western Cape, South Africa, 2010. Sketch and SketchUp render.

Sarah Calburn founded her Johannesburg practice in 1996, with an aim to 'spatialise clients' personalities and desires, whilst sustaining a creative dialogue with the social and physical environments around them.' Calburn's architectural experience has developed across international contexts. She graduated in 1987 from the University of the Witwatersrand, Johannesburg and went on to complete a Master's degree in Architecture at the Royal Melbourne Institute of Technology. She has worked in Paris, Hong Kong, Saigon, Swaziland, Lagos and Melbourne as well as her base in South Africa. Spanning three decades, the studio's portfolio includes residential, retail, offices, schools, galleries and product design.

Calburn's houses draw together the main themes in her work and show a practice at the intersection of architecture and landscape. Private residences Cuilidh, in Walker Bay, and Sea House, in Western Cape, were designed as a balance between the clients' requirements and particularities of site and climate. They extend the landscape, designed to leave it relatively uninterrupted by the house, while Sea House also incorporates a partially constructed ruin. This process exploits what Calburn calls 'the line between inside and out' – realising the physical excitement of the location and the multiplicity of views.

The process of creation is important to Calburn. She develops a sensitive relationship with the client, as can be seen in this intimate account of her imagining of Cocoon House: 'I imagined Cathy [the client] safe within an oval courtyard; the whole house a smooth passage; all of her house visible from any room.'

Fig. 2 Sea House, Western Cape, South Africa, 2010. The roof was conceived as an extension of the landscape out over the sea cliffs, providing complete privacy for the house.

She then uses sketches to spatialise early conversations with clients and the houses are built closely to these first designs.

Over time the way she works has evolved. She started working on a drawing board in 1982, becoming freehand in the 2000s. Now she directs her assistant to create walk-through movies of her projects that are structurally resolved and almost 'final' – comprising colours, finishes, painting and garden design.

Important too is a constructive relationship with the builder and site team. Calburn notes, 'There are always ways of doing things better in practice, and knowledge to be gleaned and honed.'

Calburn's practice and writing have been published in magazines and books on architecture and urbanism, and she brings this experience to teaching at local and international universities. She is also active on the South African cultural scene, most notably as Programme Director of the first South African Architectural Biennale, Architecture AZA 2010. Against the often bland, internationalising impulse in modern architecture, she values the potential of African cities to develop in ways geared to their own characteristics and eccentricities.

Fig. 3 Cuilidh, Walker Bay, South Africa, 2019. Cuilidh is built into the undulating landscape of ancient dune formations along the coast. Ocean and fynbos horizons remain uninterrupted by the house.

"I don't believe in statement buildings."

NINA MARITZ

Fig. 1 Habitat Research and Development Centre, Katutura, Windhoek, Namibia, 2003–9. The approach to the centre's two conference halls, built with alternative materials and construction methods and retaining and restoring existing vegetation.

Namibian architect Nina Maritz is the country's pre-eminent designer of environmentally conscious architecture. She has spent the past two decades creating 'sustainable community-orientated projects' across Namibia. The daughter of architects, Maritz studied at the University of Cape Town in South Africa before moving to Namibia in 1992, two years after the country gained independence, to begin her architectural career. After a brief spell working for the government, she established her own studio in 1998, at a time, she tells us, when 'sustainability wasn't on the map' in the country.

The decision to enter a competition to design the Habitat Research and Development Centre in Windhoek – as 'an opportunity to learn about sustainability' – helped to set Maritz's studio on its two-decade environmentally focused course. Built using passive design principles, her competition-winning design, which appropriately is dedicated to research and promotion of sustainable housing, bears many of the hallmarks of her low-embodied-energy approach to architecture. 'I focus a lot on issues of passive design – durability, functionality and flexibility,' she tells us.

'We don't rely on mechanical, electrical, or high-tech solutions to create sustainable buildings.'

The studio has won numerous Namibia Institute of Architects Merit Awards for its varied work, which includes schools, offices, hospitals, houses, visitor centres, libraries and tourist resorts. In all of her projects, Maritz places functionality at the forefront of the design. 'There is no point in a beautiful building that doesn't work,' she says. 'To me, the separation between aesthetics and function is the same as that between the rational and the intuitive – there is no separation. They are integrated in

Fig. 2 Habitat Research and Development Centre, Katutura, Windhoek, Namibia, 2003–9. Walkway to offices between tyre and gabion walls, built with alternative materials and construction methods to investigate sustainable construction.

our brains, so function and aesthetics should be integrated.'

One building that expresses this ethos is the Twyfelfontein Visitor Interpretation Centre in northwest Namibia, which has local sandstone gabion walls and a roof made from reclaimed oil drums cut into Roman tiles. It was designed to be completely reversible. Maritz explains, 'We made an entirely cement-free building so that it can be completely dismantled and demounted – all the things can be reused – there's no waste.'

Maritz's architecture often incorporates raw, unfinished materials, with clerestory ventilation and day-lighting a recurring theme. However, her focus on creating appropriate structures for the country's varied climatic contexts means that Maritz's buildings do not have a shared aesthetic. 'The thing that connects them is an intrinsic understanding of sustainability and contextuality, and that's why they look so different,' says Maritz. She continues, 'They are not really statement buildings, which aren't sustainable. If people want to communicate something to the passer-by through the building, that is fine. But I don't believe in empty statements – like a curving concrete wall with no practical function.' Beyond creating usable buildings, Maritz believes that this focus on functionality and climatic appropriateness also results in buildings that are in tune with their surroundings. 'I strongly believe that buildings have subliminal communication; it's environmental psychology – it's what makes people feel a certain way,' she says. 'I'm very interested in the sensory experience of buildings.'

Fig. 3 Twyfelfontein Visitor Interpretation Centre, Twyfelfontein Rock Engraving World Heritage Site, northwest Namibia, 2005.

SITHABILE MATHE

"In my mind and in Setswana culture, architecture has always been a natural domain for women."

Fig. 1 H&A Cutting Works, Gaborone, Botswana, 2008. View of the main office space.

Sithabile Mathe is an architect whose practice, Moralo Designs, is embedded within the culture of Setswana – the most widely spoken language in Botswana. The practice, based in Gaborone – the country's capital city – is multidisciplinary spanning landscape, urban, architectural and interior design. Mathe observes, 'Our work is grounded on a strong sustainability profile focusing on passive means as much as possible. The form of our buildings seeks to merge traditional vernacular forms with contemporary design.' Mathe was educated as an architect in Glasgow, Scotland, before embarking on a career that has taken her to Norway and across the African continent including South Sudan, Tanzania and South Africa. She is a registered member of no less than four professional bodies and has been the Chair of the Architects' Registration Council of Botswana, among a number of other significant roles within the profession. Yet, as Mathe notes, 'Many people in Botswana still do not consider the practice of architecture as a profession that is suitable for a woman. As a student, and now as a practitioner, upon telling someone that I am an architect, I am often met with a look of disbelief or, at best, a polite dismissive smile. In my mind and in Setswana culture, architecture has always been a natural domain for women.'

It is clear that Mathe is acutely aware of her position as a female architect and is quick to identify her grandmother, Selinah Ralefala, as her role model and ally. 'When I was growing up in Mochudi under her care, I watched and later helped her repair and decorate her home at the cattle post. The walls and floors were made of sun-baked clay, the roof made of thatch and the patterns on the walls crafted in exquisite, delicate shapes and forms.' Mathe found that her architectural training 'only partially' provided the requisite tools for making architecture in Southern Africa, telling us that 'there was very little

Fig. 2 H&A Cutting Works, Gaborone, Botswana, 2008 in collaboration with Ishmael Mosinyi and Bernard Hyde. This view of the exhibition space shows the use of contemporary vernacular form.

room to explore my own architectural identity related to where I came from and where I would ultimately practice.' And so it is that her early life experiences have provided the contextual underpinning for her body of work. Two projects that exemplify Mathe's approach are H&A Cutting Works and Hagen Residence, both located in Botswana. H&A Cutting Works is a diamond-polishing facility, formed of a collection of buildings that house an exhibition space, office, factory and canteen. These independent structures together comprise what Mathe refers to as a lolwapa or 'homestead', with the exhibition 'house' sitting at the entrance to the complex. 'In form [it pays] a direct homage to the traditional Setswana house. In its use of materials, it turns to the contemporary, with the curved cement plastered wall cut by long elements of glass.'

The Hagen Residence more obviously engages with sustainable strategies. Consisting of two independent dwellings on a single plot of land, the structures can be inhabited by two independent households or function as one household if required. Mathe describes the project as 'built over two storeys to allow as much outdoor garden space as possible. The house has a strong sustainability profile using insulated cavity walls and double glazing to reduce heat gain, with low-energy fittings.' The buildings also capture rainwater and recycle their grey water, harnessing the environmental conditions of the local landscape.

Moving forward, Mathe hopes to spread her architectural ethos to a wider audience and educate future architects in Botswana. This is crucial work if there is to be greater recognition of the role that Indigenous architectures play in the search for climate justice.

Fig. 3 Hagen Residence, Gaborone, Botswana, 2016. The north-facing living space has an uninterrupted view of the garden with deep verandas for shading from the sun.

SUMAYYA VALLY

Fig. 1 Serpentine Pavilion, Kensington Gardens, London, UK, 2021. The forms are a result of abstracting and splicing elements from architecture across London into the Pavilion structure, while the varying textures and hues of pink and brown reference changes in quality of light.

As the youngest-ever designer of the high-profile Serpentine Pavilion in London, and recently named as one of *Time* magazine's 100 leaders of the future, South African Sumayya Vally is one of the world's best-known young architects. Vally is also Honorary Professor of Practice at The Bartlett School of Architecture, University College London.
Vally grew up in Johannesburg in the shadow of apartheid. Understanding the multi-layered nature of the city, with its informal economies and segregation, was central to her early thinking while studying at the University of

Pretoria and University of the Witwatersrand. In the final year of her Master's degree, she established the studio Counterspace with four fellow students 'to continue engagement with the city'. 'When my practice started, it was very much obsessed with Johannesburg – wanting to translate the city, and find form for it, in as many different possible ways,' she tells us.
As Counterspace has evolved, her desire to use research into the intangible forces that constitute meaningful urban spaces has remained central to the studio's work. Vally

emphasises the importance of storytelling in her work: 'I want to find expression for hybrid identities and territory, particularly for African and Islamic conditions – both rooted and diasporic,' she says. 'I really aim to express place from these other narratives – and other ways of being and seeing.'
This ethos can be seen the Serpentine Pavilion (2021). The design responds to the historical scarcity of informal community spaces across the city. The forms reference existing and erased gathering spaces, which are significant to diasporic and cross-cultural communities.

Fig. 2 Fragment of Serpentine Pavilion at The Tabernacle, Notting Hill, London, UK, 2021. For the first time, the Serpentine Pavilion commission had four fragments placed in partner organisations whose work has inspired its design.

Among them are some of the first mosques built in the city – such as the East London Mosque – as well as cooperative bookshops – such as the New Beacon Bookstore, one of the first Black publishers and booksellers in the UK – and cultural sites like the Notting Hill Carnival. Elements of these were abstracted and superimposed to create the new Pavilion structure. In a further gesture to decentralise architecture, four fragments of the Pavilion were placed around London in the partner organisations whose work inspired its design. As Artistic Director of the inaugural Islamic Arts

Biennale in Jeddah in 2023, Vally has creatively shaped the Biennale – from the theme to contemporary commissions. The aim was to expand and deepen the definition of Islamic arts in an effort to embed new discourses and identities that are resonant with the philosophies and experience of Islam. Through her work, Vally aims to expand what is considered architecture, placing a 'focus on process rather than end product'. She believes that a diversity of voices is the key. 'Architects need to be tackling things that fall outside of the current, mainstream view of

architecture and that's something that people who have different perspectives can bring.' Diverse voices – the perspectives of women or different cultures – will ultimately reinvent the systems that create architecture. 'These lenses constitute something that affects the way that we see things,' says Vally. 'They produce different worlds and different forms of architecture – or they can if we let them.'

Fig. 3 Inaugural Islamic Arts Biennale, Jeddah, Saudi Arabia, 2023. Vally, as Artistic Director, worked to expand the definition of Islamic arts in way that is resonant with the philosophies of Islam.

"A lot of the spatial violence in apartheid South Africa disconnected people, and disconnected societies – so part of our work is to be aware of social networks and of what people experienced."

ILZE WOLFF

Fig. 1 Centre for Humanities Research, University of the Western Cape, Cape Town, South Africa, 2022. Lobby staircase.

Ilze Wolff runs South African studio Wolff Architects, alongside her partner Heinrich Wolff. 'I'm not one of those architects who always wanted to be an architect,' she tells us. Originally focusing on graphic design, she also considered archaeology, before deciding to study architecture at the University of Cape Town. These broad interests have impacted the multifaceted thinking adopted by the studio. 'Architecture is a nice place to begin to work in an interdisciplinary way,' says Wolff. 'At our studio, everything bleeds into everything else. We consider ourselves conceptual thinkers when it comes to art, design and architecture. We work with musicians and poets, but there's also a very strong technical side to the practice, to understand the construction of buildings.' Founded in 2012, Wolff Architects has a strong focus on advocacy, research and documentation. Says Wolff, 'I feel like I am doing archaeology through the research that we're doing; it's a lot of digging, a lot of thinking.' The practice aims to create architecture that is inclusive through considered interventions. Before starting any project, the studio looks to build a deep understanding of its potential impact. 'When we get a commission, we sit around the table as a team and I ask everybody what is the story? What do we know about this client? What do we know about where the money's coming from? I need to know about those things before I even start sketching.' The practice has a wide-ranging portfolio and has completed a series of interesting homes around Cape Town along with numerous cultural projects, including the Watershed at the V&A Waterfront in the city and

Fig. 2 Vredenburg Provincial State Hospital, Cape Town, South Africa, 2021. A healing environment is created by ensuring that all wards look out onto tranquil garden spaces free from the activity of other hospital operations.

the Vredenburg Provincial State Hospital. According to Wolff, the hospital is especially important within the Cape Town context given the history of South Africa. 'Architects were so complicit in the construction of racialised neighbourhoods and the apartheid state,' says Wolff, 'so we need to be fully aware of what we're doing. And our office really believes in immersing ourselves – being knowledgeable, being informed – and that takes a lot of work. Then our decisions are not from an ignorant position.'

A project that encapsulates the studio's ethos is the transformation of a school building into a site for arts-based education for the University of the Western Cape. The university – originally established to educate 'coloured people' – was located at the edge of the city, but the new building is central to the Woodstock suburb as a real symbol of change. 'This project allows us to implement all of our ideas about arts education,' says Wolff, 'rewriting this history of state racialised education, moving the university from periphery to centre, and also restoring an old building.' With such projects, Wolff Architects aim to repair some of the wounds and rebuild connections within communities.

Although recently shortlisted for the Moira Gemmill Prize for Emerging Architecture at The Architectural Review's Women in Architecture Awards, Wolff is keen to highlight that the studio's work is the result of numerous team members and collaborators, not least Heinrich Wolff. 'We have a really intense partnership,' she says. 'In terms of our work and in terms of life, everything is shared – but there are obviously individual ways of thinking about certain things.'

Fig. 3 Inaugural V&A Waterfront Watershed, Cape Town, South Africa, 2015. Interior view.

OLAJUMOKE ADENOWO

"Global in perspective, rooted in my heritage."

Fig. 1 AD Consulting Studio, Lagos, Nigeria, 2011. View at dusk of the restrained studio exterior, composed of 'primary' solids.

Olajumoke Adenowo is a Nigerian architect practising in Lagos. The neo-heritage architecture of AD Consulting combines Adenowo's career-long exposure to global architecture with a traditional African approach to building design solutions. Context is central to her work, be that socio-economic, cultural, climatic or technological. Also influential is the zeitgeist of the African continent, which is home to a growing and aspirational middle class, and the globe's youngest population.

Adenowo is the architect of more than 70 buildings, and specialises in master planning and projects at scale. She has received multiple awards and shares her experience as a consultant, educator, mentor and provider of opportunities for young architects. She studied architecture at Obafemi Awolowo University in Nigeria, followed by qualifications in Business Management and Leadership in Lagos, Harvard and Yale in the USA and Barcelona, Spain. Growing up on university campuses, she experienced buildings by Bauhaus-trained architect Ariel Sharon and British Architects Fry and Drew.

In her design for the AD Consulting Studio building, Adenowo demonstrates the defining principles of neo-heritage architecture. In all of her projects she deploys her practical knowledge of the climate, orientating the building to harness prevalent winds for passive cooling and to reduce the thermal load from the harsh tropical sun. Another signature practice is the use of daylight interacting with internal spaces. A circular opening above the tudio's atrium evokes the quality of daylight filtering into the assembly spaces of the central courtyards found in the traditional Yoruba architecture of south western Nigeria. Following the style of Hausa architecture in northern Nigeria, a flat roof garden allows for rainwater harvesting.

Time is central to Adenowo's work. She explains how walking through the AD Studio space reveals new views and level changes, creating the illusion of a much larger building.

Fig. 2 Render of Calabar Church, Boki, Cross Rivers State, Nigeria, 2015. A low maintenance, passively cooled, Marian Chapel for a rural rainforest community inspired by the religious spaces of traditional architecture.

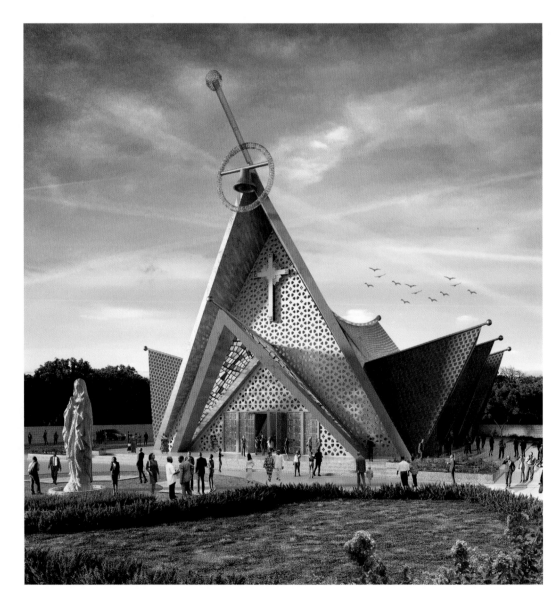

The studio changes from the daylight serenity and opacity of the envelope to a nocturnal glow and transparency as darkness falls. The skylight in the roof garden glows like an observatory at night. Neo-heritage principles are evident in the metal burglar screen she designed for the studio's atrium window, both as artistic expression and security feature. 'Functional Art', as Adenowo defines this phenomenon, is typical of traditional Nigerian architecture which eschews 'art for art's sake'.

The inherent principles of sustainability are reflected at every scale, from single buildings to the Bayelsa Eco-Industrial Park Master Plan. Features of traditional architecture provide new ways of designing climate-responsive structures. The design for Calabar Church incorporates perforated walls to provide passive cooling – inspired by the effects of daylight percolating through the grass walls of traditional meeting houses of the neighbouring Bamileke people in southern Cameroon.

Adenowo is keen to expand on the conflicts that arise between an architect's ethos and the realities of execution – especially for a young female architect. When the Guiding Light Assembly was commissioned in 1994, her design included sculptural sunscreens, visualised as hands folded in exultant prayer and reminiscent of Seraphim's wings. These acted as climate modifiers to shield the walls and windows from the sun. On completion of the frame and roof construction, the building contractor convinced the client that this defining feature was neither possible nor worthwhile. Confronted with a rectangular concrete bunker, her solution was to adorn the building with vibrant pattern, colour and texture after the manner of African traditional architecture. Neo-heritage pervades Adenowo's work from inception to date.

Fig. 3 Render of Heritage Bank Headquarters Project, Victoria Island, Lagos, Nigeria, 2016. A vented double-glass envelope provides passive cooling.

"I see my 'errant practice' as a personal and professional journey searching for meaningful references and supporting collective efforts for building community."

PATTI ANAHORY

Fig. 1 'Volumes of EMPTY Memories', installation, Tarrafal, Cabo Verde, 2017. In Águ, one installation at the former prison camp presents 96, 25l water containers filling an area the size of the former solitary confinement cell, labelled with names of former Cabo-Verdean political prisoners.

Patti Anahory is an architect, educator and independent curator based in Cabo Verde who works at the intersection of pedagogy and practice. She is the co-founder of Storia na Lugar, with César Schofield Cardoso, a storytelling platform and 'independent space for inter(un)disciplinary exchanges, creative experimentation and cross-disciplinary dialogue.'

Anahory studied for a Bachelor's degree in Architecture at Boston Architectural College and for a Master's degree in Architecture at Princeton University in the USA – an experience she describes as framed by 'symbolic and epistemological violence as we confront racist, euro-centric, elitist, patriarchal systems of meaning making and exclusion'. After college, she won a prize that enabled her return to the African continent, where she began to explore the complex cultures and geopolitics of African cities and establish their legitimacy as sites of architectural enquiry. In Cabo Verde, Anahory helped to establish a multidisciplinary research centre based at the country's first public university, with a remit to investigate issues related to the local built environment. For her, architectural practice within this context is necessarily political, engaging with the production and experience of space from an African (and in terms of Cabo Verde – African island) perspective. Anahory co-founded the art collective XU:Collective with Andreia Moassab and Salif Diallo Silva to interrogate issues of environmental and social justice outside of an academic setting. She also practises independently and her radical, interdisciplinary projects examine questions of urban dynamics. In 2017 Anahory was one of six artists invited to participate in the exhibition 'A Glimmer of Freedom', which aimed to address themes of memory and identity. Anahory's approach to the brief was to create two installations, one of which was located beyond the walls of a former prison camp in Tarrafal, Cabo Verde,

Fig. 2 'Volumes of EMPTY Memories', installation, Tarrafal, Cabo Verde, 2017. 2,000m of fluorescent fishing line enclose the perimeter of the fourth volume, entitled 'Linha Vida' ('Life Line'), located inside the latrines of the former prison camp.

allowing it to directly engage inhabitants of the dilapidated quarters of the former administrative staff of the prison in ongoing discussions regarding the renovation and memorialisation of this site. The first piece, 'Pedestals of [X]clusion', proposed alternative narratives of the museological project by appropriating existing incomplete pedestals that were destined to host information placards about the former use of the buildings while ignoring the current living inhabitants of the site. The intervention installed placards made of mirrors, blackboards and mappings on plywood bases that directly referenced the current residents.

The mirrored placards aimed to implicate the visitors of the exhibition in the voyeuristic act of visiting the site. The blackboard placards, with messages in chalk, highlighted the temporality of written words in the narration of history.

The second installation, 'Volumes of EMPTY Memories', located inside the walled camp, questioned the (im)possibilities of memory reconstruction of spaces of violence in museological projects. The installation used the dimensional reference of the solitary confinement cell of the camp, known as Holandinha – a miniscule space of approximately 90cm width, 190cm length and 180cm height. It consisted of four volumes of exactly the same dimensions as the cell, filled or enclosed with the essential material needs for daily survival, that are used by the families currently living in the camp grounds. This material narrative served to 'interconnect narratives of violence along temporal and spatial axes'.

Embedding art and curatorial practice within an architectural sensibility, Anahory's work crosses disciplinary boundaries. In her own words, it engages with the 'fugitive edge and radical margin of African worlds – the continent, its islands, diaspora and imaginaries'.

Fig. 3 'Errant Praxis' project initiated by Patti Anahory – ongoing.

errant_praxis
is a happening, a performance, an experiment, a digital gathering and an active space to interrogate our complex modes of practicing in/from and for the African world – the continent, its islands, diaspora and imaginaries...

reframing architectural practices + narratives in African worlds:

it is an unfinished manifesto, a manifesto in a multiple process of making and unmaking, stating and retracting, a/un-manifesto...

"African cities need more carefully considered architecture that can express a vision for the future."

OLAYINKA DOSEKUN-ADJEI

Fig. 1 Render of the Institute of Contemporary African Art and Film, Ilorin, Kwara State, Nigeria, 2024. View of the building situated at a corner intersection within the city of Ilorin.

Creative Director of Studio Contra, Olayinka Dosekun-Adjei, looks to the future with designs that evoke a strong sense of being rooted in culture and environment. The practice was set up in partnership with her husband Jeffrey Adjei, with offices in Lagos and a foothold in London.

One of the challenges for architectural practice in Nigeria is the legacy of colonial rule and ongoing political and economic upheaval. For Dosekun-Adjei, recognising the profound psychological impact of the built environment on a rapidly urbanising population has led her to create architecture which embodies and expresses a vision for an African future.

Dosekun-Adjei's early experience was broad-ranging and cosmopolitan – from the UK to the USA and Germany before settling in Nigeria. Her professional direction was influenced by a course on Design through Engineering, taught by Hanif Kara, at the Harvard Graduate Design School. 'It reorganised my understanding of the hierarchies between architecture and engineering. It is not always architects who challenge and push engineers, sometimes it can happen the other way around!' The outcome is a practice that seeks to test new materials and methods, and to integrate structural logics and more sustainable practices.

Dosekun-Adjei observes, 'Our instinct is to bridge the historical and cultural norms of the context and the processes and language of contemporary architecture; we consider beauty and local craft.' She continues, 'Equally important for our region are buildings that are highly robust, flexible, low-energy and responsive to local climate conditions.' Dosekun-Adjei talks about the challenges of connecting the low-tech and low-skilled labour of the construction environment of sub-Saharan Africa to ambitious, and sometimes technically difficult, designs. 'We have to find ways of doing things that are affordable, simple to build, robust and low maintenance without compromising design aspirations.'

Fig. 2 Concept section drawing, Institute of Contemporary African Art and Film, Ilorin, Kwara State, Nigeria (completion date 2023). Section showing the proportions below the undulating roof profile, designed for light and air to reach interior spaces.

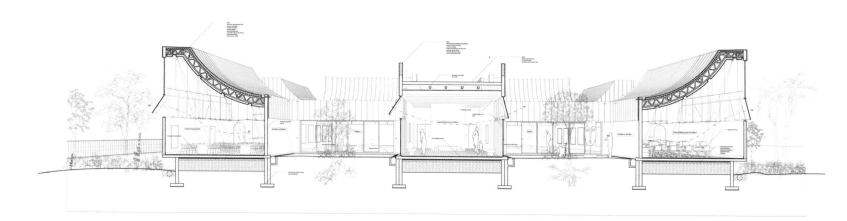

Studio Contra has developed a portfolio of work across sectors – cultural, retail, office, domestic and leisure. By far their largest commission to date is their work on the Institute of Contemporary African Art and Film. This project is allowing them to manifest their vision for the African city. An ongoing project, it forms part of a broader regeneration project creating a new creative economy for the city of Ilorin. The brief provided a chance for Studio Contra to explore how a building can be both iconic and unimposing – often mutually exclusive aims. The design provides a multi functional space with galleries and production facilities, which is distinctive on the streetscape and designed to invite the public in. Playing with some of the Islamic architecture found in north and central Nigeria, the elliptical arches of the entrance are inverted to form a distinctive roof profile that also assists with interior airflow.

Studio Contra does not always work alone. Working across industry groups and with international architects allows them to engage with projects of a greater scale and complexity. They have collaborated with Alison Brooks Architects as shortlisted finalists for a new building in central London for the London School of Economics. They also work with other kinds of designers, notably Nigerian furniture and industrial designer Nifemi Bello.

Looking ahead, Dosekun-Adjei emphasises the climate agenda. 'Environmental building standards have not yet been meaningfully adopted, properly incentivised or written into building codes in many African cities,' she explains. 'The impetus for this sort of thinking will first have to come from clients, end users and architects like ourselves; we owe a responsibility to future generations to take this seriously.'

Fig. 3 Retro Africa Gallery, Abuja, Nigeria, 2018. Retro Africa is an art platform and community. The design repurposes an old building for use as a contemporary art gallery, with a central void in the upper gallery exposed to reveal the timber roof trusses.

"Design can be incredibly dangerous – we use it as something that does not have a conscience or moral implications, but then you can do an incredible amount of good with it."

MARIAM ISSOUFOU

Fig. 1 Library and community centre in Dandaji, Niger, 2019. Working in collaboration with Studio Chahar, a mosque was converted in to a community centre.

Mariam Issoufou is an architect who is drawing global attention to Niger with her brand of locally focused, materially sensitive architecture. She founded architecture and research studio atelier masōmī, now Mariam Issoufou Architects. Splitting her time between Niger and the USA, where she completed her Master's degree in Architecture at the University of Washington, her studio is based, and entirely rooted, in the West African country.

Whether converting a mosque into a community centre in Dandaji, building a colourful market in the same village or her upcoming, high-profile Niamey Cultural Centre in the country's capital, Issoufou aims to create architecture that is appropriate for its context. 'I want to create a universal way of working that produces completely different results depending on where you are,' she tells us. 'It is attention to the local conditions – what's available locally, what the local skills are and what the local history is – then having this process that can happen everywhere.'

Issoufou was a latecomer to architecture despite aspiring to be an architect since she was a teenager. 'Growing up in sub-Saharan Africa I didn't know anybody who was an architect,' she recalls.

But she believes that the time spent away from architecture allowed her to look at the built environment of Niger and its capital, which she describes as a 'pure product of colonisation, created for exploitation', much more critically. Observing the impact architecture can have was the trigger that made Issoufou realise that as an architect she could have a hugely positive impact. 'I wanted everything about it to be local,' she explains. 'I did not want to work on projects with eyes that came from outside of the place.'

Fig. 2 The market in the village of Dandaji, Niger, 2019. The Dandaji market provides 52 enclosed stalls and colourful round canopies that shade each individual slot.

A project that clearly demonstrates this commitment to localism is the regional market in Dandaji, where the forms of the previous market were replicated in new materials to create a functional, but visually vibrant and modern, new facility. Arranged around an old and locally significant tree, the market stalls were made from a specially developed compressed earth brick and sheltered by colourful recycled metal canopies that provide shade.

'The challenge for me was how do you take something like that and create something that is just incredibly contemporary and modern, but without making people feel like they don't know how to use it – making them feel inadequate,' says Issoufou. 'This is a line that we tread very lightly in all of our projects.' Commercially the project has been a great success drawing traffic and business to the village, as well as becoming a regional tourist attraction, but for her the most satisfying element was that the users fully understood the project's aims.

Issoufou hopes for more projects that challenge her and allow her to figure out what those using it require. Her studio's name, masōmī, translates as 'the inception', and at the inception of all of her work is research into the local environment. 'I just want to continue working in a huge variety of topologies because what interests me is the process and the local conditions, understanding them and analysing them, then figuring out what can be done with them.'

Fig. 3 Before (left) and after (right): The market in the village of Dandaji, Niger, 2019.

"Architecture permits me to open my mind."

MÉLISSA KACOUTIÉ

Fig. 1 Baazar Bar and Restaurant, Abidjan, Ivory Coast, 2019. The minimalist design uses the repetition of simple elements to create complex motifs that become part of the identity of the bar.

Ivorian architect Mélissa Kacoutié studied architecture at the École Spéciale d'Architecture in Paris, where she lived for six years, before returning to Abidjan to work. While the opportunities for an architect practising in France may well be broad, Kacoutié tells us that she believed her 'impact would be small'. In contrast, she suggests, in Ivory Coast she would have the chance to make her mark. 'We have a huge amount of construction, and we are a young country, so you can change people's point of view and really make an impact,' she explains.

'In Ivory Coast, people like what I propose; it is different from the norm.'
After working at Ivorian studios Archi Concept and Koffi Diabaté, Kacoutié decided that she needed to be independent. In 2016 she established Jeannette Studio, initially working out of her apartment. Since then, the studio has expanded to take on more people and has created a number of villas and small-scale interventions in Abidjan, each conceived to have an impact on their surrounding communities. 'With my architecture I am carrying out acupuncture in the city,' says

Kacoutié. 'I don't like big things. I like the little things and feel they can add a huge amount of energy to the places around them.'
With a minimalistic style that is embedded in traditional motifs, Kacoutié creates colourful buildings that connect with people, inviting them to engage. A recent example is a bright yellow juice bar that neatly expresses her ethos. 'This little shop represents the kind of architecture that I want to do,' she says. 'It provokes a reaction and that's the point. It is very yellow – you just need to enter it.' As with all her projects, Kacoutié hopes that the

Fig. 2 Sum Good Juice, Abidjan, Ivory Coast, 2022. The yellow facade is designed to provoke a reaction and invite passers-by to engage.

juice bar will incite a reaction from locals and passers-by. 'You need to have some emotion when you see architecture,' she explains, 'even if it's not a good emotion, it just has to talk to you.'

Looking ahead, Kacoutié is aiming to develop buildings that have a modern aesthetic rooted in the culture of the Ivory Coast, with expressive facades like at her Baazar Bar and Restaurant project. Formed like traditional graphics, these facades utilise the repetition of simple elements to create complex motifs – a strategy that is instantly familiar yet visually exciting. These spaces 'are created with love and emotion, but outside I put something that I call the ID, something very graphic', says Kacoutié. 'I create my own graphics, my own way to see Africa, my own way to see symbolism, and I put it on my facades.' A facade of terracotta bricks became the identity card element for her renovation of the Danga Pavilion, a private residence in the city of Abidjan. Kacoutié continues, 'In Ivory Coast, and in many parts of Africa, we have this way of seeing things instinctively – we can call it "technology" because it is a mix of technique and symbolism.'

Kacoutié aims to spread this aesthetic internationally 'as a way to communicate it in every part of the world'. 'I want my work to be perceived as a way to show African technology,' she says. 'This different kind of assemblage that I use in my projects is an expression of a type of African cultural wealth.'

Fig. 3 Danga Pavilion, Abidjan, Ivory Coast, 2021. This 1970s house had lost its brilliance and the renovation restored its character, including a facade in terracotta brick.

"I have learnt to be creative in the confines of scarcity."

TOSIN OSHINOWO

Fig. 1 Ngarannam Village (United Nations Development Programme), Borno State, Nigeria, 2022. View of the primary school.

Tosin Oshinowo is principal architect at Lagos-based cmDesign Atelier (cmD+A), with an interest in socially responsive approaches in architecture, design and urbanism. A polymath, Oshinowo's awards reflect the breadth of her creativity – from the 'Ilé-Ilà' furniture line (House of Lines in Yoruba), through photography and public art to festival curation.

Oshinowo is equally known for the leading role she plays in the cultural landscape. She is a founding member of the African Alliance for New Design – a think-tank exploring the value of design for a new generation of creatives on the continent. Her writing and speaking address issues of public space and African identity in a modern context.

Educated in the UK, with RIBA membership, Oshinowo then returned to her home city, Lagos. 'Coming from a very sheltered upbringing in Nigeria to the UK, culturally, I was very lost. Then coming back, having left Lagos at 16, I found I was not Nigerian either.' Practice-wise, she started without the benefit of professional networks established during her training. 'There were a lot of things that I had to pick up, so it was good that I worked at a local practice, because I learned those things there – I had a cushion.'

It's evident there has been some frustration in Oshinowo's early career trajectory, which has not been helped by local challenges, such as widespread, out-of-date and unambitious building practices. 'We don't build in steel here, we still build in the materials of post-Second World War – concrete and reinforced iron rods, which are readily available and exceptionally cheap. Building finishes are added with little attention to design quality.'

Nevertheless, projects such as the Coral Pavilion in Lagos, completed in 2021, challenge this approach. This is a building that plays with the thresholds between inside and out, taking advantage of

Fig. 2 Ngarannam Village, (United Nations Development Programme), Borno State, Nigeria, 2022. One of 500 new homes.

directional winds coming in off the sea to cool the habitable spaces. Similarly, Rensource – a retrofit utilising a defunct bank to house an alternative energy company – signals Nigeria's shift away from oil production to more sustainable alternatives. In 2022 Oshinowo designed the Ngarannam Village in the Borno state of north west Nigeria to replace a settlement destroyed by Boko Haram – an Islamist militant organisation based in the north east of the country. Instigated by the Nigerian government and the United Nations Development Programme (UNDP) in order to coax people back to the region, the village accommodates a number of key community spaces at the centre of a radial layout, including a marketplace, health clinic and primary school, as well as 500 homes that occupy the periphery.

In conversation with the incoming residents, the scheme has been developed according to the community's specific needs and requests. 'It was very important that the design solutions were local and sustainable. Community engagement and researching existing housing solutions was part of the process, as well as exploring traditional materials that could be used in a contemporary approach.' For Oshinowo this project represents a shift in the type of commission she usually receives, re-articulating her role as architect/facilitator, voicing the community's own vision for their future home. 'My objective was to foster development for the community, provide a sustainable platform for economic growth and, most importantly, help the people recover with dignity by providing homes that give members of the community cause to be house-proud.'

The Ngarannam Village project seems to have catalysed Oshinowo's career. Recently chosen to curate the second Sharjah Architecture Biennale, 2023, focusing on 'sustainable architecture, urbanism and infrastructure', Oshinowo now has a platform from which to voice the hopes and ambitions of Nigerian communities on a global stage.

Fig. 3 Coral Pavilion, Lagos, Nigeria, 2021. View of the interior and bespoke table designed for the project.

AMEI

RICAS

CARMEN DÍAZ ACOSTA AND CELIA GARCÍA ACOSTA

Fig. 1 La Magnolia, Topes de Collantes, Sierra del Escambray, Sancti Spíritus, Cuba, 2019. The proposal is inserted in the characteristic topography of Topes de Collantes without 'attacking' or imposing upon it.

Carmen Díaz Acosta and Celia García Acosta are Cuban architects who are deeply invested in the idea of architecture as a collective endeavour. Working in collaboration with their colleagues at Ad Urbis (based in Havana, Cuba), as well as independently, both in practice and in architectural education, the pair are 'passionate about architecture and the city'. For both, these differing contexts suggest a common approach that is underpinned by research. 'All projects are different', says García Acosta, 'so our work process begins with the identification of the real conditions of each scenario and, based on these particularities, we prepare its *mise en place*. In this way we are enriching our

knowledge and our "tool locker" – always taking into account the binary of ethics versus aesthetics.'
Receiving a conventional architectural education, filtered through the lens of European and North American architectural role models, García Acosta and Díaz Acosta highlight the positive aspects of their learning. 'Architects, by training, are quite versatile,' suggests Díaz Acosta. 'The years in school provided an incredible foundation on which to build other things and continue to gain experience and knowledge.' Nevertheless, it wasn't until they were exposed to the challenges of professional practice – in particular managing clients

and sites – that they were able to evolve their architectural identities. For García Acosta this process was complex and two-fold. 'There was little practical preparation that I brought from the academy and that forced me to learn about the different trades involved and their production chain,' she states. Further, she was having to make her way 'in a world colonised by men, where the client, the supplier of materials, the bricklayers, plumbers, electricians, were all men and they did not easily accept a woman, much less a young woman, telling them how, where and what to do'.
Two projects that exemplify the collective approach of Ad Urbis are 'Meeting Space

Fig. 2 'Meeting Space for Urban Pedagogy', Calzada Street corner to F Street, Vedado, Havana, Cuba, 2022. Space located in front of the restrooms and over the septic tank where the waste from the restrooms and kitchen is collected.

for Urban Pedagogy' and La Magnolia. The former project is an ongoing urban intervention in the Vedado neighbourhood of Havana, using strategies of co-design with the local community in order to facilitate a transformation of the urban environment. According to García Acosta, the project implements concepts related to the principles that they defend through their work – to revalue, reuse, resignify and renaturalise urban and citizen space.

La Magnolia is a project designed to forge a new relationship between architecture and the land. It is situated in the coffee-growing, mountainous region of Cuba, which for many years has seen the steady decline of the indigenous forest habitat due to the deliberate planting of fast-growing, foreign species. Recently, the native species, *Magnolia cubensis*, has been replanted and, in order to support further reforestation, the architects were asked to renovate an existing dwelling on the site. The design makes use of local building materials and traditions in order to craft a structure that is at home in its surroundings.

Ad Urbis promote a way of using architecture as an instrument of change. For Díaz Acosta, García Acosta and their collaborators this approach has emerged from the specific constraints of architectural practice in Cuba. García Acosta explains, 'The private and independent practice of architecture was repealed in Cuba in the 1960s and even at the time of writing there is no regulatory legal framework that allows us to have a "legal personality". However, we have been able to adapt to our times and we know what we are not. We are not theoretical academics, we are not artists, or builders, or companies. We are a group of people who, as a collective, are passionate about architecture and the city and we work together for it.'

Fig. 3 'Meeting Space for Urban Pedagogy', Calzada Street corner to F Street, Vedado, Havana, Cuba, 2022. Children's play area.

PATRICIA E. GREEN

"My work process is relational and cross-cutting. I hinge my work on historic precedence with a people-centred, culturally relevant, pioneering approach."

Fig. 1 University Bookshop, University of the West Indies, Mona Campus, Jamaica, 2008.

A graduate of the Architectural Association in London, Patricia E. Green is a pioneering architect whose education and long career intersect with such globally recognised figures as Bob Marley and Zaha Hadid. A student trip to Barcelona in 1973, and in particular Ricardo Bofill's La Fabrica – a repurposed cement factory – opened Green's eyes to the architectural possibilities in adaptively reusing redundant and abandoned buildings.

Green returned to Jamaica in 1980 to practise as a government architect and 'help rebuild a nation', working on a number of restoration projects including Headquarters House – a former parliament building. During this time she was also Head of School at the Caribbean School of Architecture, working alongside architect Patrick Stanigar. This was a challenging period for Green who faced considerable obstacles in her day-to-day work because of her gender, including lobbying for permission to drive to rural site meetings, instead of being escorted there. She also recalls the time when she was 'denied the entitled government house assigned with my upcoming appointment as Chief Architect (I would have been the first woman)', resigning her post and starting her own private practice. Green was also told by colleagues to 'hide my love for architectural heritage and the historic urban environment in order to receive work', as well as being told that 'men were entitled to [architectural] contracts instead because they had wives and children to support'.

In 1985 Green was approached by Rita Marley, the widow of the late Bob Marley, about what to do with the house she had inherited from him. It was Green's idea to convert this into a museum celebrating both the life and music of Marley himself, as well as the architectural heritage of this suburban vernacular building. Conducting the historic preservation of the house, Green worked alongside sociologist Dr Eleanor Wint, Marley's creative director Neville Garrick and Rita Marley to bring the house into the public domain. The house has since been replicated by Universal Studios who approached Green to authenticate it.

Another project that illustrates Green's approach to remodelling existing buildings is the University Bookshop at the University of the West Indies, Mona Campus, Jamaica. Expanding an existing single-storey unit into the landscape beyond, the project is set against the backdrop of the Blue Mountains and sits next to the historic monument fragment of a 1786 aqueduct. 'My design concept was to push and pull the expansion as I straddled the existing building,' says Green. 'In so doing I extended the building outward into its natural and historic built environment, simultaneously bringing the environment into the building. I wanted the building to be bold because it had extra structural loading for book storage and a future third storey. I finished with vivid colours to reinforce its prominence on the main entrance thoroughfare of the university, which at the time generated much debate on a campus where most buildings were white and/or pastel shades of cream.'

Green's focus on the historic preservation of buildings, especially in Jamaica whose own architectural heritage is only now being acknowledged, has put her at the forefront of a movement where the architecture of colonisation is reclaimed. Although currently the only person in Jamaica with a PhD in Architecture, Green can foresee a future where this heritage is more widely interrogated, recognising the 'global contributions of Jamaica and the Caribbean' to architectural history, theory and practice.

Fig. 2 Bob Marley Museum, Kingston, Jamaica, 2023. Green chats with Manager Lecia-Gaye Taylor about Jamaica Reggae Month.

"Where I can, I prefer to let the materials express themselves."

LAVINA LIBURD

Fig. 1 Bayhouse Villa, Crook Bay, Virgin Gorda, British Virgin Islands, 2008. A fusion of classic Caribbean architecture and contemporary tropical design. Traditional louvred windows provide natural ventilation and shade, while rooftop louvres promote passive cooling, reducing the reliance on air-conditioning.

A native of Saint Kitts and Nevis, Lavina Liburd is principal of TigerQi Architecture, which she established in 2013. Having worked in the USA and the Caribbean, she is experienced in a broad range of building typologies and has developed an approach that is formally expressive and responsive to the natural environment. She completed her undergraduate degree at the University of California, Berkeley and is proud to have earned her professional degree from Florida Agricultural and Mechanical University (FAMU), which is a historically Black college and has become a pre-eminent institution in the USA for educating female architects of colour.

Once she established her studio, Liburd, like many of her contemporaries, experienced some misogyny and prejudice. She tells us, 'I was a bit too starry-eyed and confident in my talent and saw opportunity and freedom rather than challenges. I didn't fully realise that being a woman would be an issue until a couple of contractors turned their backs on me in front of my clients and totally ignored my instructions.' It is interesting therefore that Liburd also highlights the positive role that some contractors have played in developing her practice: 'I've found strong allies in specific contractors I've worked with and for. Some of my most interesting projects

have come to me through contractors who have built a relationship with the client and realised they're looking for something special.' Liburd also points to significant role models who have supported her – from mentors such as Mui Ho at the Organisation of Women Architects and Design Professionals in the San Francisco Bay Area, and LaVerne Wells-Bowie at FAMU, to various colleagues in practice. Her project Bayhouse Villa was completed while she was a Project Architect at OBM International. Located on the British Virgin Islands (BVI), this is a building that draws inspiration from its regional architectural history and fuses this with what Liburd

Fig. 2 Brandywine Estate Restaurant, Brandywine Bay, Tortola, British Virgin Islands, 2018. The design covered the open terrace and added protected seating. The parabolic plan of the terrace did not lend itself to a traditional roof shape.

describes as 'contemporary tropical design'. Utilising traditional louvres to facilitate natural ventilation, large openings frame views of the sea and trellised concrete canopies provide shade, creating complex shadows that shift and change through the day.

Another project illustrating Liburd's approach to making architecture that sits comfortably within its natural habitat is her remodelling of the Brandywine Estate Restaurant. Moving away from the conventions of traditional wood-framed roof construction, Liburd used an organic structure for the roof. She tells us, 'We set up an asymmetrical, leaf-shaped roof structure, which echoes the floor plan of the terrace, but is segmented rather than curved.' Moving forward, Liburd anticipates an 'increasing emphasis' on what she terms 'healthy buildings' in the Caribbean. 'The conversation around sick buildings is now starting to happen here. Multi storey office buildings in the BVI are a fairly recent development (within the last 20 years) and we are starting to see the results of uninformed building practices in terms of mould and persons with severe allergies and lung infections.' While domestic architecture is more readily able to achieve the 'Nine Foundations of a Healthy Building', Liburd believes that it is in the design and construction of commercial and public buildings where the most significant environmental gains can be made.

Liburd's design for the Eslyn Henley Richiez Learning Centre – an all-age special educational needs (SEN) school in the BVI – includes sensory and therapy rooms, as well as indoor and outdoor trampolines for rebound therapy, and outdoor classrooms. While the form and organisational layout of the proposal is inspired by the local species of iguana, the ethos of the building captures Liburd's overarching concern for making architecture that sustains and improves the health and well-being of its users.

Fig. 3 Eslyn Henley Richiez Learning Centre, All-Age Special Educational Needs (SEN) School, John's Hole, Tortola, British Virgin Islands, 2023. The design includes sensory and therapy rooms, trampolines for rebound therapy, outdoor classrooms and hoists to aid in transferring non-ambulatory students.

"A country's architecture is a reflection of its culture."

LAURA NARAYANSINGH

Fig. 1 65 Gallus Street, Woodbrook, Trinidad and Tobago, 2014. The rehabilitation of a 20th-century gingerbread home on a former sugar estate.

Trinidadian architect Laura Narayansingh aims to make architecture 'more accessible to the average Trinidadian' through her buildings, advocacy and Carnival costume designs. 'With regard to my own work, that means making myself more accessible,' she tells us. 'For me, it's critical that architects know the people – society – we are designing for, and that they, in turn, know us.'
Narayansingh studied architecture at the University of Miami, Florida, before returning to Port of Spain in Trinidad. Here she started working for ACLA Architecture – the country's oldest Indigenous architecture studio – where, eight years later, she is now a director. She explains that she always intended to practise in Trinidad and Tobago as she believes she can improve the urban fabric and change people's perception of architecture. Unlike many of its Caribbean neighbours, Trinidad and Tobago's economy is industrial, built on oil and natural gas as opposed to tourism. The post-colonial economy developed rapidly to reflect the rewards of the hydrocarbon sector and, coupled with ethnic diversity, has led to a unique and complex urban fabric. As Narayansingh describes it, 'as unorthodox as it is chaotic, with most buildings created without any guidance from architects'. She explains, 'I felt it was my duty to help Trinidadians build a relationship with architecture,' not least because 'access to architects has, throughout our history, been limited to the wealthy and educated minority'.

Despite 'theory proving far more simple than practice', Narayansingh is now working on a series of projects that aim to consider what contemporary architecture in the

Fig. 2 The Bush House, Petit Valley, Trinidad and Tobago, 2020. The 92m² home was designed to embrace the principles of traditional vernacular architecture in a contemporary, post-colonial environment.

country should be. With the oil boom over, the nation's economy needs to diversify and transition and ACLA architecture are, as she puts it, 'literally and figuratively doing the groundwork'. Narayansingh's work has focused on adapting and reusing existing structures by refurbishing colonial-era homes, revamping coastal hotels and renovating beachfront houses. She also designed her own home – Bush House – as 'a personal search for an Indigenous culture through architecture'. The design for the two-bedroom dwelling is largely a result of three culturally tied elements: intelligent burglar proofing, colonial-informed arches and 'shadow boxes' (passive cooling planters).

Alongside her work as an architect, Narayansingh designs and sells costumes for Carnival, which she describes as 'a language we speak across our diverse backgrounds'. Along with broadening the reach of her work, she believes that the annual event, which is so ingrained in the culture of the island, impacts how she views architecture. 'I've integrated what I learned about how we consume both culture and commodities to expand the discourse on our built environment,' she says. 'During Carnival, we display our inner *cosquelle*; that is, our garishness, our relentless colourfulness. What would happen if we decided to embrace our *cosquellity*, appropriating it year-round and in all facets of design? Perhaps then

we'd free ourselves to live the magical spirit of Trinidad Carnival endlessly.'
Narayansingh is one of a small number of women in senior positions at major architecture studios in Trinidad and Tobago. She aims to use this for her benefit and leverage her position at ACLA Architecture. 'Often the only woman in the room, I position myself to ensure that my womanhood is perceived as a sign of strength, which has, in turn, cultivated my hyper-vigilant approach to my practice,' she says. 'It drives me to work smarter, push the envelope and to realise and rely on the strength of other women around me.' She is using her position to develop the firm towards a more diverse portfolio, inclusive staff culture and better – more accessible – customer service.

Fig. 3 Trinidad and Tobago Carnival costume, 'Femme Fatale', Port-of-Spain, Trinidad and Tobago, 2022. Designed for Bliss Carnival's 2023 presentation, themed 'WILD'.

"Architecture is underappreciated, undervalued and not truly understood."

VICKI TELFORD

Fig. 1 Maria Holder Diabetes Centre for the Caribbean, Jackmans, Barbados, 2012.

Barbadian architect Vicki Telford aims to create buildings that are 'what the client asked for but look and function better than they could ever have imagined'. She has run her studio, Vicki Telford Architects, in Bridgetown, for the past 20 years and has the honour of being the first and only female president of the Barbados Institute of Architects (BIA) in its 54-year history. Telford studied architecture at Howard University in Washington DC, before returning to Barbados. She worked as an architect for seven years before establishing Vicki Telford Architects in 2003. This was a momentous year: she also began the first of her two terms (2003–5 and 2018–19) as president of the BIA, when the Barbados Architects Registration Act was finalised. 'Our institute and profession were ready for it and I enjoyed the post as there was a big contribution to make to the profession and industry at the time,' Telford tells us. 'The Barbados Registration Act was a long time in coming – my predecessors worked hard and I was keen to continue the cause and get the act passed during my presidency. I think it apt that diversity was added to the line of presidents.'

Over her career, Telford's multidisciplinary studio has designed numerous homes, commercial spaces and hotels across the Caribbean island using a 'tropical-modern approach' that aims to merge inside and outside spaces. The key driver in all her designs is translating the needs of the client into reality. 'I really enjoy taking a client's brief and dream, internalising it and creatively designing a product that becomes their desired and cherished reality,' she says. 'I incorporate tropical features with passive cooling and energy-saving materials and fittings into my designs. This goes a long way towards the look and feel of the project, but also the well-being of the client and end user.' Along with the South Gap Hotel, which she describes as 'a feel-good project', it is the Maria Holder Diabetes Centre for the Caribbean that best demonstrates Telford's architectural ethos. During the early stages, she spent hours meeting with the client and their team to understand the disease, the needs of the patients and how the different services, spaces and equipment was to help the end user in an open, modern design. 'Due to my keen awareness of the disease and how it is treated, I was able to create spaces that could multifunction and provide multiple treatments in reduced square footage when the budget was cut.'

Looking to the future, Telford hopes that architects in Barbados and around the world 'gain more recognition and respect'. The problem, she feels, is that architecture is misunderstood. 'Many believe it is only needed for the rich and so many clients go straight to the contractor. They do not understand what value an architect brings and the vast and varied contribution made from site selection, design, financial advice, sociology studies, psychology of the end user, construction, materials, rental potential, market trends – and so much more!'

Fig. 2 South Gap Hotel, St Lawrence Gap, Oistins, Barbados, 2018.

"I try to understand and help people to develop a dialogue with their project – a platform for them to develop their own lives."

TATIANA BILBAO

Fig. 1 Botanical Garden Laboratories, Culiacán, Sinaloa, Mexico, 2018. The building holds the scientific research centre of the botanical garden and is also the place where plants are cared for.

For Mexican architect Tatiana Bilbao 'architecture is a huge responsibility' and with her socially conscious work she aims to create spaces that will enhance people's lives. 'I was always aware that I had a very big responsibility,' she tells us. 'Architecture is about understanding the position and possibility of human life within a space – asking what is the purpose of this space for human life?'

Bilbao was born and raised in Mexico City and studied at the city's Universidad Iberoamericana Ciudad de México (IBERO)

before setting up her studio, Tatiana Bilbao Estudio, in the city in 2004. 'Everything is Mexico City,' she jokes, and the city has had a huge impact on her approach. 'Wherever you live, it shapes your imagination, your mind and soul,' she explains. 'Mexico City is the best city in the world and it's a very fertile ground because of its very intense and creative energy.'

The granddaughter of the well-known architect Tomás Bilbao Hospitalet, Bilbao 'was always an architect' although she didn't realise it when she was young. It was one of the most tragic moments in Mexico

City's history, the huge 1985 earthquake that ruined much of the city, which shaped her early thinking. Although only 11 at the time, she describes the collapse of a local housing block as 'an image that I will never, ever, ever forget', and it ingrained an understanding of the basic requirements of architecture. 'It marked a moment where I was very conscious of the impact of space on humans,' she says, continuing, 'Architecture functions as a primary necessity, when you make a space you shape a life, you allow it to be nurtured and grow.'

Fig. 2 Aerial view of Casa Ventura, San Pedro Garza García, Monterrey, Mexico, 2013.

With her work, which ranges widely in style and function, she focuses on people's real-life needs. Whether it is the studio's long-running development of Mexico City's botanical gardens, private homes like the distinctive Casa Ventura, "a chapel" on the Ameca pilgrim's route, or prototype social housing projects in Ciudad Acuña and Hidalgo, people are the priority. The houses in Ciudad Acuña, commissioned by the federal government, are part of a wider project the studio have developed following 2,000 interviews exploring housing expectations – a modular housing unit with the goal of reproducing it nationwide. Other projects are bespoke. In all her projects, Bilbao aims to collaborate with her clients and users to develop a project rather than impose her will on them: 'I think, "I know nothing, and I have no right to do this,"' she explains.

According to Bilbao, who has taught widely and is now a Professor at Yale in the USA, this approach is dramatically different from what she was taught at university when 'everybody spoke about proportions, beauty, light and different geometries'.

However, she believes that, in recent years, there has been a marked shift in emphasis within the profession. 'It's hard to think about structural somersaults when there is a complete disconnect from human needs,' she says. 'I am an in-between generation – the one after those that enjoyed exploring these fantastical moves. Things have really shifted towards a much more conscious way of understanding the built environment. Architecture is a social-human thing.'

Fig. 3 Social housing in Ciudad Acuña, Mexico, 2016.

FERNANDA CANALES

"I am interested in a future where
we can see cities designed by women."

Fig. 1 Casa Bruma, Valle de Bravo, Estado de México, Mexico, 2017. Each space is linked to the main patio and opens towards the opposite end, which allows for private views but also for spaces that open up completely to the landscape.

Fernanda Canales is an award-winning architect, curator, teacher and writer, whose work addresses collaboration and place-making. With a PhD in Architecture from Escuela Técnica Superior de Arquitectura de Madrid (ETSAM) and author of *Private Spaces; Shared Structures* (Actar, 2020) and *Architecture in Mexico 1900–2010* (Arquine, 2013), her work has been widely published. 'Books are my allies, a new world to be discovered every second,' she tells us.

Canales has also been a Visiting Professor at the Yale School of Architecture, the Architectural Association in London and the Universidad Iberoamericana Ciudad de México (IBERO) in Mexico City. She says, 'I also understand architectural education as something you find in places that are not only schools. The most important tools have come with time and through the understanding of architecture not as a method but as an intuitive process.'

An engagement with the site is an important part of this process. 'I try to collaborate with the site, my main preoccupation is to create a strong link with the existing conditions and the history of the place.' Canales looks to extract 'the natural essence of the site' – a process facilitated through collaboration with landscape designers, local builders and craftsmen whose specific knowledge offers essential insight into contexts and conditions. Turning to a seminal project, Canales tells

Fig. 2 Terreno House, Valle de Bravo, Mexico, 2018. Entrance hall.

us, 'Casa Bruma is a project that was with me years before having a site and a client. It started with a personal interest in rethinking the historical patios in domestic architecture, influenced by Luis Barragan's architecture, haciendas and convents, and an interest in collective dwelling that can retain privacy within shared structures.'

The project took on new meanings with the commission of the client, the conditions of the site and collaboration with architect Claudia Rodriguez, who designed the site's masterplan and shared Canales' profound knowledge of landscape design. Says Canales, 'The process encompassed both the specificity of the local conditions and responded to broader questions such as the relationships between the public and private spheres.'

Canales' influences include a century-old text by Paulette Bernège, *If Women Made Houses*, which challenges the relationship between architecture and inhabitants, and issues of labour and gender inequality. Canales thinks architecture will need to be completely rethought if we are to have the houses and cities we need. She explains what, for her, this looks like: 'I am interested in a future where we can see cities designed by women and we can lessen the oppositions between the public and the private realms, between owners and dispossessed, the rural and the urban, and resources and waste.'

Fig. 3 Terreno House, Valle de Bravo, Mexico, 2018. East facade showing bedrooms.

"Architecture is like a network, or a constellation, of people doing things."

FRIDA ESCOBEDO

Based in Mexico City, Frida Escobedo is principal and founder of an architecture and design studio whose work impacts internationally, beyond built projects, through teaching and commissions for biennales. Escobedo's training and breadth of experience has expanded her sense of what architecture could be. 'When you think about yourself as an architect who is limited to being specialised in one area – perhaps residential or hospitality – it becomes too transactional.' Instead, she has come to relish the 'possibility of thinking about space

in different ways; so, I can be designing an object or writing a text, and I was still constructing space.'

Like many architects, Escobedo's practice addresses the social dimension of architecture. 'This idea of the architect as this guy who is drawing on his table and bright ideas appear – I don't think that's true at all.' For Escobedo architecture is fundamentally a collaboration between many different participants and agencies.

A point of departure to other practices might be the way that she positions this work within

a theoretical framework, especially the early-20th-century philosophy of Henri Bergson, and his concept of 'social time'. 'I think about space, not just in terms of dimensions and materials, or shapes,' says Escobedo, 'but in terms of what happens in space as well as the tension between individuals and the distance between individuals.'

This thinking has been realised in conceptual works such as the El Eco Pavilion (2010), 'Civic Stage' at the 2013 Lisbon Architecture Triennial and 'Estaciones' presented at the 2017 Biennale d'Architecture d'Orléans. In

Fig. 2 Mar Tirreno 86, Mexico City, Mexico, 2016–19. Aerial view of the courtyard.

these, she explores how form can be explored and manipulated.

In her built work, this ethos can also be seen in projects such as La Tallera (the Workshop, 2012) and in Mar Tirreno, a residential scheme in a middle-class neighbourhood in Mexico City. This scheme captures a moment of transformation where gentrification, which typically has an economic agenda, is reimagined as regeneration and is more socially sensitive.

'Developers in Mexico are voracious,' she tells us, 'they want more and more square metres and often work on a copy-and-paste basis.' In this project, however, the zoning allowed for nine apartments. A typical approach to layout would have been 'to have open spaces – balconies – on the perimeter, because that gives you a very compact, very easy scheme'. But, she explains, 'we didn't want to do that, because it just becomes exterior storage space.' And, the orientation to the street would mean that, 'you would just want to have your curtains closed all the time'. Instead, the project created nine townhouses with their kitchens looking onto a courtyard that extends the house; an interior layout inspired by the Mexican patio house. 'Rather than looking outside, you would be looking inside.' Laid out in a checkerboard scheme, inhabitants never actually overlook their neighbours. 'That allows you to be very open, so you can see your children playing on the courtyard, and you can have the door open.' After the experience of lockdown during the Coronavirus pandemic and looking beyond, Escobedo suggests it is the right time to propose more projects with a sense of community like this.

Fig. 3 Mar Tirreno 86, Mexico City, Mexico, 2016–19. Kitchen and interior patio.

"I see architecture as something that is always open, and that is constantly changed through interaction."

GABRIELA ETCHEGARAY

Fig. 1 Guayacan Pavilion, Casa Wabi, Puerto Escondido, Oaxaca, Mexico, 2022. The Guayacan nursery following a few years of vegetation growth.

Gabriela Etchegaray is an architect, curator and researcher based in Mexico City and New York. Her work is interdisciplinary – from built projects to installation – and is underpinned by research that focuses on art, geography and architecture. It was Etchegaray's education that proved a point of departure from the traditional idea of architecture as a physical construct. The 'Critical Curatorial' Master's she studied in New York expanded her knowledge, 'to see architecture through different skills'. When Etchegaray co-founded Ambrosi Etchegaray with Jorge Ambrosi in 2011, the interdisciplinary approach informed the collaboration. 'Jorge is keen on the detail –

everything that makes architecture tangible. I'm more ephemeral. Sometimes I feel that I'm nurturing the design process,' she tells us. With work ranging from housing to cultural projects, the practice was the recipient of the 2015 Architectural League of New York, Emerging Voices. In her own right, Etchegaray received the Moira Gemmill Prize for Emerging Architecture 2016 and was appointed curator of the Mexican Pavilion for the Venice Architecture Biennale in 2018.
In the Mexican context, architectural practice is not as highly regulated as it is in other countries. Etchegaray believes this fosters greater collaboration between the different

parties involved. It also creates a lack of accountability. 'Because architects are not the ones signing off the construction, we can get detached from taking responsibility, thus limiting architecture to a field of aesthetics,' explains Etchegaray. Further, she believes that architectural practices should design to address social conflict or ecological urgencies like earthquakes. 'If you're not aware of specific realities during the process of design or research, there's a possibility for things to be even more biased.'
Ambrosi Etchegaray maintain control of their projects by overseeing the whole process, 'so that if we need to rethink something

Fig. 2 Section drawing of Guayacan Pavilion, Casa Wabi, Puerto Escondido, Oaxaca, Mexico, 2018. Representation of the section, showing the dislocation from ground and plant beds.

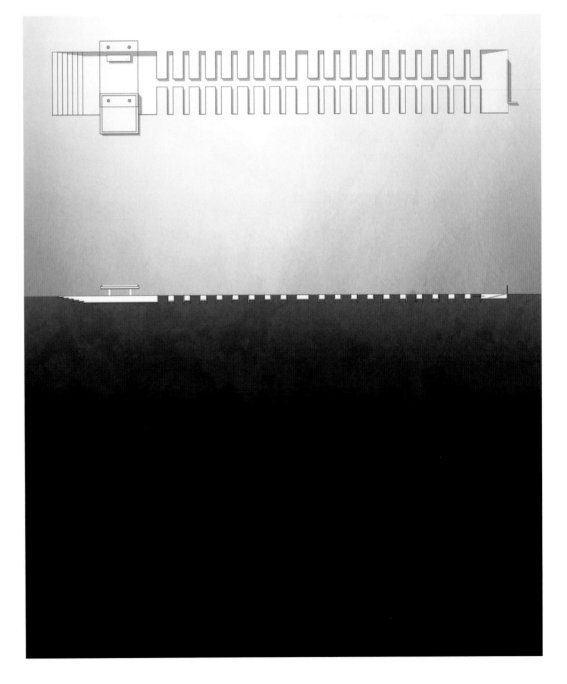

during the process – from an economical decision to a change of material – we are there'. They also keep posing the question of value. Etchegaray tells us their work is often described, in Mexico, as 'raw'. However, she says, this is because 'we work with the notion that less is enough, rethinking luxury as an imported component or something intrinsic', A project that exemplifies the practice's architectural approach is the Guayacan Pavilion, Casa Wabi, Puerto Escondido, Oaxaca, Mexico – a nursery designed to protect an endangered native tree, colloquially known as 'Guayacan'. The building is a below-ground environment, where visitors descend into the space and move through an arrangement of long tables that house the seedlings. The aim is to help people interact with the climate conditions needed for the protection of the species. The pavilion contrasts with other significant buildings in the area, including Tadao Ando's Artist's Retreat and Alberto Kalach's Brick Chimney. Where these are prominent in the landscape, the Guayacan Pavilion is 'more anonymous, merging with the earth'. The project is an excavation rather than build. The combination of retaining walls with the existing earth 'elevates the dust in the atmosphere, tinting the light and concrete'. This is an architecture created out of its context where trees are nurtured in harmony with their surroundings. For Etchegaray and her practice, this project illustrates her working methods – intersecting a deep concern for qualities of atmosphere and materiality with thinking about how people use and inhabit built space. Etchegaray combines practice with teaching in Mexico City and in New York as Adjunct Professor at Columbia GSAPP.

Fig. 3 'Murales del Territorio', exhibited at the Faculty of Architecture, National Autonomous University of Mexico, Mexico City, Mexico, 2019. The exhibition, 'A Place: Mural of a Territory', comprises a succession of voids containing murals and was originally made for the Mexican Pavilion, 'Echoes of a Land', Venice Architecture Biennale 2018.

ROZANA MONTIEL

"My philosophy is for beauty as a basic right."

Based in Mexico City, Rozana Montiel's Estudio de Arquitectura (REA) is winning global accolades for her brand of place-making and design, which offers a social impact that is also mindful of the environment.

Whether she is building public infrastructure, housing, work units, furniture or art installations, her philosophy is democratic – seeking to design inclusive, sustainable spaces. 'School never prepared me to do participative design with communities,' she tells us. 'I have learned to do that slowly in every project.' Her postgraduate training was in Architecture

Theory and Design at the Universitat Politècnica de Catalunya, Barcelona. While this sharpened her critical thinking, she argues, 'Architecture students should be taught sociological tools to understand how to manage and lead community projects.' One of her initial challenges was to gain funding for projects that were true to her interests so Montiel turned to grants from academic and cultural institutions. 'I knew that I did not just want to build, I wanted to do research and build on solid concepts and principles.' Having been in practice now for over a decade, her original research has led to new

prototypes in social housing, while her place-making agenda adds social value to urban infrastructure.

The project Court demonstrates this ethos of intervention for the social good. Here, a simple brief to put a roof on a sports ground, which was exposed to the sun and rain and so unused, was reimagined as a portico/community centre to solve a lack of public space. The programme of the portico includes multipurpose rooms, a library and playground furniture, with an agora shaded by local vegetation. 'The success of the project hinged on it being more than a

Fig. 2 Court, Lagos de Puente Moreno, Veracruz, Mexico, 2016.

roof,' she tells us. When a biologist from the nearby natural reserve set up a herbal medical clinic with a small botanical garden to teach locals the properties of medicinal plants, 'it became an ecological hub for community awareness'.
In early 2021, Montiel's Court project received an Honorable Mention in the Fassa Bartolo International Prize for Sustainable Architecture. The significance of the project, for her, is that 'Court sums up so much of our design philosophy: it makes a sustainable use of resources by offering more programme with less expenditure while answering community needs.'

Montiel's holistic approach to architecture draws inspiration from Brazilian architect Lina Bo Bardi: 'She was quite visionary in her time; a congruent thinker of architecture, urbanism and cultural landscaping. Her built projects still have a lot to teach us.'
While Montiel draws on Brutalism for its functional simplicity, her own process is one of repurposing. She collects optical objects and plant and insect specimens, explaining, 'Imagining these objects in different situations provides an archive of atmospheres and impressions to inform my design.'
Now she wants to bring this experimental approach to materials such as bamboo,

polyaluminium and recycled materials. 'I constantly re-signify industrial materials by adding different textures and expressions – for instance, by making concrete resemble wood through colour and layout.'
She concludes, 'In a world of limited time and resources, what is really worth building? At the industry level, I think we still don't get it. Architecture should work more with nature than in opposition to it. Building should become a form of ecological infrastructure.'

Fig. 3 Axonometric view of Court, Lagos de Puente Moreno, Veracruz, Mexico, 2016.

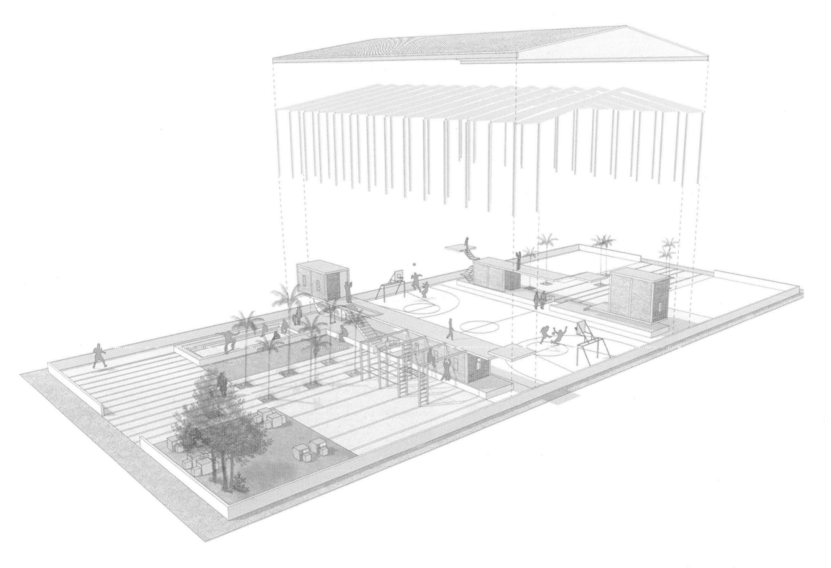

DOREL
RAMIREZ

"My architecture is highly contextual and bespoke."

Fig. 1 Casa Puente, Lake Nicaragua, Granada, Nicaragua, 2016. The domestic property, translating as 'bridge house', spans a waterway between two islands.

Dorel Ramirez is a Nicaraguan architect who sees 'architecture as being truly meaningful and having a soul'. To achieve this, she aims to involve her building's final users deeply within the design process. 'Architecture should be the reflection of an organic creative process,' she tells us, 'a fusion of ideas and solutions from the architect with the wishes and means of the client, while always capturing the spirit of the site.'

Born In Costa Rica and raised in Nicaragua, Ramirez moved to Mexico City to study at the Universidad Iberoamericana Ciudad de México (IBERO), before returning to Managua and establishing her studio in 1996. Over the past 25 years she has designed and supervised over 100 houses, commercial buildings, schools and holiday homes. 'Working in Nicaragua has given me the experience of developing projects not only in cities but also at the beach, on mountains, lakes and even on a volcano,' she says. She cites Casa Puente (bridge house), Casa del Volcán and the expansion and remodelling of Teresiano School in Managua, Nicaragua as key works.

Each of Ramirez's projects aims to respond to the, often dramatic, nature of their site. Bridge House spans a waterway between two islands in Lake Nicaragua and Casa del Volcán is sited within a nature reserve on the slopes of the Mombacho Volcano. 'Two projects should never be the same or even look much alike. We should never just plant or impose some building in a place.' Ramirez continues, 'I find that beginning an

Fig. 2 Casa del Volcán, Granada, Nicaragua, 2016. This private house was built on the slopes of the Mombacho Volcano.

architectural challenge with a strong will to build in a certain style is too limiting.' The bespoke nature of Ramirez's work is also achieved through what she describes as a 'client-centric' approach, which places importance on deep involvement of the building's end user from start to finish. 'My approach is highly collaborative,' she tells us. 'The ideas of my clients are as important as mine and they become members of the design team.' To this end, the design is made and presented in 3D from the very first meeting, to help clients understand everything from the beginning. 'From there, I make them participate actively on each stage so that, at the end, they feel like co-creators of every aspect of the project.' Speaking to the broader significance of her approach, Ramirez tells us that she hopes that this process results in architecture that is not only rooted in the landscape and responsive to the country's climate, but also translates the traditional, colonial and vernacular of Nicaragua into a contemporary design language. 'I like to believe that the architecture I make shows that it exists in Nicaragua today and not in any other place, at any other time.' It feels as if she tackles the question of what it means for architecture to have a soul in her final words: 'I think that what gives character and identity to architecture is the degree to which it manages to converse with and solve the needs of the particular cultural and physical context of its time.'

Fig. 3 Colegio Teresiano, Managua, Nicaragua, 2015. The project involved the expansion and remodelling of this elementary school.

"In terms of power, authority and importance, architects are not that senior."

KATHERINE DARNSTADT

Fig. 1 Community event at Boombox, Wicker Park, Chicago, Illinois, USA, 2015.

Katherine Darnstadt designs architectural interventions to have significant social and economic impacts on their surrounding communities.

'"How do you make the thing that makes the things?" – that is our guiding mantra,' says Darnstadt. 'How do we think systemically, not only in terms of the impact of our design on a building, but the building in a broader context so we understand who is impacted? Often that creates questions that are definitely larger than the project brief.'

Darnstadt, who describes herself as an 'accidental architect and an accidental firm owner', studied English and Philosophy before Architecture. She worked for a local firm and a developer before the recession made her unemployed and prompted her to establish Latent Design in 2010. 'It wasn't my plan to have a firm that young; I was just trying to generate work until somebody hired me – I was pregnant, I didn't have a job', she explains, 'and plan B became plan A.'

After graduating from Illinois Institute of Technology, Chicago, she soon realised the need to focus on the wider potential impact of a project, as her earliest experiences exposed her to the often-limited influence of architects. 'That's very jarring coming from school, where you feel like architecture is everything. And then you really see it in practice and it's not,' recalls Darnstadt. 'In architecture school, you learn about the complexities of a building, but you don't really understand how the built environment comes to be, you don't fully understand construction, finance, planning and policy. That doesn't come as part of that educational curriculum.'

Now, over a decade old, Latent Design has created projects that range from a cloud-like installation to an arts incubator space and housing for Habitat for Humanity, all projects that aim to leverage community and political forces to make a wider, meaningful impact.

Fig. 2 Boombox, Wicker Park, Chicago, Illinois, USA, 2015. Interior space.

'Define the context, design the content and deploy your solution, no matter what scale it is,' she tells us. 'Our objects, in terms of physical size, tend to be smaller. But I think that's where we look at the larger system that's around that.'

The project that best explains the studio's ethos is Boombox, which was designed in response to a request from City of Chicago for proposals to incorporate digital advertising into city plazas to generate income for the city. 'We gathered a team almost as a protest response to show there are better ways we can treat plazas,' Darnstadt recalls. 'There is a fundamental need for more arts and culture,

and we could generate revenue in other ways besides advertising billboards that could support local small businesses and artists.' Despite micro-retail of this type being illegal in the city at the time, the proposal won and the first Boombox was installed in Chicago's Wicker Park neighbourhood. Following its success, multiple kiosks were installed across the city and Boombox has supported over 150 businesses 'to bridge the huge gap between start-up and storefront'.

Boombox is one of many community-focused projects that Darnstadt has worked on. She believes that despite architecture's obsession with 'celebrated hallmark projects',

architects can be successful by focusing on community-led work. 'There's a constant narrative, which is totally flawed, that to do community-based work means you're going to be broke all the time. What does that even mean? Is that financially broke? Is that spiritually broke?' she asks. 'For me, creating a safe space and home for children is another piece of value; those are markers of success. As is being able to grow a firm that can take care of other people, like our staff, so that they can set themselves up on that pathway.'

Fig. 3 Boombox, Englewood, Chicago, Illinois, USA, 2015. Micro-retail space under construction.

"I invest the same intellectual energy into architecture as our experimental work in the arts."

LIZ DILLER

Fig. 1 The Shed, New York, USA, 2019. The McCourt, a space for events, is formed when The Shed's telescoping outer shell is deployed from over the base building and glides along rails onto the adjoining plaza.

The cross-genre work of Liz Diller, co-founder of Diller Scofidio + Renfro (DS+R), has led to Diller being included in *Time* magazine's '100 Most Influential People' list and receiving the first MacArthur Foundation fellowship awarded for architecture. DS+R's work explores how architecture, as a manifestation of social relationships, 'is everywhere, not just in buildings'. Some of Diller's notable projects in New York include the renovation and expansion of the Museum of Modern Art (MoMA) and the Mile-Long Opera, an immersive choral work she co-created, directed and produced, which was staged on the High Line. Diller is a Professor of Architectural Design at Princeton University, New Jersey, and a member of the UN Council on Urban Initiatives.

Polish-born Diller initially enrolled at The Cooper Union in New York, USA to study art, but later transferred to their architecture school, where she found 'there was a sense of accountability to ideas that you didn't find in the art school'. During this time, she was influenced by the cross-disciplinarity of John Hedjuk's anti-architectural practice, the experimentation of Peter Eisenman at the Institute for Architecture and Urban Studies, and New York's downtown art, music and dance scenes.

After college, Diller established a practice with Ricardo Scofidio, imagining an alternative approach that she describes as 'not an architecture practice, but a practice where we could teach, write and make installations. We wanted to create agendas that followed our curiosity, independent of the profession, which we felt was intellectually bankrupt.' Their work was informed by the institutional critique prevalent at the time, which also saw alternative spaces as a better context for new ideas, media and audiences.

Much of their early work was done on borrowed sites and was often ephemeral. As they

Fig. 2 Matchbox model for The Shed, New York, USA, 2019. One of the original models DS+R made to show the city what The Shed could be and how the footprint of the space could be doubled.

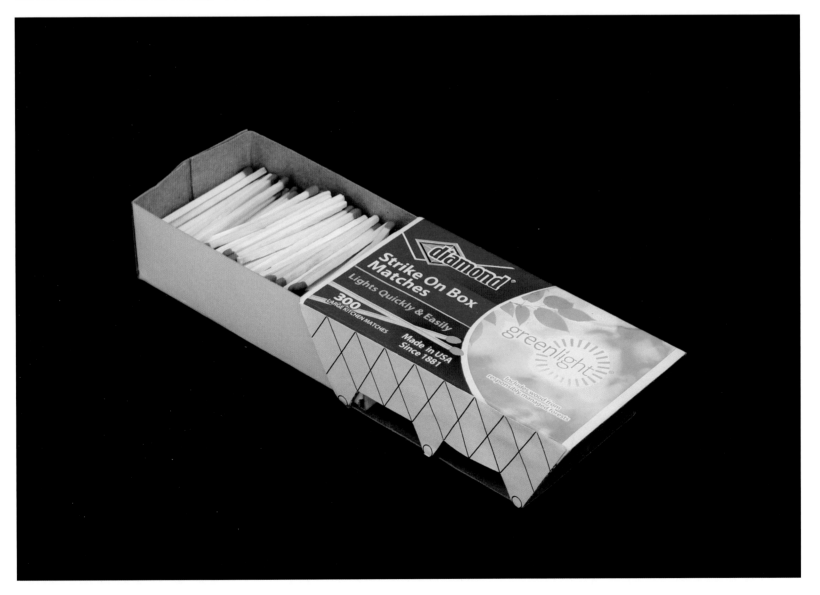

began to work in the field of architecture, their practice expanded from experimental independent work to include commissions from new institutions that fostered experimentation. Today, DS+R balance permanent building projects with independent ones and collaborate widely with practitioners across the arts, science and more. Within the practice, the partners (Diller, Scofidio, Charles Renfro and Benjamin Gilmartin) all collaborate on the concept design of every project, fostering a collective instead of the typical model of a singular heroic voice.

As our cities are being rapidly privatised, Diller has felt it important to protect the decreasing publicness of our cities. For the High Line, they used reclaimed parts of a disused elevated railway to open up new, unofficial vistas of New York. For the Lincoln Center for the Performing Arts, rather than erasing the existing centre, they turned the campus 'inside out' by extending the spectacle of the performance halls out into their previously desolate public spaces around it. Diller says she wanted to create 'a social consciousness and civic pride', creating 'a destination for the general public, with or without a ticket'.

The Shed, a nonprofit cultural organisation, is also open to the public both programmatically and physically, exposing new populations to experimental arts, with $10 tickets in every row. The building can respond to various media and scales as well as the evolving needs of artists, by doubling its footprint with a telescoping outer shell that expands over an adjoining plaza. Flexibility is at the heart of the studio's vision going forward. 'Architecture is slow, geo-fixed, heavy and expensive,' says Diller. To prevent architecture's obsolescence, she argues, we need 'to stress things like lightness, suppleness and a responsiveness to programme change, economic change and population increases. This level of adaptability is critical for the discipline to become important,and connected to what is happening.'

Fig. 3 High Line, New York, USA, starting in 2009 with phased openings in 2011, 2014 and 2019. In collaboration with James Corner Field Operations & Piet Oudolf. DS+R used the design opportunity to address multiple civic issues: unclaimed public space, adaptive reuse of old infrastructure and preservation as strategy for sustainability.

"We like to create things that people weave into their life."

CATHERINE JOHNSON AND REBECCA RUDOLPH

Fig. 1 Verve Mateo, Roastery del Sur, Los Angeles, USA, 2019. A café, coffee-roasting facility, restaurant and creative office combined in this public hub.

Catherine Johnson and Rebecca Rudolph are the founders of the unforgettably named Los Angeles studio Design, Bitches. It's a name with a very important comma, that they 'never would have come up with if we were starting an architecture firm'. But it reflects and encapsulates the ethos of doing, and the ideal of fun that runs through the studio's work.

Design, Bitches was established almost accidentally in 2010 in the midst of a recession after the duo responded to an AIA competition seeking manifestos from emerging architecture studios. The competition challenged the young architects to define what architecture means. Johnson and Rudolph's simple, and perhaps flippant, response was architecture is 'design, bitches'. This was submitted along with a portfolio of early collaborations and a series of semi-fictional projects – and the duo expected to hear nothing more. But much to their surprise, a couple of months later they received a commendation, and the studio was born. 'We didn't set out to start a practice, or a firm with client-driven projects,' the pair tell us. 'We had some art mural installation ideas in there that we then executed. We were then asked to give some lectures, we started our collaborative way of working and eventually we got client commissions.' The central themes within the duo's initial manifesto are now at the core of Design, Bitches' playful work. 'We take our work quite seriously without taking ourselves too seriously,' say Johnson and Rudolph, who both hold Master's degrees in Architecture from Southern California Institute of Architecture, USA. 'Spaces should feel like someone has thoughtfully cared for them, without them being overly orchestrated or that formal.' Working as Design, Bitches, the pair have created over 150 built projects at the time of publication – often a series of joyful spaces that combine pop references with touches of

Fig. 2 9 Dots STEM Education Center, Los Angeles, California, USA, 2018. The studio developed interior spaces and custom furniture within two 'white box' warehouses for their diverse programme.

"Indigenous perspectives are revolutionary – the way we relate to land and acknowledge equity between each other creates places that are accessible, sustainable and regenerative."

ELADIA SMOKE

Fig. 1 Centennial College Expansion, Ontario, Canada, 2020. The A-Building expansion is a six-storey, mass-timber, net-zero-carbon building with academic programming.

Eladia Smoke/KaaSheGaaBaaWeak – *lady smoke* – brings back Indigenous knowledge to contemporary architectural contexts through her practice and teaching. She set up her studio Smoke Architecture in 2014, working between institutional, commercial and residential projects at a variety of scales. The third Indigenous female architect in Canada, Smoke was part of the national team for the 2018 Venice Architecture Biennale with the multimedia installation 'UNCEDED: Voices of the Land'. She is also a founding member of the RAIC Indigenous Task Force.

Smoke grew up in the boreal forest near Sioux Lookout and is a member of Obishikokaang, Lac Seul First Nation, with family ties in Alderville First Nation. Her father was a builder and what influenced her to go into architecture 'was seeing my dad work in remote locations and telling stories about how the infrastructure is so poor and the craftsmanship of their homes is so bad'. She tells us how she 'gained a vivid understanding that the places we live have a profound effect on how we see ourselves in the world and what we think is possible. I thought architecture would be a way of influencing that.'

A liberal arts programme in New Mexico schooled Smoke in 'the underpinnings of the Western world', for the most part disseminating the dogma of high modernist design. Back at architecture school in Canada, Smoke tells us, 'Only one class in six years mentioned Indigenous architecture.' She continues, 'Canada, as part of its colonial project, has sublimated all of that history.' The colonial project severed relations between people and land, and modern design compounded this by foregrounding 'the new' and impressing upon people that 'good design' was modern design. An important part of Smoke's work is 'revisioning' – to show that good design *strengthens* relations and thus is transformational. She expands, 'Good design embodies the wisdom and principles of the community it serves and strengthens relationships between people and with the land. Good design is like water flowing, it shapes itself to what's already there and strengthens it, stimulates new growth and becomes one and the same with the life of the place.' Smoke's architecture reveals the powerful narratives that emerge when Indigenous perspectives are used to design cross-cultural spaces. A good example is the

Fig. 2 Wisdom Hall, Centennial College Expansion, Ontario, Canada, 2020. A student touch-down atrium with an interior courtyard, which includes an outdoor classroom and viewing garden visible from all levels – where pavement markers for the student gathering circle align to the noon sun for each full moon..

Centennial College expansion for the School of Engineering Technology and Applied Science, Scarborough, Ontario, Canada. Collaborating with architect DIALOG and Centennial's Indigenous Working Group, a narrative of seed-growth-culmination-balance, arising from Anishinaabe and Haudenosaunee understandings of spatial configuration and pre-contact cosmology, informed the design. The outcome was a six-storey, net-zero-carbon, timber building integrating outdoor and indoor learning spaces to support Indigenous rhythms of work and gathering.

Smoke advocates a process of land-based learning so that landscape interventions are crafted specifically for each community and place. The Naskapi of Kawawachikamach collaborated with Smoke Architecture to build a new shelter to care for members who experience family violence. As a result, the design for Naskapi Women's Shelter is informed by pre-contact, tent-like architectural forms of the Manukashunanu. To help the participatory process, Smoke uses diagrammatic and illustrative collaborative design tools to work alongside elders, knowledge carriers and other community leaders. Smoke observes, 'Now is a critical time to seek out every opportunity to transmit this knowledge to future generations.' Smoke's teaching at the MacEwan School of Architecture, Laurentian University, Sudbury, Canada, gives her an opportunity to transmit Indigenous and participatory methods. Here, students are encouraged to work on live projects like the Henry Inlet Community Centre, using engagement tools and conducting site reconnaissance through the seasons. Smoke always works with a landscape architect so that architecture and landscape design are understood as intertwined. The separation of specialisms often remains in colonial and Western architectural thinking, working against sustainable thinking, which needs to learn from Indigenous perspectives and connect architecture back to climate and context. 'What I hope to see in future is a scenario where we don't see that duality, where buildings are regenerative by their 'very nature.'

Fig. 3 Naskapi Women's Shelter, Kawawachikiamach, Quebec, Canada, 2019. Community engagement allows the architects to learn from an inherently Naskapi conception of space.

"I have an obligation to take risks."

DEANNA
VAN BUREN

Deanna Van Buren is the founder of Oakland-based architecture and real estate development nonprofit Designing Justice + Designing Spaces. The organisation aims to end mass incarceration and structural inequity by dismantling prisons and building spaces that are alternatives to incarceration, including spaces for survivors, spaces for re-entry, spaces for youth, behavioural services and more. Van Buren maintains that buildings should be a reflection of all the people in our society and not just of the powerful and the elite. She believes that 'the built environment foments, anchors and amplifies the beliefs of the elite and the powerful. Therefore, it does damage to those that aren't valued.' Van Buren's work is characterised by what she considers the task of all architects: 'To analyse and investigate what our beliefs are because we're building them, and we are responsible for that.' Van Buren has a clear commitment to 'work for people who look like me', and so students, in particular, find the integrity of her approach to be avant-garde and atypical of architecture's mainstream priorities.

Before founding her studio in 2011, Van Buren studied at the University of Virginia and Columbia University, USA, choosing to focus on designing spaces for restorative justice following a period working in the UK and Australia. She has since worked on a series of projects that offer an alternative to traditional prisons and tackle the root causes of mass incarceration. Such projects include Restore Oakland, which houses six non-profits focusing on community advocacy and restorative justice and supports a campaign to turn the Atlanta City Detention Center into a community hub. Also, the Near Westside Peacemaking Project in Syracuse, New York, which brings Native American

Fig. 2 Restore Oakland, California, USA. In 2019, Restore Oakland became the first American centre dedicated to restorative justice and economics, located in the Fruitvale neighbourhood.

peacemaking practices into a non-Native American community. This work powerfully evidences Van Buren's ability to 'support something that works rather than trying to prop up a system that is broken', while also giving restorative justice a transformative spatial dimension. In doing so, Van Buren inspires other architects to adopt a similar approach in order to address the root causes of a bigger system of oppression and transform it.

While social movements, such as #BlackLivesMatter, remind us that racial justice and equality remain shamefully illusive,

Van Buren acknowledges that as one of approximately 500 Black female licensed architects in the USA, she contends with a responsibility to use her education and professional experience in order to 'manifest ideas around ending mass incarceration and envision a system of restorative justice'. By determining to assume 'an obligation to take risks, try new things, push the boundaries and step into my leadership', Van Buren's advocacy is working. Support for restorative justice is incrementally becoming more mainstream, driven by the murder of George Floyd by Minneapolis police in 2020 and the

global #BlackLivesMatter protests that followed. However, as Van Buren points out, the cataclysmic efficacy of such events in raising collective consciousness also reveals 'just how racist the [USA] criminal justice system is. It's what we've always been trying to communicate, and people finally get it.' Unequivocally, Van Buren is both conscientiously creative and critical. By calling for more diversity in architecture, she describes the need for variations in practice models to become more prevalent 'because, just as in nature, a monocrop is not sustainable. Biodiversity is necessary for every kind of way'.

Fig. 3 Restore Oakland, California, USA. The space was intentionally designed in calming colours with bright light to create a peaceful space.

"We think of buildings as experiences, looking for ideal conditions of use and avoiding thinking of them as aesthetics objects."

SANDRA BARCLAY

Fig. 1 The Place of Remembrance, Lima, Peru, 2015. The building – a cultural centre with exhibition spaces, auditorium and research centre – is inserted into the dynamic of cliffs and ravines that ring the bay of Lima.

Peruvian architect Sandra Barclay is the co-founder of Barclay & Crousse and the recipient of numerous awards, including Woman Architect of the Year at the Women in Architecture Awards in 2018. She studied in Lima before heading to Paris where she completed her studies and established her studio with Jean Pierre Crousse.

After 16 years in France designing prestigious projects, including the Malraux Museum in Le Havre, the duo returned to Peru where they are leading a resurgence in climate-appropriate architecture in the country. 'In terms of climate conditions, working in Peru is a paradise. You don't have to protect yourself from rain or extreme temperatures; you need only to create spaces of intimacy where life can flourish taking advantage of these conditions.'

Recalling her first project in the country, Barclay explains, 'We started by thinking about the strategies that pre-Columbian people used to inhabit the desert. We applied those strategies, and they are key concepts we continue to work with today.' She continues, 'The programme, for us, is not a list of physical needs because clients don't know what the possibilities can be. We think in terms of usage and the ideal conditions needed, always taking advantage of natural ingredients like natural light, breeze, space and shade.' Expanding on their approach, she tells us, 'Buildings should be generous with their context, avoiding walls around the plot, seeking to offer connection with place and community – it can be an experience, a public space to meet and more.'

With all their projects, Barclay & Crousse aim to go beyond the building brief, to consider the spaces between and around in a way that is appropriate for the arid Peruvian climate. In the desert to the south of Lima, the studio designed the red concrete Museo de Sitio de Paracas to complement the tones and harness the natural climate of the surrounding desert landscape. At the Place of Remembrance in Lima, the studio input their research to challenge the original brief, adding a stunning public plaza on a balcony overlooking the sea.

It is at the Edificio E in the Universidad de Piura, which won the Mies Crown Hall Americas Prize

Fig. 2 Edificio E Lecture Building, University of Piura, Peru, 2016. The project comprises 11 independent buildings with open, informal learning spaces protected from the desert sun by cantilevered roofs.

in 2018, that this ideology of giving back is fully realised. Set in Peru's dry northern savannah, the campus building combines classrooms and lecture theatres connected by open, shaded spaces. 'What we called the informal learning spaces, the in-between spaces, are as important as the classrooms they asked for in the programme. They are non-hierarchical learning places where people from the city and rural areas can meet and exchange knowledge,' explains Barclay.

'To cope with high temperatures, the design created shade inspired by the trees in the surrounding dry tropical forest. Barclay explains, 'The porosity of the building embraces the breeze and helps to cool these exterior shaded spaces so they can be just open. This also reduces the cost of these essential spaces for informal learning. At the same time, for the formal classrooms, we've avoided air-conditioning by using natural ventilation.'

Barclay tells us that a benefit of the climate is that the transition between public and intimate space can be fluid and open. 'We know that we have to imagine the project as an experience, avoiding ending with an isolated object with no relation to site, community or society.'

Fig. 3 Edificio E Lecture Building, University of Piura, Peru, 2016. Stairwell. The space is designed as a threshold between the harshness of the tropical dry forest and the exterior shaded spaces inside the compound.

"We consider architecture to be a storytelling experience, respectful of place and the traces of time in buildings."

MICAELA CASOY
AND PAULA DE FALCO

Fig. 1 Rappi Argentina, Palermo, Buenos Aires, Argentina, 2019. The rehabilitation of an early 20th-century studio has created a fluid workspace.

Argentinian architects Micaela Casoy and Paula De Falco are founding partners of Buenos Aires-based Octava Arquitectura, a studio that has quickly gained wider recognition since its inception in 2014. The studio's approach uses design to reveal stories of people, place and the passage of time. 'We aim to give clients their own voice and identity through our work,' they tell us. 'We challenge "high-end" results and adapt to the limitations of site and budget.'

Casoy has a degree in Architecture, with specialisation in real estate, from the University of Buenos Aires. De Falco has a Master's in the History and Culture of Architecture from Di Tella University and has worked as an editor for the Argentinian architecture magazine *Summa+*. The two met at the University of Buenos Aires, where they both teach architectural history, becoming collaborators in 2014. Through Octava, Casoy and De Falco have worked with private clients and firms, both large and small, such as Lunigo, Linio, Tastemade, Dafiti, Rappi and Redbull.

Fig. 2 Rappi Argentina, Palermo, Buenos Aires, Argentina, 2019. Trees and plants cohabit in the space.

The way Octava works involves constant contact with clients and collaborators. For Tastemade, a gastronomic content producer, Octava converted a leather factory, in Buenos Aires' Villa Crespo neighbourhood, into offices and recording studios. The design includes a large central nave, covered by a parabolic roof with metallic structures and floors – creating an industrial aesthetic while preserving the original features. As with Octava, 'telling stories' is one of the main practices of the founders of Tastemade and thus the design intention was to respect both the history of the structure and the gastronomic traditions of the local Spanish-speaking community.

Principles of adaptive reuse can be seen in Octava's design for the offices of delivery company Rappi Argentina. Based in Buenos Aires' Palermo neighbourhood, Octava's design involved the rehabilitation and transformation of an old, early 20th-century workshop, into a fluid workspace. Most original elements were preserved and restored inside and out; doors, metal structures, marbles, glass and vegetation. The floor plan was structured to create three naves – the main one providing a spacious work area with a long acrylic vault to deliver maximum natural light. Lateral naves work as meeting rooms, small office spaces, a dining area and restrooms.

Octava's storytelling includes respect for the natural environment. In the Rappi offices, we see this in the way that existing trees and plants 'cohabit' the space in quite surprising ways.
'We learn from challenges and opportunities and look forward to working on a bigger scale,' Casoy and De Falco tell us. As Octava develops, the aim is to systematise some stages of their processes and create 'a signature identity' but, crucially, the women want to keep the company small, to preserve the distinctively personal touch for which they are known.

Fig. 3 Tastemade Argentina, Villa Crespo, Buenos Aires, Argentina, 2017. The renovation of an old leather factory shed became the recording studios of Tastemade, the online gastronomic content producer.

"Architecture is an idea of space in synthesis with a programme."

CARLA JUAÇABA

Fig. 1 Humanidade Pavilion, Rio+20 UN Conference on Sustainable Development, 2012. The scaffold building is translucent, exposed to all weather conditions.

Working across practice and academia, Carla Juaçaba is an architect with a mission to 'redesign our relationship with the environment'. Since 2000 she has been working independently on public and private commissions from her home city of Rio de Janeiro, Brazil, as well as from a base in Europe. She also teaches at the Accademia di Architettura di Mendrisio in Switzerland. In 2013, Juaçaba won the first edition of the international prize ArcVision Women and Architecture in Italy, and in 2018 she won the first prize of AREA Architectural Review Emerging Architecture Award.

Juaçaba's unique approach to architecture first captured global attention in 2012 with her Humanidade Pavilion in Rio, constructed for RIO+20 United Nations Conference on Sustainable Development. Working in collaboration with theatre director Bia Lessa, they created a large scaffold structure, reminiscent of English architect Cedric Price's highly influential, theoretical 'Fun Palace' project, which deliberately exposes the user to the weather and therefore to their 'frailty' in the face of nature.

The pavilion is comprised of five structural walls measuring 170m in length and 20m high, with a 5.4m gap in between, creating a suspended walkway over the city's landscape, punctured by spaces designed for reflection and thought. A system of ramps and sloped walkways connects the building to its visitors. A roof plaza, 'adorned with rows of flags from around the world', emphasises 'how exigent this time in human

Fig. 2 Humanidade Pavilion, Rio+20 UN Conference on Sustainable Development, 2012.

history is and how very appropriate and responsive architecture can be'. Built from recycled materials, the intention was that the pavilion itself would transform into future architectures similarly responsive to the environment.

In 2018, Juaçaba was invited to participate in the Venice Architecture Biennale with BALLAST, referencing the rope-making origins of the Corderie where the exhibit was staged. She was also one of 10 architects selected by Francesco Dal Co to design a structure around the theme 'Vatican Chapel', built for the same Biennale event on the island of San Giorgio Maggiore. Her chapel – almost invisible in its context – comprises of four polished stainless-steel beams, measuring just 12cm in length, which 'compose' the ensemble: one is a bench, the other one is a cross. The ensemble is built on seven pieces of concrete, measuring 12 x 200cm. Of the chapel, Juaçaba observes, it is 'an ethereal project that speaks metaphorically of the passage of life, of existence and of non-existence'. Juaçaba's architecture engages quietly with context – almost all of her projects are 'set gently on the ground', with the capacity to disappear completely. The Humanidade Pavilion, for example, 'comes from the observation of a place, its geography and, in the case of Copacabana, of its events. The choice of building a scaffolding building is one way to understand sustainability that is in the material itself.' Her vision for architecture in the future demands a deep contemplation of the environment and a design process that emerges from rigorous historical-ecological investigation.

Fig. 3 Vatican Chapel, Holy See Pavilion, Venice Architecture Biennale 2018. Curated by Francesco Dal Co, the chapel was one of 10 built in the woods on the island of San Giorgio Maggiore.

CATALINA PATIÑO AND VIVIANA PEÑA

"Public life determines the nature of our structures."

Fig. 1 Pajarito La Aurora kindergarten, Medellín, Colombia, 2010. A flexible and adaptive design helps confront problems of ecological instability in the valley.

quirkiness. It's this approach that led to the duo being shortlisted for the Moira Gemmill Prize for Emerging Architecture in the 2016 Women in Architecture Awards. They have also received the AIA Los Angeles Emerging Practice Award. With each of their projects, Johnson and Rudolph aim to make spaces that improve people's daily lives, telling us, 'We like to create things that people weave into their life; it's just an extra part, a place where they want to be.' These varied spaces include several houses that employ a ground-up approach, an extremely open veterinary clinic, a bold pink shop for beauty brand *Shop Good*, an eclectic LA restaurant filled with

retro video games, an ice-cream shop and numerous restaurants. It's the 9 Dots project that Design, Bitches feel sums up their ethos. This is an award-winning, computer-science-focused, nonprofit, educational facility in Hollywood for which the studio developed interior spaces and custom furniture. Through their approachable and engaging architecture Design, Bitches hope that they are contributing to making architecture a little bit more accessible. 'Part of our goal is to expand the audience of architecture,' they tell us. 'If we're really going to have a thriving profession, we need to reach more people and make it something that feels more

approachable to all different kinds of people who know very little about architecture.' In their work, Design, Bitches see their role as giving the client 'more than they could have imagined', through a collaborative approach that involves the client in the design process. 'We've become quite good at asking generative questions to our clients,' they say. 'We help them come to some other understanding of how, spatially, they can augment what they're doing. People intuitively know how they like to live, but they don't necessarily know how that translates into space. And that's our job. And that brings us joy.'

Fig. 3 Stomping Grounds concept, *Dezeen*/Adidas Originals P.O.D. System Architecture project, 2018. Design, Bitches created a park concept that brings different activities together in unusual ways.

As co-founders of Colombian architectural studio Ctrl G, Catalina Patiño and Viviana Peña work together on public educational and cultural projects as well as on their own smaller, private projects. Recognition of their work is both home-grown and international. It includes the Colombian Biennale of Architecture and the Mies Crown Hall Americas Prize, and projects have been published in numerous magazines including *Mark, Harvard Design Magazine* and *Arquitectura Viva*.

When asked what brought the women to architecture, Patiño tells us that her interest came early, through family involvement and travelling. Peña found in architecture an opportunity to combine engineering with design and cultural awareness. In 2006, the two women graduated from the Faculty of Architecture at the Universidad Pontificia Bolivariana (UPB), Colombia, and moved to Spain to pursue further studies in Complex Architecture at the University of Alicante. A period in Madrid followed and then the return to Medellín in Colombia, to set up Ctrl G in partnership with Eliana Beltrán in 2008. Medellín sustained severe damage as a result of extreme political protests towards the end of the 20th century. The 'rawness of urban culture', says Patiño, provided opportunities for architectural experiment, but also demanded a high level of social and political responsibility.

Early success came from a competition win to construct a series of kindergartens on the outskirts of the city. The approach was to create flexible and adaptive structures, allowing them to avoid segregation and confront ecological instability. For the kindergarten in Pajarito La Aurora, they worked together with Federico Mesa of Plan B. The classrooms are polygonal modular spaces, arranged like petals and integrated into landscaped gardens. Says Patiño, 'These topologically conceived structures provide nourishment and healthy environments where mothers can be trained and employed as teachers.'

Ctrl G went on to work with 51-1 from Peru on the extension to the Museum of Modern Art of Medellín. Inspired by the urban fabric – especially the informal settlement pattern and stacked houses of the barrios – the building is composed of stacked boxes,

Fig. 2 Drawing for the Pajarito La Aurora kindergarten, Medellín, Colombia, 2010.

creating terraces that provide dramatic access for the public and integrate curated events into the urban landscape. Like the provisional and mutating architecture of the barrios, the museum is a work in progress. The design incorporates a refurbished steel factory and follows an open system connected by stairs, terraces and yards. This provides potential for the museum to grow according to resources. Here we see a glimpse of how Peña's work is inspired by union and repetition as well as Patiño's interest in architecture as intervention and encounter.

Summing up their approach, Peña lists 'flexible collaboration, an acute sensitivity to site and scale, and an interest in ornament as a resource to bring together society, culture and technology'. Crucially, drawing is integral to the working process. Patiño describes the 'creative freedoms provided by making fast and free drawings before deploying informational software'. In Peña's words, the collaging and overlapping of drawings and models proceeds by what she terms a 'process of contamination'.

Since 2016, Patiño has partnered with Juan Pablo Ramos under the name CAPA. They design family houses with a dynamic relationship to landscape and an emphasis on sustainability, fair wages and working conditions. The independent studio Viviana Peña Taller de Arquitectura has been operating since 2015 between Colombia and Spain. It allows Peña to collaborate with other studios and institutions on architectural projects and competitions, academic workshops and research projects. Pajarera House provides a dramatic realisation of her early ambition to synthesise engineering and creative design. Described as 'a giant birdhouse for people', it is designed as an A-frame with an open-plan interior that rests on two thick, deeply rooted concrete columns. Through teaching at different universities, the women have been able to pass on an approach that brings creative experiment and craft skills to social and political ends. Patiño, a professor at EAFIT University, Colombia, draws attention to the need to mentor young women entering the profession and, crucially, argues, 'We need to advocate for awareness of the demands of motherhood on young architects.'

Fig. 3 Expansion of the Museum of Modern Art of Medellín, Colombia, 2015. Influenced by the cumulative brick structures of the local barrios, the building is composed of stacked boxes, which create terraces that integrate with the landscape.

VERÓNICA VILLATE

"We dare to say that we are part of a movement of architects in Paraguay, formed by many generations."

Fig. 1 Oficinas Nordeste, Curuguaty, Paraguay, 2018. Side elevation – working in the landscape.

Verónica Villate is a founder-member of Mínimo Común Arquitectura based in Asunción, Paraguay, a practice evolving an approach to making architecture that is embedded in traditions of sustainable practice. Villate explains, 'In our studio, we are constantly referencing Latin American architects such as Alejandro Aravena, Angelo Bucci, Carla Juaçaba and José María Sánchez, among others. Also, like all enthusiastic architects, we look for inspiration in the works of Le Corbusier, Paulo Mendes and Lina Bo Bardi.'

A graduate of the Faculty of Architecture, Design and Arts, National University of Asunción, Villate comes from a family of architects, growing up 'between plans and buildings'. Studying and practising alongside one another, Villate and her studio are keen to emphasise their collaborative approach to designing the environment, utilising what they describe as simple materials and local labour. These principles are especially evident in two of their projects imaged here. The first – Nordeste Curuguaty – is a 200m² office building 350km from Asunción, constructed in the middle of an agricultural landscape. Fabricated from bricks made on site from local earth and surrounded with a lattice structure made from the same soil, the

Fig. 2 Oficinas Nordeste, Curuguaty, Paraguay, 2018. Longitudinal facade, view to the south.

structure is covered by a catenary roof that becomes 'its own machine for collecting water and cooling the whole building'. Shade was and is key, both in terms of constructing and inhabiting the building, as was capturing rainwater – a precious resource.

Casa Luce y Pablo also illustrates Villate's interest in experimenting with traditional building methods. Formed using compacted earth techniques, the studio saw the project as an opportunity to develop these tried and tested methods in pursuit of a more sustainable approach to architecture. The building that we see here additionally incorporates other natural elements from the existing surroundings, such as trees, which offer both shade and form.

Considering the question of architecture's function and purpose moving forward, Vilate is reflective: 'If we don't modify our ways of living, our planet's resources are not going to be enough.' Instead, she suggests, we need to consider the wider picture, making the link between the local and the global and taking responsibility for our actions and their impact on the environment, however minimal these may be. Mínimo Común Arquitectura is looking to future-proof its approach to making architecture, while simultaneously foregrounding the role of local communities in establishing sustainable building practices.

Fig. 3 Casa Luce y Pablo, Vivienda de Tierra Vertida, Mariano Roque Alonzo, Paraguay, 2018. Side view of the house showing the compacted earth technique.

SOFIA VON ELLRICHSHAUSEN

"We want buildings to be a tool for thought."

Fig. 1 Cien House, Concepción, Chile, 2011. The architects' own home – a seven-storey concrete tower that shows how they rethink traditional arrangements and forms.

Led by Argentinian architect Sofia von Ellrichshausen, alongside her partner Mauricio Pezo, Pezo von Ellrichshausen is a studio that aims to create buildings at the border of art and architecture that question conventional thinking.

Von Ellrichshausen uses buildings as a tool for thought. 'This', she tells us, 'means one has to shift away from the prejudices and the comfort zone of how a building's function is expected to be.' She continues, 'As much as a book or a telescope, a building is a mediation device that not only allows us to be in the world but to also see beyond, to experience something otherwise hidden, to reflect about our own human condition, our values, our memories or desires, to make us aware of our own existence.'

Based in a farm at the foot of the Chilean Andes, the studio has created a succession of abstract buildings that rethink traditional arrangements and forms, including their own home, Cien House, a seven-storey concrete tower. They have also built an innovation centre with a large central void and curved walls, a semicircular wooden home on a southern Chilean island and a floating-platform off-grid residence for the Matarraña region of Spain.

An early project that demonstrates the studio's ethos is Poli House – a concrete clifftop monolith that is both a home and a cultural centre with a programme that has

Fig. 2 Poli House, Coliumo, Chile, 2005. A home and a cultural centre, curated by Pezo von Ellrichshausen.

been curated by Pezo von Ellrichshausen for the past 15 years.

'It is an autonomous concrete piece at the edge of a cliff, an opaque object without an explicit sense of scale or programme,' von Ellrichshausen explains. 'The interior is rather informal and flexible, with a thick perimeter that contains all the fixed functions such as staircases, bathrooms, kitchen and storage, liberating the spatial core for unprescribed activities.'

The studio has also created a labyrinthine-like structure at the Venice Architecture Biennale, a wooden tower of 'ambiguous' scale in Paris, and a permanent pavilion for Christian Boltaski's work. The studio's contribution to the Royal Academy of Arts, London, 'Sensing Spaces' exhibition, a timber elevated platform, encouraged people to view the gallery from an entirely different perspective. Von Ellrichshausen and Pezo co-author all their work and their lives. They have taught widely including at USA universities Harvard in Massachusetts, Cornell in New York and the Illinois Institute of Technology in Chicago. Von Ellrichshausen believes that architects need to reflect on the definition of success which, for her, doesn't mean striving for the biggest studio or the largest project. Pezo von Ellrichshausen has remained deliberately intimate, working only on a couple of buildings at a time.

'Try to understand what your principles are, what you consider to be your core values in life and share them with others through the architecture you make,' she says. 'It is not about the industry of architecture, not about an efficient problem-solving service, it is more about the ethics of a practice in search for a basic language with common meaning.' She concludes, 'We have no other strategy than doing whatever we believe works for us. Since our exploration is about spatial character and identity given by rather discreet elements, we trust this intuitive understanding should resonate with almost anyone.'

Fig. 3 Nida House, Navidad, Chile, 2014–16. A concentric and non-directional residence formed by four rigid concrete frames.

ASIA

TOGZHAN
AUBAKIROVA

"As Kazakh architects we need to find
our own identity in the world of architecture."

Fig. 1 Republic Square, Almaty, Kazakhstan, 2021. Dome and canopy designed by structural engineers Schlaich
Bergermann Partner. View of the site, with City Hall in the background.

Kazakh architect Togzhan Aubakirova aims to create architecture that responds directly to the environment the building stands in. 'The location, place, context and environment of any future building or architectural "object" already contain most of the key answers and solutions,' she tells us. 'My role in the process is to be able to see and distinguish these factors, translate them and bind together a place and programme for a future building – to understand the exchange that buildings and environments can make and unravel what they can give to one another.'

Togzhan Aubakirova studied at the Kazakh Leading Academy of Architecture and Civil Engineering in her home city of Almaty before leaving Kazakhstan to complete her architectural education at the Hochschule für Technik und Wirtschaft in Dresden. On returning to Almaty, she worked at the office of international architecture studio Aedas (later AHR) before taking up twin roles as Design Director of Atomik Architecture, Kazakhstan and Global Design Director of Adventure Architecture Group. With all her projects she focuses on the experience of a building rather than its external aesthetics. 'My main point of interest is how people experience architectural space by using it,' she explains. 'From my very childhood, I can often hardly remember how buildings looked from the outside, but know how I felt myself in the spaces.' Although she has been practising architecture for 15 years she feels that she

Fig. 2 Republic Square, Almaty, Kazakhstan, 2021. View of the newly designed café next to a playground on the plaza.

is still on a journey and is 'at the very beginning of finding my own way'.

One project where Aubakirova hopes she created a space that could be experienced and enjoyed widely was the reworking of Almaty's central plaza – Republic Square. The design activated the square, which stands alongside the former presidential building, with seating, cafés and a pair of winged pavilions surrounding a glass dome that illuminates an underground mall built in 2012. She says, 'Republic Square was not experiencing its first transformation, therefore we were challenged to release all its possible potential – while respecting its historical past and unique architectural situation – to respond to the needs of the city today.'

The square has long been a place for mass demonstrations in Almaty and unfortunately, not long after the completion of the project, it was heavily damaged during the 2022 Bloody January protests over rising fuel prices and economic inequality.

Aubakirova is part of a new generation of architects in Kazakhstan (a country which gained its independence from the Soviet Union in 1991) who are developing a style rooted in the country's past and present. Speaking of developing a Kazakh identity in the world of architecture, she says, 'Historically our country was nomadic and then part of the Soviet Union so this is a difficult and challenging task for current and future generations of Kazakh architects. The identity of a place makes it special. 'I don't want the architecture of my city or country to be interchangeable with any other buildings from any location of the world.'

Fig. 3 Republic Square, Almaty, Kazakhstan, 2021. The covered stair to City Hall has become a popular place for hanging out.

GULNARA DIYAROVA

Fig. 1 Villa Alma Plus, Almaty, Kazakhstan, 2020. This private house was designed to rethink luxury, focusing on the interaction between the interior space and natural surroundings.

Kazakhstani architect Gulnara Diyarova has built her reputation creating a succession of private houses across Central Asia over a career spanning 20 years. She has created modern, oriental, classical and American-style houses, designed 'from the inside out', along with office spaces and interiors, built with the aim of rethinking luxury. 'I can design a house in any way the client sees it,' she tells us. 'I do not need to say something new, what is important to me is that people feel comfortable in their homes.'
Although her architecture does not have a shared aesthetic, it does have a uniting ethos. Each home is designed with a focus on the client's 'dream', how they will use the house and Diyarova's emphasis on internal space. 'Internal connections, family and its patterns are the most important things I consider in the design process,' she explains, and it is these that inform the internal and external space of the architecture.
Another key emphasis of her work is the climate and landscape of Kazakhstan. Her houses pay particular attention to the transition from outdoor to indoor, making the most of often-impressive views and 'each finished with a dramatic touch'.

Diyarova cites Villa Alma Plus and Villa Georgia as being two of the clearest examples of her ethos. 'The main thing is that a project converges with my principles – fullness of light, unity with nature, harmony and ergonomics,' she says. 'Because of the local climate, merging inside and outside usually becomes a marked threshold but I always try to make it a smooth and controlled transition – through deep shadows, covered terraces and glass passages.' The design for Alma Plus directs the building around a courtyard to create an enclosed, comfortable environment in the semi-

Fig. 2 Villa Alma Plus, Almaty, Kazakhstan, 2020. Common modernist shapes are paired with materials chosen to have a perception of the 'natural'.

wild context, with openings to the views. Common modernist shapes go along with materials that emphasise the perception of the natural: hand-treated limestone and metal-pigmented concrete are rough, unique and imperfect. Villa Georgia is a large-scale house, so the mission was 'to bring human scale to the building without losing respectability'. Thus, the design used a composition of fragmented facades and plans with materials like limestone and travertine being used – both 'noble' and able to bring the appearance of lightness despite its dimensions.

Graduating from Kazakh Leading Academy of Architecture and Civil Engineering in Almaty in 1983, Diyarova had a career as a fashion designer before refocusing on architecture at the turn of the century. She established her practice, D.Studio, in 2001 which she now runs in partnership with her son Chingiz Batyrbekov. She describes the time when she began practising, soon after the country gained independence from Russia, as 'low on architectural ambition and production'. As the country stabilised, the rise of a nouveau riche led to a demand for large houses as 'people wanted great palaces and villas,

not to gain comfort, but to show wealth'. It was against this muscular culture that Diyarova was able to develop a niche creating more sensitive homes for businesspeople and often female clients who allowed her to develop her skills as an architect. 'It was then that the demand for people like me appeared,' she explains. 'I was lucky with my customers – businesspeople are sober-minded, smart people. There was a synthesis of desires that allowed me to prove myself as an architect.'

Fig. 3 Villa Georgia, Almaty, Kazakhstan, 2006. This large house – which includes a swimming pool, winter garden and five bedrooms – was designed with the intention to bring a human scale to the building.

"The architecture of Tajikistan should be inspired by our unique geographical position, beautiful nature and traditional forms, proportions and textures."

SHAHNOZ RAHMATULLOZODA

Figs. 1 Exterior of school No.8 in Dushanbe, Tajikistan, 2014.

Over the past 20 years, Tajikistani architect Shahnoz Rahmatullozoda has designed over 200 buildings across Central Asia, and in 2019 was made an Honorary Architect of the Republic of Tajikistan. 'Architecture is about ideas. It is very important that the idea carries something special, can surprise people, evoke emotion in them', she says. Shahnoz Rahmatullozoda graduated from the Polytechnical Institute of Tajik Technical University in 1992, just after Tajikistan became an independent nation, and went on to gain a PhD from the Moscow Architectural Institute. When she began designing, she aimed to create buildings that stood out from the prevailing post-Soviet architecture. 'I think that my projects were bold, innovative to some extent and significantly different from what happened in the architecture of Tajikistan in the 2000s and early 2010s', she tells us. 'The scientific approach – the eternal search for inspiration in not just architecture but also from different kinds of art – led to interesting ideas that could truly touch people.'

In her government roles as Chief Architect of the State Institute of Fine Arts and Design of Tajikistan and Deputy Chairperson of the country's Committee for Architecture and Construction, Rahmatullozoda has created dozens of schools and residential blocks across the country. She has also worked on high-profile buildings in the capital including the Russian-Tajik Slavonic University, reconstruction of the Avicenna Tajik State Medical University, the National Museum of Tajikistan, the headquarters for Tajikistani mobile brand TCell and the country's largest bank, Amonatbank.

Developing architectural identity in Tajikistan is an overarching agenda for all of these projects. Rahmatullozoda believes that 30 years after independence, the country is at a juncture with 'Tajik architecture in search of answers to its most important questions'. Expanding on her agenda, she says, 'Only as a result of the quintessence of nature and architecture – taking into account the environmental factor – is it possible to create an original, national Tajik architecture, and

also ensure the sustainable development of the cities of Tajikistan.' In her own projects, she achieves this aim by leading her clients and, at times, overruling their desires. 'I do not seek to match projects to the requirements of the customer but offer them options that seem interesting to me', she says.

Despite Rahmatullozoda holding numerous senior roles within government, architecture in Tajikistan is dominated by men, with the number of women practising able to be 'counted on fingers'. However, she has aimed to turn this to her advantage. 'Throughout my career, I was the "black sheep" at all meetings and conferences, I was always the only woman', she tells us. Contrary to many of the women interviewed in the book, she explains that she 'never had a problem with it – on the contrary, it only made me stronger. Perhaps there are even some advantages because it is the female nature that allows me to treat projects like children, with "motherly" love, which sometimes results in specifically beautiful projects.'

Fig. 2 Russian-Tajik Slavonic University, Dushanbe, Tajikistan, 2016.

Fig. 3 National Museum of Tajikistan, Dushanbe, Tajikistan, 2014. Winner of the Grand Prix for best project 2009.

"A place suggests what should be built there. The architect should only hear, feel and then bring this out."

TAKHMINA TURDIALIEVA

Takhmina Turdialieva is an Uzbek architect who believes that 'just as nature heals and empowers us, architecture should do the same. Architecture, first of all, is creating harmony within oneself.' She recently established her studio, Tatalab, in Tashkent, but earlier in her life 'hardly believed that being an architect was possible'.

As 'architecture wasn't really available for women' in Uzbekistan, she initially focused on graphic and interior design, before attending the Tashkent Institute for Architecture and Civil Engineering and then heading to China to study at the Huazhong University of Science and Technology. After working in China and Italy she returned to Uzbekistan, where the serendipity of a failed job interview and the Coronavirus pandemic lockdowns led her to establish her own studio. 'I couldn't make my way abroad again so I decided to stay and start my own studio,' she tells us. 'I always had this idea but didn't see it was coming so soon – it was a risky leap.'

As a young architect, Turdialieva aims to make an impact in Tashkent through both her work and advocacy. Her studio is engaged in numerous projects including the refurbishment of the offices of the government's anti-corruption agency. The studio recently created an outdoor events space at the city's Centre for Contemporary Arts (CCA), which is located in an early 20th-century diesel power plant. 'We developed a shadow structure from flags that shades an area from the extremely

Fig. 2 Uzbekistan Anti-corruption Agency, Tashkent, Uzbekistan, 2022. The building envelope was covered with travertine, imitating local architecture.

hot sun to allow the CCA to hold outdoor public talks, film screenings and activities for children,' she says.

Turdialieva is part of a new generation of architects in Uzbekistan who are pushing to have greater involvement in the development of the country's cities, which she believes are 'suffering from disorderly construction'. To push this agenda, she co-founded Shaharsozlik To'lqini – an organisation dedicated to 'raising the voice of young architects'. Established in the wake of the demolition of Tashkent's Navrōz marriage registrar office, the group aims to contribute to preserving the city's unique architectural heritage while developing its future. 'We young architects had to do something,' she explains. 'The reason why architects lost their social authority in Uzbekistan lies in our passive or indifferent attitude to our cities. Young architects are brave and bold and full of aspirations – this is necessary to achieve progress.' Since its foundation in 2021, Shaharsozlik To'lqini has organised protests in the form of flash mobs, public talks and a government-backed architecture competition to redesign the Al-Khwarizmi square in Tashkent – the winning scheme is set to be realised this year.

As well as younger architects, Turdialieva also believes that women need to have a greater voice in the development of Uzbekistan: 'Women make up half the population of Uzbekistan, so as long as we restrict women we're developing only half the potential of our nation and this is the same in architecture.'

Fig. 3 Uzbekistan Anti-corruption Agency, Tashkent, Uzbekistan, 2022. The reconstruction of the facade was carried out in collaboration with the engineers Original Project.

ASEL YESZHANOVA

"Through dialogue and participatory design we can get much better, sustainable and effective decisions and results for our cities."

Fig. 1 (left) Applying a traditional Kazakh construction technique using mud and felt. (right) Art installation 'Rhythms' for a project curated by Etage Group, Almaty, Kazakhstan, 2021–22. The installation designed in collaboration with Chingiz Batyrbekov, D.Studio, Rhythms-Art, is made from an abandoned Soviet bus stop.

Asel Yeszhanova is a Kazakhstani architect and urban activist whose participatory approach led her to establish a first-of-its-kind urban forum for city makers and city users. Their aim is to discuss the urban situation and urban development of Almaty, the country's largest metropolis and cultural hub.

Although Yeszhanova wanted to study politics, she was encouraged by her parents to become an architect and has never looked back. 'From the moment I got into school, from the very beginning until today, I think it was the best decision I could have ever made,' she tells us. Yeszhanova first studied in Astana when the city was 'booming' as it had recently been announced as the new capital of an independent Kazakhstan. She later moved to study in the USA as part of a government programme that sent the country's most promising young people to the world's best universities.

After studying at the University of Maryland, USA, Yeszhanova moved to the UK where she worked at global studio Aedas Architects before returning to the USA to complete her studies at the Pratt Institute in New York. She finally returned to a rapidly changing Kazakhstan where she set about engaging the public to determine how the country and its cities should be developed. 'There was no tradition in Kazakhstan, or the whole post-Soviet region, of discussing urbanism, of making open and transparent decisions or involving people in this process,' explains Yeszhanova. 'As a newly independent country, we want to build a new image, we want to build a future vision for the country and architecture is part of this agenda. But this doesn't mean that all old architecture should be knocked down. We can remember the past and look to the future.' While heading up Atomik Architecture's Kazakhstan studio, Yeszhanova founded

Fig. 2 Sketches for the art installation 'Rhythms', curated by Etage Group, Almaty, Kazakhstan, 2021–22..

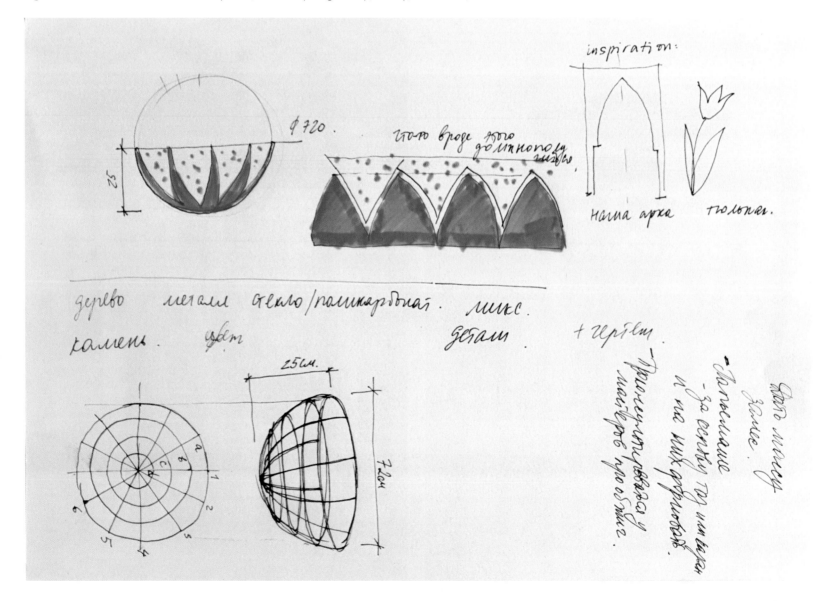

Urban Forum Almaty, a platform 'to make sure that people's ideas are represented in this new future'. She says, 'There was no platform for dialogue between different city stakeholders and so people, activists and experts were unhappy with the changes happening, while the city administration was just doing their work and didn't think they needed to communicate with the rest of the city.' The mission was to establish and encourage ongoing dialogue between different stakeholders. It started as a grassroots movement and now it has become common in Kazakhstan and Central Asia to talk about urban development and new urbanism. After two years the organisation expanded its remit and now operates as Urban Forum Kazakhstan, which conducts workshops, lectures, little interventions, roundtables and research across the country. Alongside this advocacy, which Yeszhanova describes as 'urban activism', she has worked on a diverse range of architectural projects – physical manifestations of her activism. Often collaborations, they include 'Experimental Parklet' with the Goethe-Institut, and the art installation 'Rhythms' which applied traditional Kazakh construction techniques. An early scheme, conceived while at Atomik Architecture, was the creation of the Artpoint Pavilion in collaboration with the British Council as part of the ArtBat Fest festival. The summer pavilion was a new concept for Almaty but was embraced by the city's population. 'It was pure experiment, it was something completely new for Almaty, but people really loved it,' Yeszhanova says. 'They would do with the architecture what they wanted. Sometimes I thought they were ruining it, but they felt like the owners of the space.'

Fig. 3 (left and right) 'Experimental Parklet', Almaty, 2021. Designed by Yeszhanova for a project in collaboration with the Goethe-Institut.

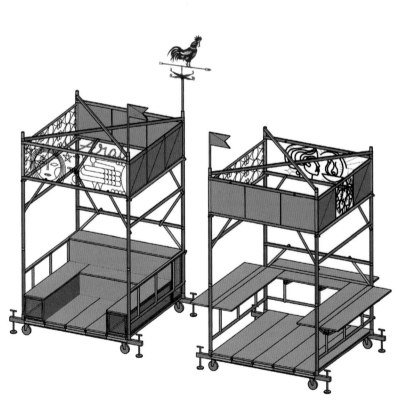

"I care more about the experience of buildings than the form."

SOOK HEE CHUN

Fig. 1 'Dialogue in the Dark', Buchon, Seoul, South Korea, 2015. The cultural centre is built on an awkward sloping site.

Sook Hee Chun is an architect who was one of the first cohort of women to graduate in architecture from Ewha Womans University in Seoul. She then moved to the USA to complete her Master's at Princeton University, New Jersey.

Along with partner Young Jang, she now leads South Korean studio WISE Architecture, which has become known for its thoughtful, sensory architecture with a strong focus on materiality – something that she believes is only truly possible to appreciate in person. 'Spatial and sensory experiences are the most important thing for me to design, using the texture of materials,' she tells us. 'A design critic once told me, "Your building is not photogenic, but it is better in person", and that was the biggest compliment for me.'

Chun had the perfect opportunity to interrogate how people experience space in her 'Dialogue in the Dark' project. Built on an awkward sloping site in the north of Seoul, the cultural building was designed to house an exhibition where visitors experience everyday activities in complete darkness. 'You go inside of the building, you see nothing, but you can hear something, you can smell something,

Fig. 2 'Dialogue in the Dark', Buchon, Seoul, South Korea, 2015. The building houses a sensory exhibition where visitors experience activities in darkness.

you can touch something.' As many of the people working within the exhibition are blind, Chun aimed to create a building that could be navigated and understood through sense and touch. For example, the floors are connected by a curved stair that gets tighter higher up the building and has steps of different textures to indicate what storey you are on. 'I tried to design the whole building to give people signs with the architectural textures,' she tells us. 'There are many indicators for the users so that they will experience the space better than any other building.' WISE Architecture have created a succession

of buildings – from domestic architecture to offices and public spaces – that often use texture and perforation to evoke strong emotional responses. One of their best-known projects is the War and Women's Human Rights Museum in Seoul, which is dedicated to the story of 'comfort woman' who were forced into sexual slavery by the Japanese military during the Second Word War. Set in a suburban house in Seoul, wrapped in a screen made with 45,000 bricks, the small museum contains a series of carefully structured spaces deliberately designed to make visitors feel 'uncertain'.

Chun hopes that the museum's 'strong presence' can help convey the women's horrifying experiences, stimulate discussion and make a lasting impact on visitors. The depth of Chun's work has recently been recognised by being shortlisted for the Women in Architecture Moira Gemmill Prize for Emerging Architecture. She believes that having more women architects will help create a world that is better able to reflect the people that inhabit it. 'Would the world be more balanced, the physical environment more balanced and the living environment more balanced? Absolutely.'

Fig. 3 Suan Coffee Company, Busan, Pusan-jikhalsi, South Korea, 2019.

JUAN DU

"Co-design can advocate
for communities on the margins."

Fig. 1 Friendship Homes: Transitional Housing for Working Homeless, Hong Kong, 2019. A pilot project allowing residents to form a six-member co-living community with semi-private sleeping spaces.

Fig. 1 Friendship Homes: Transitional Housing for Working Homeless, Hong Kong, 2019. A pilot project allowing residents to form a six-member co-living community with semi-private sleeping spaces.

Architecture and teaching combine to define the career of Juan Du, who has gained recognition for work that is informed by the social and ecological processes of the city. Juan Du grew up biculturally and bilingually, having been born in northern China and then moving to the USA at the age of 12. She has worked in China, the USA, Italy, France and Switzerland, gaining experience in designing museums and performing arts centres, as well as bespoke and luxury commercial projects. In 2006, shortly after moving to Hong Kong, she set up her own office, IDU_architecture. While there, Du taught at the University of Hong Kong, where she also founded the school's Urban Ecologies Design Lab and served in a number of academic leadership roles. In 2021, she was appointed Professor and Dean at the John H Daniels Faculty of Architecture, Landscape and Design at the University of Toronto.

A career-defining moment came early on: 'I was frustrated by the limitations of conventional architectural practices, especially after a 2003 Fulbright Research Fellowship in Shanghai exposed me to the escalation of social inequity and

Fig. 2 Hakka Village Commune Community Centre, Shenzhen, China, 2017. A new centre of culture, arts and community services that enhances the existing architectural heritage.

environmental problems of China's rapid urbanisation,' Du says. 'From then on, I started to speak with and learn directly from residents, migrant workers and various people in the broader socioeconomic communities.' In her work, engagement with disadvantaged communities and social sustainability have become consistent motivations. Friendship Homes – co-living flats for homeless residents – were the outcome of long-term collaboration with the Society for Community Organisation, a Hong Kong NGO, to renovate long-vacant flats and create transitional housing and community spaces for the city's working homeless population. The vacant flats were rented for HK$1 per year.

In 2006, Du won first place in an international urban planning competition for the redevelopment of Shenzhen's 50ha urban village of Huanggang, a migrant worker enclave in the city's 'special economic zone'. Her approach – to learn from local knowledge – included drawing on the Indigenous history and narratives of the city's unacknowledged process of urbanisation. The 2017 project is an exercise in transforming and renovating an abandoned, centuries-old village housing compound into a community centre and night school. The existing Hakka architectural heritage is preserved and new spatial elements, such as circular skylights, were added.

For Du and her practice, repairing historic structures and installing contemporary design elements is an approach to urban renewal that works with the existing architecture through a strategy of adaptation. Her design, research and curatorial work over 15 years in Shenzhen has contributed to significant changes in public and media representations and shifts in governmental and institutional attitudes towards Indigenous communities. In 2020, she authored *The Shenzhen Experiment: The Story of China's Instant City*, which documents the rapid urbanisation of this former rural hinterland. Says Du, 'I'm looking forward to applying many aspects of what I have learned from the urbanisation processes of Asian cities in the North American context.'

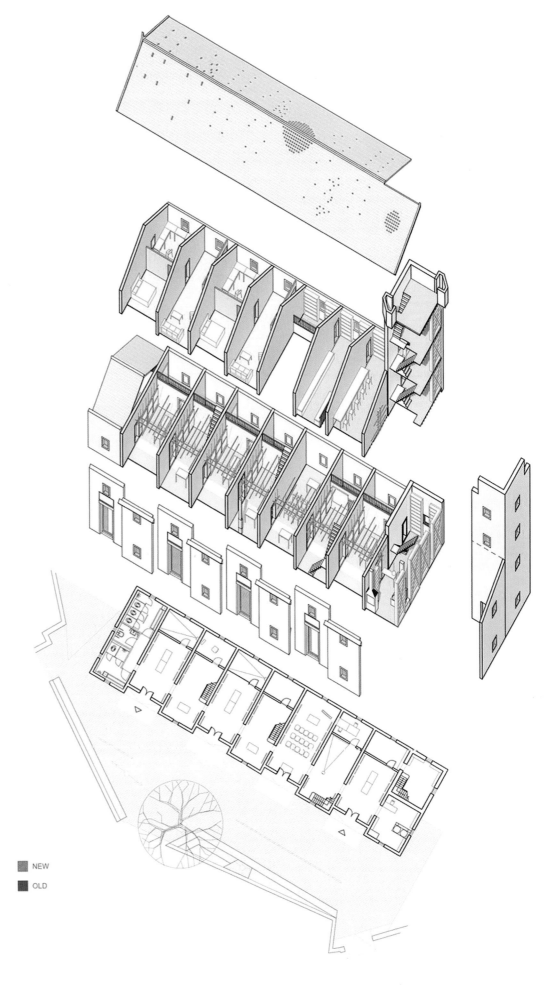

NEW

OLD

Fig. 3 Drawing for Hakka Village Commune Community Centre, Shenzhen, China, 2017.

"Research tells us certain things that help us rethink the whole process of design."

ROSSANA HU

Fig. 1 The Waterhouse, South Bund, Shanghai, China, 2010. The four-storey boutique hotel is built into an existing Japanese Army headquarters building from the 1930s.

Rossana Hu is founder of Shanghai-based Neri&Hu, which has distinguished itself for interdisciplinary research and design. 'We see design as part of a holistic discipline,' Hu tells us. For the studio this means working against the usual economic agenda and time constraints of architecture which, she says, 'leave little room to think about design in a comprehensive way'. Architecture and design can be more of a potent cultural force, Hu argues, when they are based in research: 'We have to ask ourselves what is the meaning behind the things we do.' Her approach is investigative: 'It's researching from all directions – looking for traces and signs – that gives inspiration to form.'

Neri&Hu was founded in 2004 and, over 20 years, an ethos has emerged that responds to a culture in flux with hybrid typologies and multidisciplinary practice. '15 years ago, we were practising in a city where "the old" was not taken very seriously. Everybody wanted new buildings. The old neighbourhoods were being demolished and it made us feel uncomfortable.' The underlying sense here is that gentrification too often demolishes and rebuilds for simple commercial gain, or takes a defensive, gated approach. In contrast, Neri&Hu's work explores contrasts of old and new, public and private, and sustainability through reuse.
The studio's ethos can be best understood through their redevelopment and historic

renovation projects. The Waterhouse is a four-storey boutique hotel built into an existing three-storey Japanese Army headquarters building from the 1930s which, at one time, was used as a warehouse. The design is a good example of adaptive reuse, where old and new interact and are dramatised by contrasting treatments to existing brick and new walls, and whether furniture is loose or built-in. Sited in the traditional, *Longtang* (narrow lanes) of Shanghai, the design takes a cue from the 'unique spatial flavour of the city' – but not, says Hu, in a touristic way. The architects created visual connections between spaces to force hotel guests to confront local conditions on the street, using 'blurring and layering to

Fig. 2 The Waterhouse, South Bund, Shanghai, China, 2010. Courtyard area. The design blurs interior and exterior spaces and creates unexpected visual connections.

provoke people to think about the spaces they occupy'. Here we see how contextual research can feed into practical design decisions to prompt the bigger quest for meaning. Neri&Hu have won multiple awards and yet Hu is keen to talk about the challenges she faced as a woman during her training at Berkeley and Princeton in the USA and in China. 'My early work in the US brought me to construction sites where pornographic posters were everywhere. They made me uncomfortable, especially when I was usually the youngest and only female on site.' When she set up office in Shanghai in 2004, 'the market was not mature and appreciation for design professionals nonexistent'. She explains, 'In Asian projects, you often get the sense that clients prefer to have a man in control. They speak to you, but they don't have the same confidence in you.' Today, Neri&Hu is proactive in advancing change for the younger generation coming to work at their practice. They have more female senior architects and a constant on the agenda is the need to achieve work-life balance.

Fig. 3 The Waterhouse, South Bund, Shanghai, China, 2010. Stairway. The renovation rests on a clear contrast of old and new.

"We need to change mindsets about how we live – taking care of place and network instead of space and time."

MOMOYO KAIJIMA

Fig. 1 Internal view, Momonoura Village, Ishinomaki, Miyagi, Japan, 2011–17. A collaboration with Satokura architects and dot architects. Post-tsunami reconstruction of accommodation.

Tokyo-based Atelier Bow-Wow was set up by Momoyo Kaijima and Yoshiharu Tsukamoto in 1992. Their ground-breaking and widely published work is based on a personal philosophy of '*architectural behaviourology*' – understanding architectural forms in terms of everyday experiences, from people's habits to climate realities, as well as the use of local building materials. Kaijima tells us, 'We can read architectural form to understand what has changed in the 200 years since the Industrial Revolution.' Over 30 years, the studio's work has ranged from private houses to micro-public spaces – interventions in the city at a small scale – and, more recently, they have engaged with rural contexts as well. Signature projects include 'Made

in Tokyo', 'Pet Architecture' and Kaijima's curation of the Japan Pavilion for the Venice Architecture Biennale in 2018.

Kaijima graduated from the Department of Housing and Architecture, Faculty of Human Sciences and Design at Japan Women's University in 1991, where women were only allowed to study 'the home', not architecture per se. Kaijima has used the perspective of lived experience, which she gained through her education, to develop new ways for architecture to transform society. 'A house needs a life. Life is the centre of the study,' explains Kaijima. 'Everybody has a life and, for most, a house. Therefore, the study of architecture expands from the experience of the body to the outside.'

This patterning instinct has led Atelier Bow-Wow to focus on long-term projects creating replicable urban social typologies that involve learning about local culture and, where possible, staying in touch with communities post-completion. Their work in Momonoura Village, a collaboration with Satokura architects and dot architects, exemplifies this approach. After the tsunami and earthquake of 2011, Atelier Bow-Wow began working with a group of fishermen in the village, using drawings to understand and explore their needs moving forward. This process revealed anxieties around migration, the loss of a new generation and the subsequent impact on the economic sustainability of this rural community.

Fig. 2 Momonoura Village, Ishinomaki, Miyagi, Japan, 2011–17. Post-tsunami reconstruction of accommodation and a new fisherman's school.

Initial outcomes included a fisherman's school, precipitating population growth, and expanding the scope of the project to provide homes for newcomers as well as relocating locals. Atelier Bow-Wow also collaborated with less experienced architects to develop a summer school dedicated to building these new homes, harnessing the expertise of local carpenters and the proximity of a local timber mill. Thus, the project became a hub, intersecting local knowledge with both embryonic and established architectural thinking and practice.

At the heart of Kaijima's vision for a better society is a commitment to communal public space. Atelier Bow-Wow's private housing work provides an especially interesting backdrop to this vision in its breaking down of the conventions of the single, family home. Located in Chigasaki, Kanagawa, Japan, ANI House offers an early example of this approach. Embodying the principle of *sukima*, which translates as 'in-between space', ANI House preserves the space between adjacent houses for shared use. In high-density neighbourhoods, Kaijima argues, this is a good solution to lack of space and/or amenities. HaHa House, in the same location, evidences the ongoing replication of this idea.

Alongside her work as part of Atelier Bow-Wow, Kaijima has taught at the University of Tsukuba and, in 2017, she was inaugurated as Professor of Architectural Behaviourology at ETH Zurich, Switzerland. For Kaijima, the process of zooming in on attitudes and behaviours within the built environment helps architecture to address complex global issues such as the climate crisis. 'We need to change mindsets about how we live, how much we eat and how we create our boundaries around what we consume and how we build society,' she argues. 'For architecture, this goes beyond limiting what we build and the materials we consume, to limiting our boundaries – taking care of place and network instead of space and time.'

Fig. 3 Internal view, HaHa House, Chigasaki, Kanazawa, Japan, 2021.

"To be contemporary the countryside needs to be delicately stitched back to a wider human and infrastructural network."

XU TIANTIAN

Fig. 1 Tofu Factory, Caizhai Village, Dadongba Town, Songyang County, Lishui, Zhejiang Province, China, 2018.
The factory is conceived as a flexible and adaptive public facility responding to the rural village context.

Xu Tiantian is the founder of DnA (Design and Architecture), Beijing, China. The practice is known for cultural and educational projects in rural communities including the Hakka Indenture Museum in Songyang and a number of quarry projects and production factories that have been created for local sustainable agriculture.

Xu's training developed in an international context, having qualified with a Baccalaureate in Architecture from Tsinghua University, Beijing, and with a Master's in Architecture and Urban Design from Harvard University. She practised in the USA and the Netherlands –including time spent at the Office for Metropolitan Architecture (OMA) – before returning to China to establish DnA in 2004.

While Xu's architectural education largely focused on urban contexts, her work with rural communities has required a more complex, flexible and anthropological approach that addresses cultural heritage and belonging, as well as ways of understanding traditional modes of working with materials. With a rigorous process of research, listening and dialogue her practice is able to implement new forms that are neither modern nor historically derivative. The projects in the Songyang river valley in Zhejiang province, south of Shanghai, are characterised by what Tiantian calls 'architectural acupuncture'. She describes this as making incisive, small-scale interventions that are not about form or iconic image, but which act as translators of diversity and heritage, working to increase opportunities and create sustainable developments relevant to the participants.

Fig. 2 Tofu Factory, Caizhai Village, Dadongba Town, Songyang County, Lishui, Zhejiang Province, China, 2018. Semi-open terraces accommodate visitors and socialising.

The aim is to develop an economy of competence and hope.

Many of DnA's projects contextualise traditional building techniques and display them to visitors. Bamboo Pavilion, Xu Tiantian's first commission – a modest structure intended as a resting pavilion for tea farmers and a viewing platform for visitors - is exemplary. Employing local contractors and traditional ways of working with bamboo, it incorporates the value of communal spaces for local people and an anticipation of the touristic potential vital for the future rebalancing of urban and rural life. The same year she also created a Bamboo Theatre. Brown Sugar Factory and Caizhai Tofu

Factory are opportunities to upgrade production quality and improve the value of local agricultural products. Both factories incorporate museum-like opportunities to witness work – the Tofu Factory features semi-open terraces that can accommodate visitors and convivial activities. The aim is to make local history and traditional values apparent to the villagers, as well as to tourists. Xu argues that 'architecture engaging local life/resources could be much more effective and efficient'.

All of DnA's work can be seen as experiments in hybrid economic formats that operate as exemplary projects to encourage other villages to interpret and imitate them.

Reflecting on her work, Xu suggests that architecture in these rural contexts is not primarily about space, materials or details, it is an attempt to maximise the social, cultural and economic impact of the project, learning from local creativity and traditional wisdom. DnA's work is celebrated in the RIBA video 'Rural Renaissance', and in the book *The Songyang Story: Architectural Acupuncture as Driver for Progress in Rural China* (2020). In 2006 Xu Tiantian was awarded the World Architecture China Award, and in 2008 the Young Architects' Award from the Architectural League of New York. In 2019 she won the Moira Gemmill Prize for Emerging Architecture.

Fig. 3 Bamboo Theatre, Hengkeng Village, Songyang, Lishui, Zhejiang Province, China, 2015. Each year, old bamboo can be removed from this informal leisure space and new bamboo is integrated into the existing structure.

ELEENA JAMIL

"Looking at local typologies responsive to context is a starting point for innovating architecture at all scales."

Fig. 1 The Bamboo Playhouse, Perdana Botanical Gardens, Kuala Lumpur, Malaysia, 2015. Being a lightweight material, the structure was built very quickly without the use of heavy machinery.

In 2005, Malaysian-based architect Eleena Jamil established her practice in Kuala Lumpur, developing buildings rooted in context – in terms of climate, culture and local community. She combines architecture with research, showing the relevance of traditional craft techniques to contemporary sustainable architecture.

Jamil graduated from the Welsh School of Architecture, Cardiff University, UK, in 1994. She went on to complete her PhD, 'Rethinking Modernism', on architects Peter and Alison Smithson. Her work was particularly influenced by ideas of the 'as found' and 'ordinariness', and a combination of modesty and sophistication, as an alternative to the reductive limitations of modern architecture. Those elements are evident in her engagement with traditional Malay architecture.

On returning to Southeast Asia, she tells us, 'I soon realised that the solution to developing Southeast Asian cities doesn't always have to be along the lines of Western, modernist, functionalist principles. An approach based on regional sensibilities is more apt as the way forward.'

In the early years, she worked on extensions and single-family dwellings. 'During this time', she tells us, 'I came across many people who considered my work a "hobby" rather than a serious professional career.' Winning the Millennium School Bamboo Classroom

Fig. 2 The Bamboo Playhouse, Perdana Botanical Gardens, Kuala Lumpur, Malaysia, 2015. The bamboo culms (canes) were put together using traditional methods of jointing where friction and lashings create strong connections.

competition in the Philippines established the studio's significance and renown for using sustainable materials.

Jamil's work is attentive to the social and climatic imperatives of each brief within a broader cultural framework. It is dedicated to passive design strategies and pleasurable experiences. Notable buildings include Karwa Mosque Temple in Penang and the ambitious, 1,200-student Desa Mahkota School. The latter comprises of classrooms, laboratories, administrative offices and a canteen, with its ingenious architectural promenade oriented through northern exposed corridors and courtyards – all cross-ventilated and cooled by fins and overhangs. This provides a model for improving the typology of local schools by creating comfortable conditions with the least amount of energy and lowest carbon footprint. The typology of the traditional timber pavilion – with its raised platforms and local natural materials – has also acted as a starting point for innovation. The temporary Shadow Garden Pavilion innovates with a vernacular timber jointing method called *tanggam*. The Bamboo Playhouse project is a large island structure in a public park. Built up on raised cantilevered decks, traditional timber platform elements are juxtaposed in convivial and playful relationships featuring creative planting and shaded communal spaces. They constitute a model for bamboo building on a grander scale, using industrialised, prefabricated components. Jamil was shortlisted for the 2017 Firm of the Year by the Architecture Master Prize and in 2018 she was shortlisted for Dezeen Architect of the Year. Her project End-lot House won the German Design Council's Architecture Award in 2021. Her research on making techniques has been published in *Architecture Malaysia* and informed a short film, *Tukang*, funded by the British Council. Modelling a new way of working for the future, Jamil says, 'I think my practice's role will overlap with that of an initiator, architect, maker and builder, as we try to look for different solutions for reducing carbon footprints and increasing energy efficiency.'

Fig. 3 (left) Shadow Garden Pavilion, Petaling Jaya, Malaysia, 2016. The movable shades made from galvanised steel panels are connected to planters via a simple pulley system and make interesting shadow patterns during the day. Drawing for the Shadow Garden Pavilion, Petaling Jaya, Malaysia, 2016. (right) The drawing shows a demountable vernacular timber jointing method called *tanggam* from traditional stilt houses where *tukang* (craftsmen) fit beams together without fasteners, using only tension and friction.

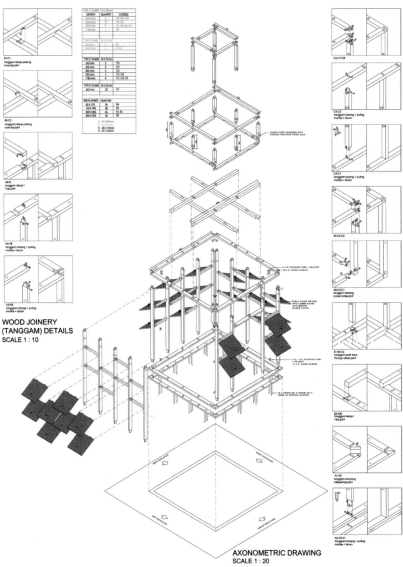

WOOD JOINERY (TANGGAM) DETAILS
SCALE 1 : 10

AXONOMETRIC DRAWING
SCALE 1 : 20

PATAMA ROONRAKWIT

"The most important thing is to get people involved in every step of the process."

Fig. 1 TEN Bangkok, Thailand, 2006.

Patama Roonrakwit is a Thai architect whose core ideal of community architecture has led to the development of tools and systems to improve underprivileged communities across Southeast Asia for over 20 years. For this work, she won the Silpakorn Award by Thailand's Ministry of Culture in 2010 and the Global Award for Sustainable Architecture in 2016.

Roonrakwit gained her undergraduate degree from Silpakorn University in Bangkok and a Master's degree from Oxford Brookes University in the UK, before returning to Thailand to work in an informal settlement in the south of the country. Here she quickly discovered that her academic training was only the beginning of her education. 'It was learning by doing,' she tells us. 'I was really interested in small-scale architecture, but when I went to the slum it blew my mind – I was impressed by the details, materials and problem solving. We had to really consider what we could add to better serve the needs of the community, which made me entirely reconsider the role of the architect.'

At this first project, located alongside the Borwa Creek, Roonrakwit worked closely with the existing community – as she would in many subsequent projects – to create a detailed development plan including walkways, bridges, drainage systems and lighting to improve the living conditions of the entire community.

'My way of working is to communicate with the user as much as I can, so that I can understand them, they can understand me and we don't waste anything, as we cannot afford to make mistakes,' Roonrakwit says. 'To place a bridge you need to understand the local conditions. That may be the soil, but it also might be a mean man in a neighbouring house who's going to charge to use the bridge – you've got to speak to people to understand.'

Following the completion of the infrastructure upgrades at the Borwa Creek slum, the

Fig. 2 TEN Bangkok, Thailand, 2006. The rooftop is a common area for all household members.

knock-on effects of this participatory approach soon became clear. 'After the community finished the project, they started to feel more confident and began improving their own homes,' Roonrakwit explains. In addition, the collaboratively created development plan had been used to gain local government funding. 'Other slum communities on the creek asked how they got this, so people started to share information on funding and teach how to prepare a plan and make proposals to the government.' Following this initial project, Roonrakwit established her studio, Community Architects for Shelter and Environment (CASE), in 1997.

This is dedicated to improving informal settlements in the country. Along with the country's poorest communities, she has also turned her attention to the middle classes, who she refers to as 'informal poor'. CASE's TEN Bangkok pilot scheme saw land acquired by CASE and divided into ten plots for self-build houses. The model has since been rolled out across the city. Her latest project aims to develop modular homes for Thailand's middle classes. 'Poor people can do anything with a little bit of help from us architects, so I thought why not the middle classes who have a better background, better education and better income.'

Although Roonrakwit has spent her entire career working to improve housing, she believes that influencing government and housing policy can make the greatest change. One way of doing this is by demonstrating better solutions than the clearance of informal slum developments. 'We need to look at the root of the problem,' she says. 'What we can do is encourage the government to listen and explain that you can spend *less money* to make better solutions.' For Roonrakwit, such solutions are not top-down: 'Putting people in housing provided by the government doesn't end the problem, and sometimes it creates more problems.'

Fig. 3 TEN Bangkok, Thailand, 2006. Design development was aided by models and discussion.

"Technology and humanism will be more relevant than ever in the next few decades."

CATHY SALDAÑA

Fig. 1 Ayala Serin Mall, Tagaytay City, Cavite, Philippines, 2014. The design uses contemporary structures and rustic designs to give a vibe of 'quaintness' to the mall, which also includes a garden in the atrium.

Cathy Saldaña is an architect, builder and master planner who specialises in sustainable development. She is CEO of PDP Architects (founded in 1992), a firm based in the Philippines, which employs mostly women. She tells us, 'We inspire and mentor the younger generation to engage in this otherwise male-dominated industry.' Saldaña graduated from the University of the Philippines' School of Architecture and the Asian School of Management, an education that fostered resourcefulness and a global outlook. Says Saldaña, 'Resilience was expected as the Philippines went through and surpassed natural disasters and sociopolitical upheavals.' Her architectural education started in her school days when she accompanied her engineer father – who worked for the National Housing Authority – on site visits. This provided her with valuable insights into the importance of inclusive architecture and the building of communities. At PDP Architects, Saldaña has overseen innovative developments of hotels, residential and corporate projects, including Ayala Serin Mall, Tagaytay City and Fe Del Mundo Medical Centre, Quezon City. She stresses the importance of forming effective teams. She also emphasises the need to be accepted as a woman in a world dominated by men – establishing international respect by moving beyond traditional residential projects to large, prestigious commissions. A role model is Zaha Hadid, whose 'strength and courage allowed her to stand among international design giants' and to create original, landmark projects.

Specialising in sustainable island development, Saldaña is committed to

Fig. 2 Damosa Diamond Tower, Damosa IT Park, Lanang, Davao City, Philippines, 2019. The 17-storey office building aims to address the growing demand for corporate spaces and features sustainable technology such as LED lighting, solar panels and eco-friendly insulation.

a comprehensive approach to projects, considering the character of the brand, the site and surroundings and the imprint of the Philippines and its indigenous resources. She stresses the importance of combining ancient, traditional strategies with cutting-edge technologies and convincing clients that green practices generate more yield, both for them and the environment. Damosa Diamond Tower (2019) is a 17-storey building that prioritises sustainability. It emphasises efficiency in the use of energy, water and construction materials. It also uses eco-friendly insulation and low E-glass, which increases access to natural light while minimising the penetration of ultraviolet and infrared light. It deploys fins to deflect heat, harvests and recycles rainwater and uses LED lights and locally sourced construction materials. Saldaña says of the building that the intention was to render it 'photo dynamic' so that during day and night it becomes a beacon and landmark in Davao City. Saldaña advocates for international collaboration that does not compromise the importance of national characteristics.

She insists on the need for innovation and storytelling as well as learning how to 'trickle down' the characteristics of luxury buildings into a wider range of projects and going beyond building codes to 'do better'. To back up this work, she serves as a trustee on the Board for the Urban Land Institute. Saldaña concludes, 'The Coronavirus pandemic has taught us that, in all things, we have to provide for health and wellness first in the buildings and spaces we design.'

Fig. 3 Fe Del Mundo Medical Centre, Quezon City, Philippines, 2016. The design aimed to upgrade and refresh the patient experience as well as attracting new business.

> "I believe that it is time for architects to become brief-makers and stakeholders."

DALIANA SURYAWINATA

Fig. 1 Micro-library Bima, Bandung, Indonesia, 2016. The first micro-library in the series, reusing 2,000 ice-cream buckets on the facade to filter daylight and allow cross ventilation.

Indonesian architect Daliana Suryawinata founded SHAU Rotterdam-Bandung together with Professor Florian Heinzelmann to pursue a cultural-environmental agenda for architecture. It was during her postgraduate study, at the former Berlage Institute in Rotterdam in the Netherlands, that she met Heinzelmann. 'We do everything together,' she tells us. 'Having a partner who can challenge your ideas is very important. Then you have cooked ideas together rather than raw ones.' SHAU designs public facilities, housing, parks and masterplans, but it's the series of micro-libraries, run by communities for low-income neighbourhoods, that best represent her ethos. This endeavour demands a reframing of the way briefs operate. Suryawinata tells us, 'Projects that are initiated and led by architects – not only "commissioned" to architects – tend to answer more societal issues.' She continues, 'Moved by the fact that Indonesia is one of the worst countries for its reading interest, we envisioned the micro-libraries to be special, custom-designed, one-of-a-kind for every neighbourhood – making reading more attractive.'

The libraries are multi-programmatic and use sustainable materials and passive design strategies. Each building has a reading space and book racks, community space and sometimes play spaces, a stage or a roof garden. Each uses reused plastic, certified wood and locally available materials. The first library, which includes a pop-up baby clinic, has a facade constructed reusing 2,000 ice-cream buckets – becoming a neighbourhood icon and pre-wedding photo venue.

Suryawinata emphasises the collaboration involved in her work. 'SHAU sees clients as

Fig. 2 Micro-library Warak Kayu, Semarang, Indonesia, 2020. Using the traditional house-on-stilts typology, the reading space is housed on top with community activities below.

equal partners whenever possible,' she tells us. A good example is Micro-library Warak Kayu, funded by the Arkatama Isvara Foundation, where they worked with PT Kayu Lapis Indonesia, a large-scale wood prefabrication factory. The structure encloses a net floor and swing to make reading more playful. 'We worked out all the wooden joints with the research team in the factory, built a 1:1 partial model and came up with detail solutions together.' Across the whole project, multi-stakeholder collaboration was made possible by tapping into Corporate Social Responsibility and sometimes state funding.

The wide-reaching impact of their work can be seen in SHAU's awards, which include the Archdaily Building of the Year, Architizer A+Awards, INDE Awards, Lafarge-Holcim Asia Pacific and an Aga Khan Award shortlist. Suryawinata is keen to credit Ridwan Kamil, Governor of West Java, who she sees as an exemplary politician-architect, creating parks and public spaces in a way that gives architects agency as stakeholders in public life. 'It is important that design briefs are made together.'

Looking forward, Suryawinata comments on the way 'sustainability will be the new normal.

The next thing is to use architecture and urban design to promote healthier, less consumptive and more meaningful lives.' She also sees new hybrid practices emerging: 'Instead of one-by-one custom building design that is constructed on site, architecture will be seen as a product line with engaging modular systems, 3D printing and robots. Local craftsmanship will still be valuable – but highly priced – so a combination of hardcore factory production with custom artisan work is foreseeable.'

Fig. 3 Micro-library interiors. (left) Bima, Bandung, Indonesia, 2016, designed for neighbourhood children and schools without libraries. (right) Warak Kayu, Semarang, Indonesia, 2020, with the wooden library on top and a net for casual seating and a swing below.

TRẦN THỊ NGỤ NGÔN

Fig. 1 Long An House, Mỹ Hạnh Nam, Ho Chi Minh City, Long An Province, Vietnam, 2017. Ventilation efficiency is increased by dividing the roof into two parts and having a courtyard.

'Architecture is my passion,' says Vietnamese architect Trần Thị Ngụ Ngôn. She runs Ho Chi Minh City-based studio Tropical Space alongside Nguyễn Hải Long, creating sculptural, climate-appropriate architecture that celebrates the simplicity of raw materials.

Ngôn, who graduated from Ho Chi Minh City University of Architecture, established her studio after being frustrated with the ethos of large practices in Vietnam. 'I felt fed up; I had not arrived in my place,' she said. 'Some studios just earn money but bring nothing meaningful to society. I established my own studio to work for my own vision.'

Since co-founding Tropical Space in 2011, Ngôn has designed a series of homes in and around Ho Chi Minh City that are sculptural responses to the country's climate. 'The climate is very important for architects to understand, because if they don't, they will ignore the local characteristics of the building,' she says. 'If architecture is built against the local climate, they have to use technology, like air-conditioning, and it's not good for the environment.'

For Ngôn, this means designing buildings from local materials that do not require large amounts of mechanical heating or ventilation. With a focus on achieving natural air flow and shading, Ngôn likes building with clay bricks, which incorporate a distinctive, signature perforated section. Ngôn's architecture

Fig. 2 Long An House, Mỹ Hạnh Nam, Ho Chi Minh City, Long An Province, Vietnam, 2017. The private house is inspired by the traditional structure of Vietnamese housing, with a layout that utilises the wind direction of the local area in different seasons.

is nevertheless responsive to locality, referencing Vietnamese culture. The dwellings that her studio has worked on, which include Termitary House, Cuckoo House, Long An House, NDC House, LT House and Wasp House, all also establish a connection to and with the natural world.

While the humid climate drives much of her design thinking, Ngôn also wants to create fun, intriguing structures. Perhaps this is most obvious in the Chicken Case – the structure designed in the garden of Long An House.

Built from left-over building materials, the structure is both a cage for chickens and ducks and a climbing frame for the owner's grandchildren.

Overall, Ngôn believes that architects need to make sure that they use technology in appropriate ways to create environmentally responsible architecture. 'We are living in the age of technology and it's bringing us a lot of pleasantness and safety,' she explains, 'but we have ignored the negative impact on the natural environment.' She continues,

'Architecture should be a combination of modern technology and sustainable, environmentally friendly design solutions that are focused on how to reduce construction materials and energy consumption.' Ngôn is also reflective on her status as a woman architect, especially one who is also a mother. She is only half-joking when she says, 'It's very challenging, I don't know if I would encourage more women to become architects!'

Fig. 3 Long An House, Mỹ Hạnh Nam, Ho Chi Minh City, Long An Province, Vietnam, 2017. The sloped roof informs a contemporary and strong architectural language.

SUHAILEY
FARZANA

"I love to see the world through the people of different communities and co-create with them."

Fig. 1 Visualisation of collective dreams and aspirations in low-income communities, 2015.

Suhailey Farzana is an architect searching for stories. She is a founder member of Co.Creation.Architects alongside her partner and husband Khondaker Hasibul Kabir. Based in Jhenaidah, Bangladesh, the practice largely works alongside and within communities to facilitate the reimagining of their environments. Farzana graduated from BRAC University, Bangladesh, where she also completed her Master's degree in Development Studies – an experience augmented with training in Youth Leadership at the University of Vermont in the USA. Much of Farzana's early career was spent undertaking action research and volunteering in low-income settlements as part of the Community Architects Network (CAN) – a modus operandi that underpins her approach to practice. 'How can I be useful with my skills?' Farzana asks. 'In our team I do not wear the hat of an architect at the beginning, so my identity is: I live in the city, so it's my own city, it's my own village, and then I try to be useful in the process.' She expands, 'Often we sit together and talk about how we can develop our city or village. There is no actual project; I would rather say it's a process because it's evolving every day.' Working with communities and as part of a team of people with different areas of expertise, as well as the city authorities, Farzana sees the role of an architect as one of 'facilitator'.

Contrary to the typical architectural procurement process, Farzana describes the work she is engaged in as 'very organic', co-designing and co-creating with communities who are mostly self-funding any building that takes place. 'In the co-creation process everyone will find their own role,' she says, describing how it is often the women within a community who instigate projects, asking questions such as 'How can we build a good house?' Farzana's mode is to 'learn it together and in the process, we try to

Fig. 2 Designing the urban open spaces together, Mohishakundu community in Jhenaidah, Bangladesh, 2019. The community built 20 houses with their own money, with Co.Creation.Architects facilitating the co-design process.

be invisible. 'When we work, it's always the people's project, not our project.'

Within their home city of Jhenaidah, in the southwest of Bangladesh, Farzana and Co.Creation.Architects work to collectively improve the local ecology as part of the Jhenaidah Citywide People's Network. The city sits across both sides of the river Naboganga, which performs a number of functions from bathing, washing and fishing to drainage. Local initiatives to reactivate the socio-cultural potential of the river require Farzana and her team to liaise with the local authorities by making models and drawings. One project – to design a female public toilet (very rare in the city) – will also link to a restaurant and shops to be run by local women. Another will extend the network of pathways along the river, introducing municipal facilities along the way such as an amphitheatre, public toilets and river steps (*ghats*). Farzana describes these projects as a 'purification' of the river and its environs, both literally in that they contribute to the cleansing of the river itself and metaphorically in that these projects indirectly address the broader concerns of climate justice.

Returning to her working process Farzana is emphatic that she is continually learning. 'In this process I always feel there is an equity,' she comments. The relationships that Farzana has brokered are built upon trust and care. 'I see the future as community led. I keep sharing what we are doing here and students often come to work in the community and get to know the people and their lives.' For Farzana, the women of these communities have many wisdoms and sometimes greater practical understanding. 'Even if you are not there, women explain their design and they can build as well.' For Farzana, a powerful aspect of co-creation is the interesting sense of aesthetics that emerges.

Fig. 3 Realisation of people's dreams, a public open space by the Naboganga River in Jhenaidah, Bangladesh, 2020.

TAKBIR FATIMA

"Accessible and responsible design is ensured using participatory, site-responsive and data-driven processes. A benefit is that results are not predetermined, but evolutionary."

Fig. 1 Bright Horizon Academy, Hyderabad, India, 2014. The ancient sheet rock that formed a cliff cutting through the site was incorporated into the building to become the wall in some spaces.

Architect, educator and entrepreneur Takbir Fatima is the Director of the Hyderabad studio DesignAware, with Abeer Fatima and Asna Moazzam Khan. They take a special interest in leveraging experimental and interdisciplinary processes for socially relevant and community building projects. The studio's ethos – to create awareness through design – was a response to the widespread belief, when Fatima first entered the profession, that architecture and design were exclusive and out of reach of the general populus. 'I wanted to dispel this myth, by making architecture and design universally accessible and applicable.' Whether engaged in small-scale collaborations with individuals

or organisations, to city-scale government initiatives, accessible and responsible design is ensured using a mix of participatory, site-responsive and data-driven design processes. Fatima tells us that a benefit is that results are not predetermined, but evolutionary, unpredictable and serendipitous.

A recent project in Hyderabad, the Bright Horizon Academy for children from disadvantaged backgrounds, illustrates the potential and impact of their ethos. Built at the heart of the 800-year-old Golconda Fort and set on a rocky cliff at the highest point in the city, the principles were to preserve the existing terrain, to respect the built heritage of the fort and to ensure the sustainability

of the project in the future. 'The resultant process was collaborative and participatory, involving teachers, students, masons, fabricators and carpenters, who provided our architectural team with inputs, creating a sort of design-construction feedback loop.' The project has attracted international attention including an A' Design Award, but for Fatima, the real impact is in its effect on the community: 'The building has taken on a life of its own, defined by the users themselves: open-ended spaces are used for functions other than intended and the school becomes a makeshift neighbourhood clinic during holidays, bringing the entire community together.'

Fig. 2 Bright Horizon Academy, Hyderabad, India, 2014. A perforated wall of lightweight concrete blocks brings in cool air; the boundary between indoors/outdoors is blurred, allowing natural light and ventilation and sometimes rain and pigeons.

Fatima's emergent approach to problem-solving was shaped early on: 'In school we are taught that there can be only one correct answer. I call this the single-solution syndrome, but this is false and any problem can have multiple approaches and solutions, each equally right.' And yet, she tells us, 'sometimes the tools we need may not exist and we need to invent them'. Fatima's response during her time at the Design Research Lab at the Architectural Association, London, was to develop computational tools – both analogue and digital – allowing results to adapt and evolve by the tweaking of parameters. Since 2011, she has developed this process into a generative computing educational initiative – Fractals Workshops – held at architecture schools internationally.

'FLOCK: Interlocking assemblies' was an exploration of a kit of parts that could be assembled in many different ways, resulting in a new outcome every time. The parts were made up of digitally fabricated 2D shapes with grooves that interlock with other units. At art festivals in Dubai and Hyderabad, art installations made up of kit parts were designed and assembled entirely by the public. Urban installations have followed, and it is being taken forward as a research project in the Department of Design at CEPT University, Ahmedabad, India. Fatima has now proven that the system is adaptable across scales, materials and applications. Looking forward, DesignAware wants to use these processes to scale customisable architecture.

Fatima's work is what she calls 'architecture without architects'. It emphasises an open-source, participatory design process, where anyone can apply the system. Now DesignAware are researching how these theories can be applied to recyclable architecture, using processes that are circular and sustainable.

Fig. 3 Bright Horizon Academy, Hyderabad, India, 2014. The computationally designed geometric skylight spans 24m, bringing sunlight into the heart of the school. This was a structural experiment, designed using 3D prototypes instead of drawings, tested directly on site.

"We are a species that is always evolving, not only biologically but also ideologically. Our habitat has to reflect this evolution."

ANUPAMA KUNDOO

Fig. 1 'Unbound: The Library of Lost Books', BCN RE.SET, Barcelona, Spain, 2014. The Pavilion was proposed as a place that celebrates reading and expresses freedom for the 300th year celebration of Catalunya.

Working out of both Berlin, Germany and Pondicherry, India, Anupama Kundoo is an architect whose work has evolved in response to the contexts and people with whom she works. She began her career in 1989, at the age of 23, after completing five years of study at the Sir J.J. College of Architecture, University of Bombay – the city name she still prefers.

From early on, Kundoo operated independently, with a philosophy of 'learning through doing'. She explains, 'I always felt that I didn't want to reduce my practice to what I know. If I didn't know something, I would reach out to people who did, ready for their input.' This includes working with craftsmen and women as she developed an architectural practice that is embedded in vernacular tradition. Says Kundoo, 'When I look at a material, I don't see only the material, I see the people who engage with it.' She is keen to point out this isn't an act of 'social work', rather an approach designed to get the best building with the resources available.

Kundoo positions her thinking in a broader materialist tradition that understands architecture and materials in an ecology. 'Architecture is an extension of the invisible laws of the universe,' she explains, 'where the passage of time is recorded in the material conditions of a building.' She argues that architecture must also respond

Fig. 2 (top left) Wall House, Auroville, Tamil Nadu, India, 2000. The architect's own residence, situated on the outskirts of Auromodele, an area designated for research and experimentation. The design is responsive to context, making use of local materials and skills. The interior has narrow, long, vaulted spaces with activities arranged in rows, like a train. (bottom right) Replica of Wall House constructed at Venice Architecture Biennale 2012.

to the biological and emotional needs of different species. For her, a problem with contemporary architecture is that it is increasingly commodified. 'I like the challenge of using materials judiciously,' says Kundoo, preferring to approach architecture as bricolage, assembling the various material components from what is locally available. 'My work is like that of a contemporary chef, putting together what's around me in a certain way.'

The Wall House is a project that represents Kundoo's spirit as an architect. Located on the outskirts of Auroville in Auromodele, India, it is both a home for the architect and a testbed for other projects. A site of research and experimentation, the building explores spatial boundaries and transitions, addressing their materiality and energy efficiency. The Wall House is responsive to context, making use of local materials and skills. In 2012, a full-size replica of the house

was constructed in the Arsenale at the Venice Architecture Biennale. It was built by a team of Indian craftsmen who understood the conditions and technologies used to construct the house originally. This moment offered a different lens through which to view Kundoo's architecture – as 'modern' rather than 'simply vernacular'.

In 2021 Kundoo was the recipient of the RIBA Charles Jencks Award.

Fig. 3 Sharana Daycare Centre, Pondicherry, India, 2019. Designed for the critical educational needs of socioeconomically disadvantaged children and communities.

YASMEEN LARI

"I was living in a kind of dream world like all architects do – and I think that the work I was creating then is no longer relevant to the reality that now exists all over the world."

Fig. 1 Zero Carbon Cultural Centre, Makli, Pakistan, 2021. Close-up view of the entrance domical structure.

Yasmeen Lari is an architect and humanitarian whose work challenges us to reconsider what constitutes architecture and what it can do. She was the winner of the 2020 Jane Drew Prize for using her work to raise the profile of women in architecture. Educated in the UK during the 1960s, Lari returned to Pakistan to set up her practice in Karachi, becoming the first female architect in the country's history. Although her early career included some social housing projects, she is better known for her imposing and uncompromising commercial architecture including the Finance and Trade Centre (1989), and the Pakistan State Oil House in Karachi (1991).

In a radical shift, Lari retired from practice in 2000 to reorientate her energies towards humanitarian work. She established the Heritage Foundation with her husband – the historian Suhail Zaheer Lari – a move precipitated by a growing discomfort with working for corporate clients. As an architect 'we always feel that somebody has commissioned us', says Lari. 'We serve their purpose; we are not independent. To think that we are free to do what we want is a bit of a fallacy.'

An earthquake in northern Pakistan in 2005 was a pivotal moment in Lari's career, sparking a long-term effort to use her architectural knowledge and networks to assist in rebuilding rural communities in crisis. Although an outsider, Lari has found herself working predominantly alongside women – something that continues to shape and define her recent career. Lari explains that most of her work, 'whether in construction or training, is mostly with women. They are

Fig. 2 Zero Carbon Cultural Centre, Makli, Pakistan, 2021. Entrance structure viewed from inside.

the ones who are spearheading everything.' Pakistan Chulah Cookstove, a mud and lime plaster cooking stove developed by Lari and the Heritage Foundation, is a project that readily illustrates this. Made from locally available materials, the design of the stove addresses both the carbon footprint of open-flame cooking and the impact such cooking has on women's health. For Lari, this project asks, 'How can you provide dignity for women through architecture?' Not only does the redesign of the stove improve the health and well-being of the women who use it, it

has become a place to socialise. Lari notices that, in particular, the posture of the women has changed: 'They're no longer crouching; they don't look downtrodden anymore.' Lari's 'barefoot social architecture' develops through experimentation with traditional building methods and local materials. Moving away from the Western building practices usually employed by international aid agencies, Lari began to work with bamboo in 2009. The Zero Carbon Cultural Centre in Makli, Pakistan, built by local people alongside the Heritage Foundation in 2021, stages

workshops for the community to develop their skills in crafting a variety of products from local materials. Understood to be the largest bamboo structure in Pakistan, and one of the largest in the world, it draws on Lari's own research into the history of bamboo buildings and the development of prototypes at her 'base camp' in northern Pakistan. For Lari, architecture can be transformative, but fundamentally it is about empowering people to build for themselves.

Fig. 3 Pakistan Chulah Cookstove, Pakistan, 2014. Village women cooking food in an eco-friendly way on this smokeless stove made from mud and lime plaster.

"Arts and crafts can mitigate the crisis of identity and hyper-perfection of globalised architecture. Design and construction need to be humanised to create unique and meaningful works."

HABIBEH MADJDABADI

Fig. 1 (left and right) Approximation House, Tehran, Iran, 2021. The facade is a penetrable green micro-ecosystem.

Habibeh Madjdabadi, born in 1977, is a prominent Iranian architect. Her work has been widely acknowledged by local and international media and exhibited at the Venice Architecture Biennale. It is distinct for an exploratory approach that goes into the realms of conceptual art and design. Madjdabadi tells us that it was her upbringing that informed this approach. Born a year before the Islamic Revolution, she was three when the Iran-Iraq War started. 'I wasn't scared of bombardment, but I was an introverted child and created an imaginary world inside my paintings. This idea – of creating an alternative world in art – subconsciously led me to architecture later on.' Madjdabadi established her own design studio in Tehran in 2003, after winning first prize in a design competition for restoring a historical building in Iran. Since then, she has received the Tamayouz Women in Construction Award 2019 and has been shortlisted for the Aga Khan Award and the International Brick Award. She was also shortlisted for the Chicago Award for Mellat Bank's corporate facade. She won third place in the Memar Award 2014 for House of 40 Knots and first prize in 2021 for Approximation House.

Madjdabadi prioritises the role of culture and innovative explorations of indigenous elements in her attention to the materials and methods of fabrication. Materials, deployed in expressive and poetic ways, are an important means of expression. She explains, 'Since materialisation is very important, I don't consider the design finish of a project until we design the construction method.' The role of labour is emphasised, with controlled imperfections of hand-work intentionally integrated into the creative process. 'In Iran there are very few specialised companies who support an architect through construction,' she says. 'In my work, all the details are like an invention – nothing you can buy on the market – so I need to work very closely with the workers.' Synthesising local and global elements, Madjdabadi's creations are the result of meticulous research into how an artistic approach can be both contemporary and rooted in traditions. In recent works, she evokes the poetic side of materials by underlining their natural attributes and interaction with the human body.

House of 40 Knots, designed together with Alireza Mashhad Mirza, is characteristic of her approach. It was a very low-budget project in a middle-class area of Tehran. The five-storey building's facade is based on a Persian carpet design. It is made of locally available bricks, assembled by unskilled craftsmen, working from construction data transformed into simple instructions. This was inspired by the written instructions used in handmade-carpet workshops.

Fig. 2 Approximation House, Tehran, Iran, under construction in 2020. The design involved training workers and involving them in the creative and construction process.

In Approximation House, we see how Madjdabadi's way of humanising relations between materials and construction is imagined as a kind of participatory art. A terraced house with two duplex apartments, the facade consists of thousands of round, wooden battens to mitigate the strong sunlight and provide privacy. Honouring the tradition of craftsmanship, the architect invited workers to cut and shape the wood pieces with approximated sizes and organic shapes – giving the building its name. Madjdabadi reflects, 'When installed on the facade, the result is an artwork belonging to all the people participating in the construction.' Here, greenery also became an elemental aspect: 'I designed a path that starts from the courtyard and goes up the facade to the roof garden. This green area is also an objection to devastation of gardens in Tehran.' Internationally recognised, Madjdabadi collaborated on the design of the Norwegian embassy in Tehran with French-Italian engineering company, Artelia-Italy. A leading and original voice for Iranian architecture, she has lectured widely in countries including Italy, Austria, Greece, Serbia, Bulgaria, Bosnia-Herzegovina and Albania. Her work has been exhibited in the Venice Architecture Biennale, Vienna University of Technology, Austria and Melbourne University, Australia.

Fig. 3 House of 40 Knots, Sattarkhan, Tehran, Iran, 2014. Madjdabadi in collaboration with Alireza Mashadimirza. The facade was entirely covered with a mesh of bricks impaled on rod bars inspired by historical traditions of Persian carpets.

MARWA AL-SABOUNI

"I'm interested in the role of architecture in creating conflict and how to reverse that – how to make architecture a tool of peace instead."

Fig. 1 The American Riad project, Detroit, USA. Facade design for a row of housing with shops on the ground floor for an art and housing justice project in collaboration with Ghana Think Tank, The American Riad.

An architect from Homs, Syria, Marwa Al-Sabouni is internationally acclaimed for her contribution to architecture through practice, writing and exhibition-making. She is co-founder of the architectural studio and portal, Arabic Gate – the world's first and only website dedicated to architectural news in Arabic.

She says, 'I don't know if I ever started practising as an architect, to be honest. When the war started here in my country 10 years ago, I was still studying for my PhD.' Since then, Al-Sabouni has become an expert on reconstruction in Syria and has participated in UN-organised conferences and workshops in Syria, Berlin, Beirut and Geneva. Her practice work has featured in documentaries by the BBC and UNESCO as well as in international journals. She was the Prince Claus Laureate 2018 for outstanding achievement in the field of culture and development and was named by *Prospect Magazine* in the UK as one of the world's 'Top 50 Thinkers'.

Unable to practise her profession in war-ravaged Homs, her home city, Al-Sabouni started to use writing as a powerful tool to interrogate how architecture has been (ab)used as a tool of war. 'Writing about architecture', she tells us, 'is the mirror to building architecture.' Her memoir, *The Battle for Home: The Vision of a Young Architect in Syria* (2016), won international acclaim. Subsequently, *Building for Hope: Towards an Architecture of Belonging* (2021) looked at the impact of the French occupation of Syria in the 1920s. She explains, 'It is about how architecture was used to unravel the social fabric by dismantling the urban fabric.' Through writing and practice, Al-Sabouni aims to recover 'the kind of architecture that we had before the French occupation in the 1920s – and radically different from the imposed style that came with colonisation.' The agenda is to reverse this process, 'bringing back a sense of neighbourliness and a nurturing built environment'.

Fig. 2 'The *Riwaq*', Hove, UK, 2022 by Marwa Al-Sabouni and Ghassan Jansiz as a commission for Brighton Festival 2022. The colonnade was assembled from CNC-cut plywood and realised in collaboration with structural engineers Webb Yates, fabricated by setWorks.

In 2014, Al-Sabouni won first place at national level in the UN-Habitat Competition for the rehabilitation of mass housing for a proposal to rebuild Baba Amr, Homs, Syria. As reported on international news feeds, 60% of the district had been destroyed by shelling. Her design aims to help people maintain the existing fabric of their communities – a hybrid of rural tradition and urban infrastructure. Referencing Arabic architectural traditions such as courtyard housing, the design is based on the principle of a 'tree unit' with a block that unfolds in four directions. An additive pattern allows each section of housing to connect with neighbouring units so that the urban area grows organically, in the manner of local precedents. For Al-Sabouni, the brutality of war has created an opportunity to begin again, not as a *tabula rasa*, the 'clean slate' modernist approach – as this would erase all memory of conflict – but through the careful reconstruction of place.

In *Building for Hope*, Al-Sabouni reflects on lessons on belonging and place-making that Western societies might learn from Islamic culture. For the Brighton Festival 2022, she worked with fellow Syrian architect Ghassan Jansiz to create a pop-up installation on the seafront in Hove – a *riwaq* (crescent-shaped colonnade) to be used as an events space. As part of a housing justice project in Detroit, USA – working for the organisation Ghana Think Tank, The American Riad – Al-Sabouni has proposed living quarters based around a colonnaded courtyard. Her design brings together inspiration from Detroit's wooden bay windows and an Islamic *muqarnas* ornamented vaulting structure. Beyond a simple aesthetic exercise, this hybrid form created nooks for assembling and frames for doorways and shop windows.

If architecture is to be a tool of peace, Al-Sabouni argues, urban regeneration needs to be based on extensive research: 'Understanding how communities work needs to be integral to strategies for a sustainable future.'

Fig. 3 'The *Riwaq*', Hove, England, 2022 by Marwa Al-Sabouni and Ghassan Jansiz as a commission for Brighton Festival 2022.

"My inspiration mostly comes from the built environment itself, understanding its current situation and how minimal acts of architecture can improve the urban context."

NOURA AL SAYEH-HOLTROP

Fig. 1 House of Architectural Heritage, Muharraq, Bahrain, 2018. Designed in collaboration with Leopold Banchini, the main facade of the building opens up to connect the building with its urban context.

Since 2009, the Palestinian architect and curator Noura Al Sayeh-Holtrop has been working at the Bahrain Authority for Culture and Antiquities (BACA) as Head of Architectural Affairs – highlighting the importance of heritage and culture, old and new. This role has provided Al Sayeh-Holtrop with the opportunity to commission architecture, curate it and, in some instances, design it. Just prior to starting, she gained her Master's degree in Architecture from the École Polytechnique Fédérale de Lausanne, Switzerland. Looking back, she tells us that this training furnished her with problem-solving skills and lateral ways of thinking, which she could bring to her work, as well as with a belief in 'the responsibilities and potential of architecture'.

Over a decade on, Al Sayeh-Holtrop's work has encompassed architectural preservation, exhibition and pavilion curation and competition commissioning, working across a range of scales. An early highlight was co-curating 'Reclaim', Bahrain's National Pavilion at the Venice Architecture Biennale in 2010, which was awarded a Golden Lion. Since 2015, she has led the 'Pearling, Testimony of an Island Economy' project, based on a UNESCO-listed World Heritage Site. It takes in multiple buildings and sections of the coastline, including the offshore pearling economy, and was awarded the Aga Khan Award for Architecture in 2019.

Al Sayeh-Holtrop's ethos of minimal intervention can be seen in the House for Architectural Heritage, a cultural centre in the historic heart of Muharraq, Bahrain, designed in collaboration with architect Leopold Banchini in 2018. The building houses

Fig. 2 House of Architectural Heritage, Muharraq, Bahrain, 2018. When both facades are open, the building connects each side of the road, making the project a public passage.

the archival collection of sketches and drawings by the architect John Yarwood, as well as serving as an exhibition space dedicated to architecture. The project is conceived as a simple beam structure that frames the existing adjacent walls of the two neighbouring buildings. Both facades of the building – back and front – open up to connect the building with its urban context and make the project a public passage. This approach makes visible traces of the different phases of construction as well as the architectural heritage of the city.

Al Sayeh-Holtrop says, 'The project, rather than imposing its own conditions on the city, attempts to reveal specific aspects of the local context, in a process of reduction rather than addition.' The ethos reverses the minimalist approach of much modernist architecture, where the eye was drawn, self-preferentially, to the form of the building itself. Taking a holistic approach to the built environment makes Al Sayeh-Holtrop well placed as a cultural leader in times of climate insecurity. The House for Architectural Heritage still uses carbon-heavy concrete,

but impact is minimised by the reductive approach to materials and urban intervention. She says, 'My hope is that sustainability becomes an intrinsic part of the industry. Starting with questioning what we need to build, to integrate sustainability in architecture – not as a catchphrase or a technological gimmick but as an intrinsic part of the design and building process.'

Fig. 3 House of Architectural Heritage, Muharraq, Bahrain, under construction in 2017. This image illustrates the project's intention of conserving the surrounding walls.

MELIKE
ALTINIŞIK

"We create space with the dialogue
between nature, technology and people."

Fig. 1 Çamlıca Tower, Istanbul, Turkey, 2011–20. Main foyer. While wind testing was employed by RWDI to confirm the structure's overall stability, it was also used to develop the unique interior facade design for the foyer to provide design continuity from ceiling to wall and furniture.

Melike Altınışık is a Turkish architect who recently completed one of the country's most distinctive new landmarks – Çamlıca Tower in Istanbul. Standing at 369m tall, the futuristic telecommunication tower is typical of the advanced technology-led work created by Altınışık and her studio Melike Altınışık Architects (MAA).

Altınışık studied architecture at the Istanbul Technical University. Moving to London, she gained her Master's degree at the Architectural Association Design Research Laboratory. This was followed by seven years at Zaha Hadid Architects, which she describes as 'the centre of knowledge and know-how', identifying Pritzker Prize-winning architect Hadid as her mentor.

Setting up her own architectural practice back in Istanbul allowed Altınışık to reflect on her architectural ideology – it starts on a 'blank, white page' and she believes in designing every step of the process. 'I really took a risk, because you go from the top to zero – but of course I believed in my own vision to achieve a sustainable revolution in architectural pedagogy.' She continues,

'Trying to spread my know-how here in Istanbul was an opportunity, because MAA is dedicated to developing innovative and visionary projects, but it was also extremely challenging to achieve this revolution because there is a common approach in traditional architecture.'

To establish the studio, Altınışık has participated in various national and international architectural competitions, winning an Istanbul Metropolitan Municipality commission to design a telecommunication tower on Çamlıca Hill, unique for overlooking

Fig. 2 Çamlıca Tower, Istanbul, Turkey, 2011–20. Istanbul's futuristic 369m tower required advanced engineering techniques, both in terms of architectural design and construction methodology, developed with the structural engineers Balkar and for the structural peer review with Thornton Tomasetti.

both Europe and Asia. The structure is not only her most significant project to date, but also demonstrates her ethos towards architecture. With the project, Altınışık combined technology and engineering to create an overtly futuristic form developed from investigations into how wind would strike the tower. 'From an architectural point of view, it represents a dialogue between the nature of Istanbul and the future of technology,' explains Altınışık. 'We didn't design a typical lollipop-shaped telecommunication tower. We put together

a contemporary structure, in which it is impossible to tell where engineering ends and architecture begins, to get this design approach based on wind data. If the wind of Istanbul was articulated in an architectural language and turned into a tower design, it would become the silhouette of Çamlıca Tower. And that is precisely what happened – wherever you look at it from the city, you will see a different silhouette.' Using an innovative construction methodology, Altınışık describes the building process of the tower as an 'urban performance', as

each four-storey section was constructed on the ground before being hoisted up to 200m into position.

This echoes her design for the Seoul Robot and AI Museum in South Korea, which is being partially built by robotic smart technologies. The museum has enabled Altınışık to establish MAA Seoul Office, and she has ambitions to expand her presence further with a London office in the future.

Fig. 3 Render of Seoul Robot and AI Museum, Seoul, South Korea, 2019–23. The design required advanced engineering techniques both in terms of architectural design and construction methodology, developed with the architect and facade design engineers WithWorks.

"There is a lack of diversity in the profession. This is a global phenomenon; however, for the Gulf region, it means the community loses when one segment of the population is largely responsible for building our cities."

SUMAYA DABBAGH

Fig. 1 Mleiha Archaeological Centre, Mleiha, Sharjah, UAE, 2018. Aerial view of the visitor centre and its surroundings.

With women banned from studying architecture in Saudi Arabia in the 1980s and 1990s, Sumaya Dabbagh is one of only a handful of Saudi women running long-established architecture practices in the Gulf. She is also one of the few women to have designed a contemporary mosque in the region, the Mohammed Abdul Khaliq Gargash Mosque in Dubai (2021). Wrapped in white GRC cladding with engraved calligraphy and decorative cut-out elements, this building is typical of Dabbagh's sensitivity towards place, identity and heritage within the Gulf. 'When architecture establishes a dialogue with its setting, when it speaks to the land and to the people, it starts to create meaning. Then, it is a primal connection evoking feelings and emotions between it and the people,' she tells us.

Born in Saudi Arabia and educated in the UK, where she studied architecture at the University of Bath, Dabbagh returned to the Gulf in the early 1990s. After working on a number of cultural projects, she established her Dubai-based practice, Dabbagh Architects, in 2008 when the UAE was dominated by commercially led, international architectural practices. 'At that time, there wasn't really the cultural sensitivity in the region or an understanding of the value that quality design can bring to a community. I felt this was a gap that needed to be filled.' She adds, 'As a Saudi, I felt a deep calling to do so by starting my own practice.'

Working across diverse sectors of the industry including hospitality and housing, Dabbagh Architects is involved in the design of several cultural projects within the UAE. 'Saudi Arabia has been going through a major transition over the past few years. In terms of culture, there is a massive effort to showcase the history and heritage of the country that

Fig. 2 Mleiha Archaeological Centre, Mleiha, Sharjah, UAE, 2018. View of the entrance and tomb with Fossil Rock in the background.

have been mostly hidden until recently.' According to Dabbagh, it is the Mleiha Archaeological Centre, a curved visitor centre situated in the Sharjah Desert, that launched the practice's trajectory in this direction. This structure, she suggests, 'signalled a new approach to architecture in the region'. The building's form – generated from the circular Bronze Age tomb that sits at its centre – is constructed from sandstone and is materially continuous with the surrounding landscape. Dabbagh believes that the Mleiha Archaeological Centre, along with the

recently completed Mohammed Abdul Khaliq Gargash Mosque, form part of an emerging architecture that is 'contextual' – 'one that pays attention to the memory of place and addresses ideas of identity and belonging'. Such values also provide the framework for Dabbagh's own philosophy of architecture. 'My personal quest is to bring awareness to the value of good design,' she says. This 'quest' led her to co-found the RIBA Gulf Chapter Committee in 2009, and as her personal mission was in alignment with that of the RIBA, she was elected as Chair of the

committee from 2015 to 2019, allowing her to extend her reach within the region. Dabbagh is also keen to highlight the importance of enabling local architects to flourish within the area: 'It is really encouraging to see that a new generation of female architects are appearing there and forging their way into the industry. My dream to see homegrown talent – both men and women – build our cities is becoming a reality.'

Fig. 3 Mohammed Abdul Khaliq Gargash Mosque, Dubai, UAE, 2021. View of the mosque from the street.

"Architecture is an intellectual process that weighs itself onto the traces of the past, to project them into the future."

LINA GHOTMEH

Fig. 1 Stone Garden, Beirut, Lebanon, 2020. The facade, with its multisized openings, invites nature to frame its view onto the city. This image shows the building after the explosion in Beirut port in August 2020.

Born in Beirut, Lebanon, the now Paris-based architect Lina Ghotmeh was first a founding member of Dorell Ghotmeh Tane (GDT) Architects (2006–16) and later of Lina Ghotmeh – Architecture. Her eponymous practice has, since 2016, allowed Ghotmeh to pursue her unique take on architecture as an 'archaeology of the future'.

Ghotmeh's projects vary across scales and geographies – from single objects to museum architecture, and from France to Japan. Her most acclaimed projects include the Stone Garden housing project in Beirut, Lebanon, the Estonian National Museum in Tartu, Estonia, Ateliers Hermès in Normandy, France and the Serpentine Pavilion in London,

UK, 2023. Awards include the Schelling Architecture Prize 2020.

It is the temporality of architecture, Ghotmeh tells us, that distinguishes her philosophy. She likens the process to a palimpsest, where new elements are inscribed onto – and bear traces of – earlier forms on a site. Translating this to practice, she approaches 'each project as a quarry, researching its contexts thoroughly, identifying local traditions, stories, materials. Like archeological finds, these are extracted into an architecture that draws an intrinsic synergy with the environment.'

This ethos is embodied in her Stone Garden housing project, completed in 2020 and

named Architecture Project of the Year at the Dezeen Awards 2021. Located near the industrial port of Beirut, the building is a response to growing up in war-torn Lebanon, where violence is evident in the very fabric of the city. The building is intended as both a memorial to the impact of such brutality and a structure that makes room for nature to take back control. The facade is made of thick plaster, reinforced by fibre additives and waterproofed. Ghotmeh designed a special steel comb to create the final texture, saying she intended the facade to feel as laboured soil – 'an agricultural field just before planting, where the earth is overturned in preparation'. The project was featured as part of the

Fig. 2 (top and bottom) Serpentine Pavilion, London, UK, 2023. The design emerges from Ghotmeh's aspiration to develop our primal relationship with the Earth into a sustainable one.

Venice Architecture Biennale in 2021, as an illustration of resilience in the face of crisis. The 1:30 scale model of Stone Garden on display captured both the craftsmanship involved in fabricating the building as well as the wider context of Beirut's recent history. The building itself withstood the explosion that destroyed a large part of the city in August 2020, when the traditional reinforced-concrete shear wall system acted as a shield for inhabitants and neighbouring buildings. Ghotmeh's Estonian National Museum is another building that is imposing in scale. A compelling aspect of Ghotmeh's winning competition proposal was the decision to suggest a different site for the museum – near a former Soviet military base – to allow for direct engagement with a dark period in the country's history. The new building was designed as a continuation of the airfield, with its high, protruding roof inviting the visitor 'to enter into the landscape and into the heart of the museum'.

Ghotmeh's approach to architecture is research driven. During her training at the American University in Beirut, she also followed courses in biology, sociology, anthropology and gender studies. This gave focus to her understanding of 'architecture as a profession that is intrinsically connected and that could impact the dynamics of the world'. Although admiring the work of many of her peers, she sources most of her ideas from her immediate environment: 'I find that my most frequent sources of inspiration lie in my surroundings: in history, art, literature, nature, material understanding.'

Looking to the future, Ghotmeh argues for science and technology to be in service of an architecture that is more sensitive to its immediate environment. This includes embracing vernacular construction with locally sourced materials and bioclimatic passive design in dialogue with nature. She tells us, 'Technology is allowing us to reinvent these methods of construction more efficiently and, I hope, will make them more common and possible.'

Fig. 3 Estonian National Museum, Tartu, Estonia, 2016. Designed by Ghotmeh and DGT Architects, the sloping glass building is 355m long and rises from the runway of a former Soviet airbase near the city of Tartu.

ELENA K. TSOLAKIS

Fig. 1 Troodos Observatory, Cyprus, 2022 (under construction). The star observatory is 'implanted' into the peak of the mountain without altering the landscape while the planetarium, which is located in the lowest level of the building, is submerged underground.

'Architecture should be the new food,' architect Elena K. Tsolakis tells us. The founder of London- and Nicosia-based Kyriakos Tsolakis Architects focuses on projects that have a direct impact on communities and believes that the value architects provide needs to be championed. 'Access to information is so plentiful now that people appreciate aesthetics, but they really don't have an understanding of what we do as architects – how we work or what inherent, integrated value we give to the life of buildings,' she says. 'I want this to change, I want to be a part of this change through advocating the culture of architecture.'

The daughter of a Cypriot-Australian architect who 'selflessly contributed to society', Tsolakis aims to create social and culturally purposeful spaces. 'We have found that a common thread amongst many of our clients is the mission to make the world around us a better place,' she explains. 'This sense of purpose and responsibility rubs off onto us. In our studio, we help animate our client and collaborator's ambition into a built form – places that support their mission and, above all, bring people together.'
Tsolakis' studio recently completed the first purpose-built women's shelter and crisis centre in Cyprus, which offers bi-communal

accommodation to both the Greek and Turkish Cypriot communities. The unique building was designed to be an uplifting home for up to eight women and their children to repair their family life, as well as accommodating a crisis centre and the headquarters for the charity the Association for the Prevention and Handling of Violence in the Family. The project was nominated for the 2017 European Union Prize for Contemporary Architecture, Mies Van der Rohe Award. The studio has also recently created a wellness resort for athletes on the Greek island of Mykonos and is designing a star observatory on Cyprus in the Troodos

Fig. 2 Troodos Observatory, Cyprus, 2022 (under construction). The 'Astromarina' (a telescope platform for stargazing) sits on one side of the building wedge as it hangs over the mountain; the roof's rotating dome sits on the other side. Between the two is a void that bridges the solar telescope room and the main telescope room.

Mountain range. 'The aim of this project is to attract astronomers, researchers and astronomy enthusiasts from around the world,' Tsolakis tells us. 'Its social ambition is to stimulate public curiosity in what lies beyond. It needed to be unlike any other building we had seen,' she continues. 'In the end it came from a place of wonder and imagination. The outcome was beyond anyone's expectations, even our own. It is a foreign object within a very natural organic setting perched on the peak of a mountain.

The idea is that it should inspire and excite anyone who sees it from close or afar.' According to Tsolakis, studying architecture 'requires a complete rewiring of the brain', but the results and the positive impact it can bring make it extremely rewarding. 'Creating architecture takes a huge amount of time, the work consumes you, it's very personal,' she says, continuing, 'At the same time, architecture is thrilling and wonderfully rewarding, allowing you to submerge yourself into a different subject every five minutes.'

For Tsolakis, each project requires a unique solution and it is the architect's job to figure that out: 'Learn the rules, break them, break them again and then put it all back together. Every project is a new jigsaw puzzle – where we are just trying to find the right solution.' Compellingly, she says, 'If you believe that you are adding to the world positively, that your approach is worth being heard or seen, then keep going, keep fighting, every day.'

Fig. 3 Troodos Observatory, Cyprus, 2022 (under construction).

EURO

"I don't see myself as a female architect. I'm just a human being who happens to do architecture."

OANA BOGDAN

Fig. 1 COOP, Anderlecht, Brussels, Belgium, 2016. The building provides a landmark in the relatively flat urban fabric of the canal.

Romanian-Belgian architect Oana Bogdan wants to fix the world: 'I'm someone who, wherever I go, if things are not okay, I try to fix them.' Until 2022 she was operating as Bogdan & Van Broeck with co-founder Leo Van Broeck. The Brussels-based practice is reconfiguring under the name &bogdan, which, she tells us, stands for cooperation and promotes the 'follow me, I'm right behind you' type of leadership.

In her work, Bogdan's problem-solving mentality and cooperative ethos come together to create 'spatial conditions for collective life'. Here she questions the architect's traditional role, believing that the profession's skills can be used to navigate the complexity of many areas of life. Embracing this ability to translate to other contexts, Bogdan took on the role of Secretary of State for Cultural Heritage in

the Romanian government, which assumed leadership of the country in 2016, following a scandal surrounding a nightclub fire. In 2022 she was appointed Chairwoman of the Expert Committee in charge of the reform of urban regulation in the Brussels Region. Together these roles provide experience that, she says, 'has proved to be most valuable'.
'Architects are generalists,' she says. 'Just think about what it means to be an architect,

Fig. 2 Exploded isometric of COOP, Anderlecht, Brussels, Belgium, 2016.

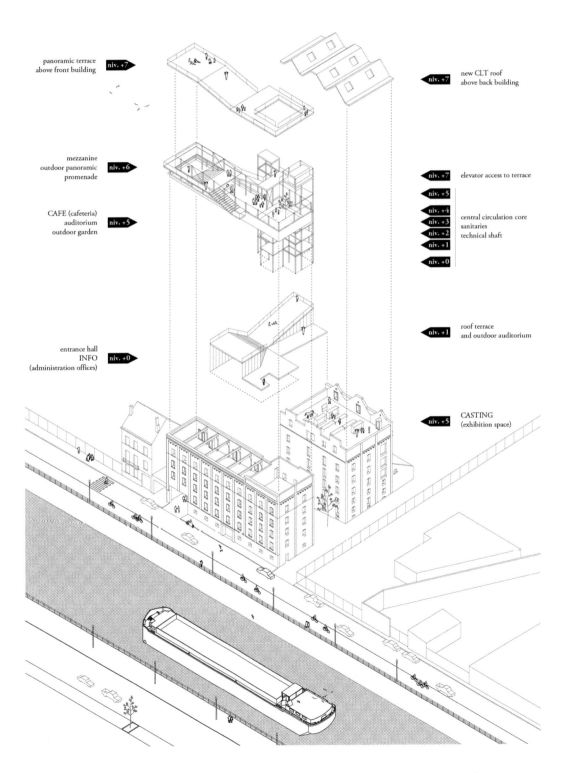

panoramic terrace
above front building niv. +7

new CLT roof
above back building niv. +7

mezzanine
outdoor panoramic
promenade niv. +6

elevator access to terrace niv. +7

CAFE (cafeteria)
auditorium
outdoor garden niv. +5

niv. +5
niv. +4 central circulation core
niv. +3 sanitaries
niv. +2 technical shaft
niv. +1

niv. +0

roof terrace
and outdoor auditorium niv. +1

entrance hall
INFO
(administration offices) niv. +0

CASTING
(exhibition space) niv. +5

what it takes to be an architect, you have to coordinate so much. I realised how useful architects could be in organising anything. Because you can architect the government, you can architect so many things. So, it's really about organising things ... improving systems.' In government this meant pushing back on overdevelopment, which saw cultural heritage 'as the enemy', and introducing legislation to prevent 'ecological disaster'. As an architect she aims to bring systems thinking and intense organisation skills to find workable solutions to complex briefs involving multiple stakeholders. Several of these projects, including three conversions – De Mouterij in Leuven, COOP in Anderlecht and, most recently, The Cosmopolitan in Brussels – have seen the studio nominated for the prestigious Mies van der Rohe Award.

'We do all of our projects because we believe in them,' she says (something that led to the studio being driven to the brink of bankruptcy following the financial crash in 2009). Winning the COOP project, which demonstrates many of Bogdan & Van Broeck's core ideals, saved the studio, explains Bogdan.

'We designed COOP as an engine for the neighbourhood,' she says. It is a museum combined with an incubator for small and medium enterprises, built within a mill along a canal. Its complexity involved coordinating multiple organisations, something that aligns with Bogdan's skills as an organiser, leader and doer.

Bogdan prefers not to call herself a woman architect. 'I don't see myself as a female architect,' she says. 'I'm just a human being who happens to do architecture.' However, she has seen that men take her more seriously since she became involved in politics. 'I became visible when I went into politics. Previously I was in situations where I would just say something and then people would react to my [male] associate... Since I became Secretary of State it was like I was suddenly 10 times more intelligent. It was as if I became a man saying the same thing.' Looking forward, Bogdan believes that the Coronavirus pandemic will give architects the emphasis and excuse to create more responsible buildings as she believes that the pandemic has made people reassess their priorities. 'There is a lot of pressure among architects to make cheap and fast architecture look expensive so that private clients can make lots of money,' she says. 'Now there is a window of opportunity to go back to our social mission because I see architecture as a responsibility. We have to be doctors of space. I believe that there will be much more attention to quality housing.'

Fig. 3 COOP, Anderlecht, Brussels, Belgium, 2016. Conversion of an old mill into an interpretation centre and working spaces for start-ups or cultural organisations.

"We are searching for poetic experiences in the process of design that slow down the use of everyday objects and spaces and open them up to moments of silence, immediacy and wonder."

ANCA CIOAREC
AND BRÎNDUȘA TUDOR

Fig. 1 The Loom, Mesteshukar ButiQ, Bucharest, Romania, 2018. 'A workshop more than a shop': interior design project for a social enterprise that links Roma craftspeople and contemporary designers.

Stardust Architects, founded in 2011 by Anca Cioarec and Brînduşa Tudor, has established an identity for place-making that impacts positively on the life of the community. The two architects studied, and now teach, at the Ion Mincu University of Architecture and Urbanism in Bucharest, Romania. Their work draws on both Cioarec's training – accrued across time in Genoa, Amsterdam and Bucharest – and Tudor's research into the neo-vernacular practices in Bucharest. Both look at local typologies to identify relevant patterns from which to innovate and improve.

'Our challenge has always been the lack of space in industry for small-scale, experimental design that questions habits and needs time for research,' they tell us. Their project, The Loom, won a 2018 design competition for Mesteshukar ButiQ (MBQ). This Bucharest craft store represents a network of social economy enterprises dedicated to revaluing traditional Roma craftsmanship. The brief was for a place that invites visitors to learn and engage. Their approach was to reimagine the shop as a workshop, creating a tactile and

convivial experience that encourages engagement and conjures up memories. The key component is a long central table where objects can be displayed and touched, with visitors guided through craft processes while experiencing the 'tool space' in ways that are reminiscent of inhabiting a loom. The walls were designed to reveal the trace of hands and the silhouette of tools and materials. Copper joints and plates were inspired by the jewellery exhibited in the shop. Innovations include the making of the columns: they were co-designed with Atelier Vast, who devised

Fig. 2 Wood and copper interior detail, The Loom, Mesteshukar ButiQ, Bucharest, Romania, 2018. Wood and copper detail. Timber sticks are held together inside the wood structure by small copper joints inspired by the jewellery exhibited in the shop.

a hybrid lathe/CNC prototyping process for them.

Collaboration has become an important way of working for Cioarec and Tudor, and Atelier Vast have been their most important collaborator since 2017. Projects are co-designed from the first conceptual processes, through the experience of using materials and tools.

In the early years, the studio specialised in interior design and clients were mostly private. Later projects have been commissioned by institutions and organisations. Work has been self-initiated or carried out collaboratively with architects, designer and artists. For the 2020 Timișoara Architecture Biennial in Romania, Stardust Architects collaborated with architect and editor Ilka Ruby and with two landscape designers to create 'Enough is Enough', modelling a responsible design for a large-scale exhibition.

The two are also generous in naming their role models, some of whom feature in this book: Anna Heringer, Flores and Prats, Case Design, Terunobu Fujimori, Anna Puigjaner, Flavien Menu, Aamu Song, Atelier d'Architecture Autogeree and Yona Friedman.

At the heart of their own work is a desire to use design to slow down habits and, they hope, allow the time and space needed to create more meaningful connections between people, place and the environment.

JULIA GAMOLINA

"My goal is to profile more clients and patrons of architecture who can verbalise the value of investing in design services."

Fig. 1 Julia Gamolina, founder of digital magazine *Madame Architect*, interviewing Molly McGowan at the RBW Showroom in SoHo, New York, USA, May 2022.

Julia Gamolina, founder and editor-in-chief of *Madame Architect* and associate principal at Ennead Architects in New York, has carved out a unique and successful career combining journalism, activism and architecture. Born in Novosibirsk in Siberia, Russia, Gamolina moved to Canada with her family on 8 August 1999 – the day before Vladimir Putin took office as Prime Minister. Gamolina felt that only architecture could offer her 'the best synthesis of her multidimensional interests', choosing to study at Cornell (2008–13), then interning at architectural practices in Brazil and Austria, before settling in New York in 2013.

As an architecture student, Gamolina found the performative demands of design reviews just as enjoyable as the production of drawings. As such, communication and articulating the merits of good design came naturally, while her writing earned her the Charles Goodwin Sands Memorial Medal for exceptional merit in the thesis of architecture.

Gamolina considers her early years in architecture practice as 'typical' – with 'poor mentorship, low pay and routine sexual harassment' to deal with. When applying for jobs, more than once, she was commended for 'enthusiasm' while being told to 'go and work somewhere else to gain experience and then come and work for us'.

In New York, Gamolina saw a need for a support network for women – not limited to connecting professional allies, but also providing mentoring and practical support. Her international moves had made Gamolina skilled in creating her own communities. She used these skills to found the, now renowned,

Fig. 2 Frank 57 West, New York, USA, 2013. Studio V Architecture for the Durst Organisation. A mixed-use development completed in multiple design phases, in symbiosis with other buildings.

digital magazine *Madame Architect*, which celebrates extraordinary women in architecture. Featured women range from established practitioners to up-and-coming innovators, architecture patrons, advocates and educators and, refreshingly, architects who have left the profession but apply their architecture skills in other sectors and sites of impact. The interviews avoid separating 'work' from 'life' – striking a balance between women's lives as architects and their broader activities and characteristics.

Gamolina has garnered a number of awards, including being named one of *Apartment Therapy's* 'Design Changemakers', one of *Commercial Observer's* 'Top Young Professionals' in 2021 and the Special Citation from the AIA New York for her work with *Madame Architect* in 2019.

In American slang, 'Madame' is a term of offence, historically used to describe a woman who runs a brothel or organises prostitutes. When asked why she chose the name *Madame Architect*, Gamolina points to the USA Presidential election race between Donald Trump and Hillary Clinton in 2016, when the term 'Madam President' felt like a real possibility – albeit with a painful election result, particularly in terms of women's rights. Gamolina added a Francophile 'e' to create *Madame Architect* – implicating architecture's persistent prejudice in exalting only the 'masters' of architecture.

At Ennead Architects, Gamolina plays a strategic role in developing the practice's educational, cultural and healthcare projects both nationally and internationally. A significant project came early in her career when working on Frank 57 West for the Durst Organisation with Studio V Architecture. At a time when mixed-use developments were still increasing in the city, the building combined residential, medical and retail programming. Understanding the client and navigating the array of city-specific protocols required Gamolina to draw upon her education's emphasis on the rigours of iteration, addressing project complexity with creativity and the balance between significant investment and infinite ambition. What she felt her education didn't equip her with was effective time management – and by implication stress management – negotiation skills or best business practices.

As well as freelance journalism, Gamolina teaches in the USA and internationally. Concerned about the 'lack of value of architects' – and pointing to 'the contribution of small budgets and low fees to poor labour practices' – she argues for 'recognition of architects and their work in mainstream culture and media, helping to connect the general public to the importance of good design'.

Fig. 3 Frank 57 West, New York, USA, 2013. Interior view. Studio V Architecture for the Durst Organisation.

MARLENA HAPPACH

"I have always thought about space as a constant relationship between humans and nature."

In 2016, Marlena Happach became chief architect for the city of Warsaw and was awarded the Silver Cross of Merit for her work. Happach originally studied at the Faculty of Architecture at Warsaw University of Technology, University of Technology La Villette, Paris and TU in Berlin, Germany. She went on to lead H2 Architekci design office with Marek Happach, specialising in public building design. Her roles also encompass Director for the Department of Architecture and Planning and President of the Warsaw branch of the Association of Polish

Architects. She is co-founder of the Odblokuj Association, which focuses on public spaces and revitalising urban areas.

Happach's approach is to apply participatory processes through which the Warsaw citizens she serves can shape the city. Her vision is consistent with her experience in working for an NGO, which promoted participation in architecture and the planning process. The priority is to design people-centred cities, with imaginative public transport, deploying processes that react and adapt according to social needs. 'Copenhagenising' is the

word she uses to describe her re-planning of Warsaw: removing mono-functional commercial structures in favour of multi-functional social amenities and green space. This was a process expedited in some ways by the pandemic.

The relationship Happach forges between humans and nature in her work can be best seen in two signature projects. The aim of the M3 apartment module was to create a symbolic reconciliation of a typical estate of 1970s M3 apartments, to exploit the surrounding Służew nad Dolinką's greenery.

Fig. 2 Apartment module, Stowarzyszenie Odblokuj, M3, Służew nad Dolinką, Warsaw, Poland, 2011. The aim was the symbolic transfer of a typical estate from the 1970s M3 apartments into the Służew nad Dolinka's greenery, which surrounds the estate.

The structure creates a frame for many kinds of cultural and architectural events, exhibitions and meetings. The juxtaposition of an interior of that kind of standard building, more suitable for a concrete desert, with the wild nature of the Służewiecki stream gave her opportunities to reimagine housing in cities. The wooden pavilion Pokój na lato is a more complex project. In the Polish language, *pokój* means 'room and peace'. This wooden pavilion was built next to the Warsaw Uprising Museum, which commemorates the history of this uprising against oppressive Nazi power in August 1944. Those two buildings create an intriguing tension between the symbolic context of the museum and the entertainment functions of the pavilion as a bar and social space. The pavilion is located on challenging, sloping terrain, close to the street and summer café. It provides space for outdoor museum activities, workshops, concerts and screenings in ways that realise the social potential of the site.

In her work, Happach is inspired by architects who think about context and nature. She names Edouard Francois' showcasing of nature and Kazuyo Sejima for putting humans at the centre of geometric architecture.

The work of Janette Sadik-Khan, who revolutionised ways of thinking about roads and cars in New York, is a model for Happach's transformation of Warsaw. Rare when her career started, woman have since made an impact in Poland, particularly in making people aware of issues relating to human needs. 'It is very hard to predict the future in such a dynamically changing world,' she tells us, 'but I am sure that women have the potential to revolutionise cities and make them better for living in so many ways.'

Fig. 3 Pokój na lato, Warsaw Rising Museum, Warsaw, Poland, 2015. The facility serves as a summer café and space for outdoor museum activities including workshops, concerts and a summer cinema.

"Every project is like a puzzle: some of them are easy, some are difficult, but there is always a perfect, unique solution that needs to be cracked."

SVITLANA ZDORENKO

Fig. 1 Office building in the Unit City Innovation Park, Kyiv, Ukraine, 2018. The deconstructed geometry, highlighted with bright colour, creates a prominent iconic corner.

Ukrainian architect Svitlana Zdorenko describes herself as a 'functional-contextualist'. As co-founder of one of Ukraine's best-known studios – A. Pashenko – Zdorenko aims to create buildings that work for both the people that use them and the context they are built in. 'I am good at designing buildings and places that work well, but I also believe in the uniqueness of each project as context plays a defining role in a project's space-planning, its composition and image,' she tells us.

Educated at the National University of Construction and Architecture in Kyiv,

Zdorenko worked for the Kyivproekt State Design Institute after graduating. In 1996, following the fall of the USSR, she set up a studio with her husband Andrii Pashenko. Over the past 30 years she has designed over 100 buildings, including the Innovation Park in the centre of Kyiv. She has grown A. Pashenko into one of the country's largest studios employing a total of 70 architects.

With her work, Zdorenko aims to find a balance between what a client wants, what the city wants and what constitutes good architecture in the Ukrainian context. The

studio's growth hasn't compromised this approach: 'We still care about each project as if it was our first,' she says. 'We probably can be classified as commercial architects, but we treat each constructed square metre with great responsibility, making sure it delivers the commercial, social and aesthetic return on investment. Good things take time and it took us over 30 years to build up the experience and reputation that we have.' Russia's invasion of Ukraine in 2022 changed everything. 'Before the war, our company was like a rushing train where all the details were running smoothly, but it suddenly came

Fig. 2 IQ Business Center, Kyiv, Ukraine, 2013. The composition is made of stack cylinders topped with a cantilevered helicopter pad.

to an abrupt halt,' Zdorenko tells us. When the war started, the lack of work meant they considered closing the company, 'but we felt responsible for all our employees and their families,' she says.

'Some of our colleagues left for the front, some went to Europe with their children and many remained in Kyiv.' Although it was 'painful to see some of our recently completed projects being shelled', Zdorenko believes that the war has created a 'sense of closeness and belonging' within her team. Despite the war continuing, some projects are now restarting. 'Some of the clients have resumed construction and some have helped us out of goodwill, which allowed us to partly pay salaries and transfer money to our army,' she explains. 'It is amazing how this horrible disaster has rallied people.'

Zdorenko is already considering how best she can contribute to Ukraine's reconstruction following the war. 'There are some positive glimpses of light in the darkness of the war, for example we have just won a European Investment Bank tender to design prototypes of social infrastructure.' After a pause, she says, 'Our train, although slowly, has started moving again.'

Fig. 3 Nikolsky Shopping Mall, Kharkiv, Ukraine, 2021. (left) On opening, the mall immediately became the heart of public life and a source of pride for the city. (right) The mall was bombed in the first months of the Russian invasion, destroying the building.

"To be a good and ethical architect,
I learned to become an agitator, an
innovator and an orchestrator."

YẸMÍ
ALÁDẸ́RUN

Fig. 1 Masterplan model, 1:1250, Meridian Water, London Borough of Enfield, UK, 2017. Karakusevic Carson Architects worked with Enfield Council to develop strategic urban principles to repair and transform the complex urban site.

Working between architecture and activism, Yẹmí Aládérun is a Nigeria-born, UK-educated architect and development manager who advocates for equality within the profession and housing justice. It was at Kingston University, London, she tells us, that she learnt to question what is considered 'acceptable' architecture and 'the need to disrupt typologies, such as housing'. By the time she graduated in 2010, Aládérun had already gained national recognition with *Blueprint Magazine's* 'Best Student Project in Britain' award and *The Architecture Review's* Top 10 London Units Prize for her diploma graduation project. Just two years later her work was profiled in the special edition of the *Architect's Journal* in 2012, which highlighted

'Women in Practice'. It was this edition that effectively kickstarted the *Architect's Journal* 'Women in Architecture' visibility and recognition campaign.

Aládérun identifies the art and culture of the Yorùbá – a group of West African first people divided through colonial partition – as the source of her passion for design and creativity. As an advocate for education, income and housing equality, she has committed her career to matters relating to social mobility and broadening access to the built environment. Since 2019, following a period as an associate at Barbara Weiss Architects, Aládérun has worked on large-scale projects for a number of London's local authorities and housing associations. In 2021,

she took on the role of Head of Development at Meridian Water, one of the London Borough of Enfield's flagship regeneration programmes. This is a project without precedent, as the council assumed the role of 'Master Developer' for the site, with a commitment to ensure its community has access to well-designed environments that enable its residents to prosper. This project offered Aládérun the perfect opportunity to bridge her expertise in the design of spaces and the design of value proposition, for example, the economic viability and sustainability of the development.

Aládérun has long been involved in equality-driven activism within the profession through high-profile roles in existing organisations

Fig. 2 Meridian Water, London Borough of Enfield, UK, is a flagship, 25-year regeneration programme, whose masterplanning designs for Phase 1 were completed in 2019. Enfield Council took the unusual step of assuming the role of Master Developer.

and setting up new initiatives. She is a non-executive board member of the Women's Pioneer Housing Association and was Co-chair of Olmec, championing race equality though economic and social justice. Aládérun credits British-Ghanaian architect Elsie Owusu as one of the inspirations behind her co-founding of the Paradigm Network in 2017 alongside fellow practitioners Chris Nasah, Lanre Gbolade, Roberston Lindsay and Tara Gbolade. Paradigm exists to support, profile, celebrate and help talented Black and Asian students and practitioners from Black and Asian backgrounds in education and as they progress in their careers, placing strategic importance on promoting the development of Black and Asian-led practices, challenging perceptions that they don't exist within the UK built environment.

Aládérun's àctivism has also included tackling the issue of women's comparably poor prospects and experiences in architecture. As a founder member of Part W – an action group calling for gender equity in the built environment – Aládérun helps to highlight issues ranging from the perennial problem of 'manels' (male-dominated architecture review and judging panels) to the lack of childcare at key architecture community events. Throughout all her activist activities, Aládérun feels that, 'it is just as much a matter of celebrating those on the margins and giving them visibility and agency as it is calling out inequities and fighting for justice'.

When considering the future of the construction industry, Aládérun feels it remains too fragmented and adversarial. She tells us there is a need for 'greater collaboration between client, constructor, consultant team and end user to achieve better project outcomes'. It requires a more serious commitment to building trust, keeping the lines of communication open, being transparent about failure and the investment and implementation of technology. But Aládérun is hopeful. 'Architects can tackle any injustice by turning our attention to reimagining existing systems and economies that prioritise profit for the few at the expense of people and climate.'

Fig. 3 Meridian Water, London Borough of Enfield, UK, 2017. Working with Periscope, the Meridian Water team developed place visions that capture core elements of Meridian Water past, present and future. Left to right: mixing uses and animating streets; park life on your doorstep; your place to make and create.

"I am inspired by creatives in other fields – like fashion, film or music – where I appreciate an experimental attitude with different sources in time and cultural context merging into something new."

RAHEL BELATCHEW

Fig. 1 Knäckepilen Residential Project, Uppsala, Sweden, 2019.

Rahel Belatchew is an award-winning architect who believes in the transformative potential of architecture. Founder of the studio Belatchew, she works at the cutting edge of residential, workplace and community design, delivering outcomes that impact the quality of life of all users. Belatchew was born in Addis Ababa, Ethiopia, and gained a Master's degree in Architecture from the École Spéciale d'Architecture in Paris in 1996. Of her education, Belatchew notes that it 'provided me with the skills to understand a broad context and to be able to form strong concepts'. However, she is also critical of her educational experience, emphasising that a more 'transdisciplinary training would be beneficial to have a better understanding of a rapidly changing world'. For Belatchew and her studio, architecture is more than simply building buildings.

Having worked in Paris, Luxembourg and Toyko, Belatchew established her eponymous studio in Stockholm in 2006. Initially 'the lack of a network in Sweden was a challenge', she tells us, 'since I had studied and spent my early years as a professional outside of the country it took me some time to understand the ecosystem and identify the stakeholders.' Nevertheless, the studio rapidly evolved and now incorporates Belatchew Labs, which works on experimental projects 'to investigate and test new approaches and solutions to urban and architectural challenges'.

The two signature projects that Belatchew highlights are both residential. The first –

Fig. 2 Render of Grønn Residential Project, Stockholm, Sweden, 2021. The project is scheduled to commence construction in 2024.

Grønn – won first prize in a competition in 2021 and will be located near Stockholm (construction is scheduled to begin in 2024). The proposals look to 'merge urban environment with nature', says Belatchew. 'In this timber-frame construction, all apartments have access to greenery, regardless of size, and the entire roof is a series of outdoor spaces and terraces expanding the interior.' Social spaces are shared within this apartment complex, the architecture facilitating community cohesion. The second project is Björk, a housing complex located in Norra Djurgårdsstaden, Stockholm and completed in 2017. Belatchew describes the building as having 'a strong sculptural character, in dialogue with the adjacent nature', with a typology borrowed from the industrial buildings specific to this area of the city. The design incorporates large balconies, which are angled to allow residents views in all directions, with the effect that the building changes character from wherever it is seen.

Contemplating the future of architecture and her place within it, Belatchew states, 'Climate change is by far the biggest challenge today for architects. We need to find means to reuse components and materials as well as keep track of and reduce the carbon dioxide footprint of buildings in every step of the design process.' Acknowledging the difficult times ahead, she continues, 'We live in times of rapid technological innovation that affect our lifestyle. What we design and build today must be flexible enough to adapt to future needs.'

Fig. 3 Björk Residential Project, Stockholm, Sweden, 2017. Close-up view of the exterior.

YVONNE FARRELL AND SHELLEY MCNAMARA

"The responsible use of resources, the way we build and the environments we create are all under review."

Fig. 1 The Marshall Building, London School of Economics, London, UK, 2022. Elevation onto Lincoln's Inn Fields.

Yvonne Farrell and Shelley McNamara are co-founders of the Dublin-based practice Grafton Architects. Since 1978, the practice has established a reputation for architecture that engages meaningfully with place, to advance social and environmental agendas. An invitation to curate the 2018 Venice Architecture Biennale provided the opportunity to distill their thinking into the 'Freespace' manifesto, proposing architecture as a space of opportunity. 'Our architectural education started in 1969,' they explain. The two women joined the School of Architecture at University College Dublin (UCD) at a pivotal time: 'It was just after a revolt in the school, which resulted in all the staff being fired and a whole new set of teachers appointed'. This included architect Ivor Smith and many younger teachers. 'We had a strong collaboration with our peers and formed relationships with our professors,' they tell us. 'The tools provided were a belief in architecture combined with an ambition and belief in the future.' Grafton was set up just one year after graduation, initially with three other architects. 'We were driven by a need to make a place for ourselves, where good work could be produced and hopefully make some contribution to the culture of architecture.' With no experience of building, contracts, or managing finances, they tell us, 'Our biggest challenge was to secure projects and to learn fast enough so as to survive.'

Two buildings give us a sense of Grafton's approach from macro planning to micro detail. The Marshall Building – a new development for the London School of Economics – is designed as a microcosm of what we perceive a city to be. They explain, 'The structure mutates from large to small spans, and rotates from diagonal to orthogonal geometries, all acting

Fig. 2 The Marshall Building, London School of Economics, London, UK, 2022. Stairwell design.

together as the cartilage, which ties the spaces into one legible, rich sequence of experiences.'

The Anthony Timberland Centre for the University of Arkansas engages in timber research and innovation. Built of wood, the building combines a large fabrication workshop with a multistorey teaching building. An undulating roof rises from ground level to the seventh floor as a 'tent-like' space unifying all the various activities. The design celebrates the structural capacity and nature of different timbers, while combining ancient craft with current technology.

Grafton's work has won the highest accolades and, in 2020, Farrell and McNamara became Pritzker Prize Laureates, as well as being awarded the RIAI James Gandon Medal for Lifetime Achievement in Architecture. The architects see their work in a lineage, in debt to the sensitivity and invention of Irish modernist designer Eileen Gray, whose work, 'from the design of a table to the design of buildings... engages so sensually with the landscape'. They also are inspired by the radical social agenda of Brazilian architect Linda Bo Bardi. In 2015 the two women took up positions as Adjunct Professors at UCD

'to distill our experience and gift it to other generations'.

Looking forward, Farrell and McNamara see another pivotal moment full of potential for real change. 'We see the prevailing climate of uncertainty as a positive force, which will make more space for architecture to take up a key role in rebalancing the current very serious imbalances in our society.' But only, they add, if 'innovation is accompanied by a re-evaluation of all our practices'.

Fig. 3 Render of the Anthony Timberland Centre, University of Arkansas, Fayetteville, USA, 2020-ongoing. Built to celebrate the beauty of wood, it combines a large Fabrication Workshop with a teaching building.

SAIJA HOLLMÉN, JENNI REUTER AND HELENA SANDMAN

Fig. 1 Kilimanjaro Women Information Exchange and Consultancy Organisation (KWIECO), Moshi, Tanzania, 2015. Shelter house designed for victims of domestic violence.

Saija Hollmén, Jenni Reuter and Helena Sandman are Finnish-based architects setting the agenda in humanitarian architecture through the nonprofit organisation Ukumbi, offering architectural services to communities in need. 'We use architecture for empowerment. A good environment is a basic human right. At best, architecture can create the hope that is needed for a better life.'

Their humanistic approach to architecture was sparked during their studies at Helsinki University of Technology (now Aalto University). At this time, the architect-philosopher Juhani Pallasmaa was a professor at the university and as an enigmatic proponent of the lived experience of architecture he influenced their thinking. In 1995 Hollmén Reuter Sandman Architects collaborated with the Women's Centre project in Senegal. This was followed by other international projects, as well as those in their homeland of Finland. The NGO Ukumbi was set up in 2007. Their process is context sensitive in the broadest sense. 'We believe in innovations by investigation, where the landscape, sensitivity towards materials, site-specific interventions and involvement of the inhabitants in the design process form a new architecture.' Collaboration at the grassroots level is also key. The group try to find local NGOs, experts and builders to collaborate with wherever in the world they are acting – as well as the people who will actually use the building.

Ukumbi's process is necessarily iterative.

Fig. 2 KWIECO, Moshi, Tanzania, 2015. In the building process, local materials, labour, know-how and renewable energies were used.

Collaboration and fundraising are part of the execution of every project, and getting to the build stage is difficult – if it happens at all. 'Every executed project has been a long journey and we have many projects that have never been constructed because of lack of funding or a lack of a sustainable future for the project,' they tell us. 'Communication challenges always seem to be a part of our work in low-resource settings.'

A signature project that embodies their approach is the shelter house, designed for victims of domestic violence in Moshi, Tanzania for Kilimanjaro Women Information Exchange and Consultancy Organisation (KWIECO). Here, Ukumbi worked with the organisation to fundraise for a suitable plot and sought financial support from the Finnish government. To provide clients with a safe environment for protection and healing, the building was situated in the inner half of the grounds.

On the main gate the Swahili words read: 'Equal rights for all are the basis of development'. This mirrors a culturally important habit among Tanzanian women: to wear kanga skirts printed with messages – subtle, but important.

Co-designed with the KWIECO personnel, the architecture is designed to respect the Tanzanian culture, climate and spatial hierarchy. Using an inclusive planning process ensured a feeling of shared ownership among the people involved. In the build, local materials, labour, know-how and renewable energies were used. To take just one example, coloured glass bricks made out of recycled bottles bring ambient light into the bathrooms.

'We feel that a large part of our work is to share and develop our thoughts with others,' the architects tell us. The impact of Hollmén Reuter Sandman's work can be gauged, in part by, the awards they have received. Yet what really matters to the team is the role that publishing, exhibiting and teaching can playing in imparting their vision of humanitarian architecture for the future. 'Among emerging architects and students there is a positive thirst towards a well-crafted, equal and socially sustainable future in architecture. Here we feel that we can play an important role.'

Fig. 3 Main gate of KWIECO, Moshi, Tanzania, 2015. The gate mirrors a culturally important habit among Tanzanian women: to wear kanga skirts printed with messages.

"What is most important to me is that the building and the place form a synthesis."

DORTE MANDRUP

Fig. 1 Ilulissat Icefjord Centre, Greenland, 2021. The aerodynamic, light structure of the building levitates over the magnificent, rugged terrain like an outstretched wing of a snowy owl gently touching the bedrock.

The studio of Danish architect Dorte Mandrup is distinct for its highly sculptural architectural proposals that foreground their environment and the complex conditions from which they arise. This includes climate innovation projects located in environmentally sensitive UNESCO World Heritage Sites and memorial projects, negotiating culturally difficult historical sites. Competition wins and projects in the pipeline at the time of writing include The Whale, 300km north of the Arctic Circle in Norway, and the Exile Museum, at Anhalter Bahnhof in Berlin.

Mandrup drew on her background in sculpture and the natural sciences to inform her practice, 'which has always been "hands-on", materialising in deep, contextual analysis and explorative prototyping'. And yet, when Mandrup was forging her creative path in the late 1980s, a context-driven approach was not the dominant mode. Between the aesthetic mantra of European and American postmodernism and the 'one-size-fits-all' of rampant 'modernising' developers, buildings had often become decoupled from the people and landscapes they served.

The studio was founded in 1999 and has grown to include 80 staff members. Over two decades, Mandrup has honed a unique approach, which combines both a scientific-analytical and artistic-intuitive process. 'It is based on an exploratory and experimental methodology that recognises the technical and scientific conditions and the importance of gathering knowledge.' Each new project, she tells us, 'begins with an attempt to be as unbiased as possible – with no fixed goal. Every place has inherent qualities that can be evoked – whether historic, scenic or societal.' The Icefjord Centre in Greenland, which opened in 2021, exemplifies her approach. It is the first visitor centre telling the story of the importance of ice and the Greenlandic culture, and also a glacier viewing platform for local residents, tourists and

Fig. 2 Ilulissat Icefjord Centre, Greenland, 2021. The roof provides a natural extension of the hiking routes and is created as a public space – a kind of gateway between Ilulissat and the wilderness beyond.

climate researchers. Sited on the edge of the UNESCO-protected Kangia Icefjord, in freezing temperatures and harsh winds, the aerodynamic, light structure reduces snow build-up and creates a refuge and gathering place. 'We have aimed to create a place that provides protection on a human scale in an otherwise scaleless landscape – a kind of gateway between civilization and wilderness.' Having worked with such a high profile has led Mandrup to publicly comment on the problematic siloing of 'women' architects through prizes and exhibitions – and books! Nonetheless, she recognises a real need for a clearer articulation of the specific challenges that women face in a still male-dominated profession. 'When you embark on your career, you lack a network and it is not easy to join the men's club as a young female architect. Feeling supported is crucial ... We need to create networks. Not because we are women but because they are the only networks we have.'

Looking forward, Mandrup argues, 'Interdisciplinarity is the key to designing for complexity.' For her, 'Architecture is a field that requires an increasing amount of knowledge and expertise. We are highly dependent on having great collaborators; engineering and construction specialists but also scientists, artists and writers.' And yet, she reminds us that 'companies are getting bigger, or else are swallowed up by bigger engineering firms, to be able to handle increasingly complex situations.' She argues that it is the architect's holistic design skills that are needed more than ever as 'a design specialist who is able to collaborate and synthesise with other specialists.'

Fig. 3 Ilulissat Icefjord Centre, Greenland, 2021. Aerial view showing how the boomerang shape frames the views towards the fjord, while preventing snow build-up and creating a shelter from the snow and the freezing winds.

"I am interested in designing buildings as open platforms that people can appropriate in different ways."

FARSHID MOUSSAVI

Fig. 1 Museum of Contemporary Art, Cleveland, Ohio, USA, 2012. West-facing facade.

British-Iranian architect Farshid Moussavi is one of the UK's most prolific and preeminent woman architects practising today. Her impact spans practice, pedagogy and also publications, exploring the philosophy as much as the pragmatics of place-making and public engagement.

Moussavi studied architecture from the mid-1980s at Dundee University, Scotland, then at The Bartlett School of Architecture, University College London and Harvard Graduate School of Design in the USA, where she has held a professorship since 2005. Returning to London, Moussavi cofounded Foreign Office Architects (FOA) in 1993 and the studio soon gained renown for an innovative, interdisciplinary approach, integrating architecture, urban design and landscape architecture in a wide range of projects internationally. Subsequently, she set up her own practice, FMA (Farshid Moussavi Architecture), in 2011.

What makes Moussavi's work both distinct and compelling is the way it delves into disciplinary research to create buildings that perform as 'open platforms'. With this approach, she pushes her buildings beyond

Fig. 2 Îlot 19, La Défense-Nanterre, France, 2017.

preset requirements or programming to offer 'open-ended opportunities for experiential engagement by the users'. In the case of the Museum of Contemporary Art, Cleveland, Ohio, USA, Moussavi was able to play with notions of public and private, cultural and even domestic – successfully convincing a typically revenue-dependent cultural institution to blend free, open-access gallery environments, evocative of 'urban living rooms', with ticketed exhibitions. This blurring of the identity and purpose of key spaces allowed her the freedom to design the art-handling entrance to accommodate a small outdoor theatre. Such devices allow the museum to enhance its role as a 'centre for the community around it'. Crucially, it allows the public to experience art in the museum beyond the limitations of curatorial ambitions and prescriptions.

This approach was similarly deployed in the residential block Moussavi designed in Nanterre on the periphery of Paris. The Îlot 19, La Défense-Nanterre residential block is arranged as an assemblage of elements that allows its diverse residents the possibility of determining how they inhabit the building – the relationship between the inside and the outside of their apartments, and their sense of privacy or of community with other residents.

The Ismaili Centre, Houston, USA, the seventh in a series of iconic cultural buildings commissioned by His Highness the Aga Khan, is a community centre for the Ismaili community but is designed with indoor and outdoor spaces that anyone in the city can enjoy, therefore becoming a destination for dialogue and an exchange between different communities. In all these works, we see how a building designed as an 'open platform' becomes, for everyday users, a place of possibility.

Over the past three decades, Moussavi has been awarded a remarkable array of prizes, and was appointed Officer of the Order of the British Empire (OBE) in 2018 for services to architecture. In 2022 she won the Jane Drew Prize for demonstrating innovation, diversity and inclusiveness, and elevating the profile of women in architecture.

Fig. 3 Ismaili Centre Houston 2, Houston, USA, 2025. Approach from south to main entry.

"The best buildings are the ones that are realised. Only then does a building – together with its users – start its own journey, independent from the architect."

VEDINA BABAHMETOVIĆ

Fig. 1 Small Administration House and Big Pine Trees, Entasis, Zenica, Bosnia-Herzegovina, 2018. The main entrance is accentuated with verticals from nature.

Vedina Babahmetović is an architect with over 30 years of experience. Educated at the Faculty of Architecture in Sarajevo in the former Yugoslavia, she wasn't able to begin practising until after the end of the 1990s Balkans War. Babahmetović recalls, 'The challenges were incredible, and the disorientation in the new economic conditions even greater. I was in my 40s and had a family and an architectural practice.' Babahmetović travelled to Italy and the UK in the early part of that decade. These experiences offered insight into the history of Western architecture, as well as witnessing first-hand the rapid transformation of London Docklands. Yet it was within her home country of Bosnia-Herzegovina that Babahmetović found the right place to begin her career. Here she could contribute to the reconstruction of the architectural landscape in the aftermath of conflict and reshape its identity as an independent Balkan state. The early years of Babahmetović's career were impacted by the availability of building materials and the shift to digital technologies, requiring what she describes as 'a lot of improvisation and passion'.

Fig. 2 Hiža Mišljenova, Entasis, Puhovac, Zenica, Bosnia-Herzegovina, 2022. The element of the central fireplace is taken from the traditional Bosnian house, while old bricks from the existing house were used as a reminder of past times.

Babahmetović's approach to making architecture is initially characterised by the 'simultaneous struggle between function, location, volume, colour, texture and aesthetics'. She tells us that the tensions within this process sometimes manifest later in the design process – 'very often in the following stages, some spatial or functional relationships reveal themselves as gifts, because we received them instinctively, we did not think about them. I call it metaphysical gain. Although, after years of work I know that these sudden "gains" are a consequence of the first and most important design step.'

Three of the projects that represent the scope of Babahmetović's philosophy of architecture are Small Administration House and Big Pine Trees, Hiža Mišljenova and Makovi. Built on the ruins of an existing building, Small Administration House is a structure that is continuous with the natural landscape. Vertically arranged sheets of timber around the perimeter of the building mimic the form of the pine trees that surround it. Hiža Mišljenova is a structure built out of reclaimed bricks and oak beams, which offers 'a modern interpretation of the old Bosnia-Herzegovina house'. For this building, Babahmetović used traditional devices including a central fire space and hipped roof, as well as reinterpreting the separation of private/female and public/male spaces within the home.

The Makovi residential complex is situated above the city of Zenica. The scheme consists of a series of interconnecting 'lamellas' that offer safe spaces between domestic interiors. Babahmetović tells us that the use of black paint 'dematerialises the highest part of the building', reducing its impact on the skyline. While Small Administration House and Hiža Mišljenova play with traditional building materials and methods, Makovi reflects the contemporary urban context that it inhabits.

Having launched her architectural career during a period of uncertainty, Babahmetović has endeavoured to make architecture that offers stability through times of change. Sensitive to context and history, her architecture extends from a deep understanding of place, that is nevertheless determined to represent the contemporary cultural spirit of a nation.

Fig. 3 Hiža Mišljenova, Entasis, Puhovac, Zenica, Bosnia-Herzegovina, 2022. The front facade opens up to the public 'male' courtyard.

"I nurture practice led by the idea
of collectiveness and solidarity."

IVA ČUKIĆ

Fig. 1 Street Gallery, Belgrade, Serbia, 2011. Before reconstruction, this passage became a street gallery.

Serbian architect Iva Čukić is an academic and activist. She earned her PhD in urban planning from the Faculty of Architecture in Belgrade and is the co-founder of the inter- and cross-disciplinary collective Ministry of Space, with the 'aim of pursuing spatial justice'. 'Together with four other fellow activists, we set up Ministry of Space in 2010, eager to work on activating unused spaces for the needs of local communities, through direct action and occupation, as well as through municipal negotiations,' she tells us. 'Since then, I'm proud to say, the collective has transformed and grown to a relevant organisation of 10 devoted people.'

With her work and research, Čukić aims to contribute to the democratic and fair development of urban environments with the lofty goal of 'collectively constructing a just city that is yet to be'. She envisions a city where decisions are made through open discussion and dialogue for the benefit of communities rather than for private individuals' concerns. At Ministry of Space she focuses on activating abandoned spaces, urban 'commoning' practices and urban transformation. 'We nourish critical thinking and reflection, multidisciplinary approaches and practical engagement as fundamental to creating and responding to the current

political and economic challenges from the spatial perspective,' she says. 'Within this framework, we closely collaborate with numerous civil society organisations, grassroots groups, neighbourhood initiatives and individuals from diverse professional backgrounds and carry out projects in cooperation with domestic and international academic and research institutions and organisations.'

A project that demonstrates these ideals and her do-it-yourself philosophy is the Street Gallery in Belgrade, of which she has been the Head Curator since 2012. The open-air gallery was created in a dark alley in the

Fig. 2 Street Gallery, Belgrade, Serbia, 2015. Exhibition of illustrations, 'Krem de la Krem' by Miron Milića.

city centre, an alley that, according to Čukić, was primarily used as an 'informal urinal'. The gallery acted as a way of reappropriating the space for communal, public use. Following an initial photography guerrilla exhibition of 'urban outcasts' being torn down after only a few hours, the group spent two years negotiating with the municipality to formally take over the space. Since then, 150 individual and group exhibitions have been hosted in the open-air gallery. 'Through the years, the purpose of the Street Gallery long surpassed its main function – not only was the exhibition space an open-access space hosting critical artistic expressions and socially and politically engaged topics, but it was also run as a

commons,' explains Čukić. 'During this time, the gallery showed collective capacity to confront commodification of space, to tackle dialogue and create new forms of socialising in public space.'

Čukić believes that architects need to expand their view on what architecture is to encourage a wider perception of the profession. 'In my professional career, on certain occasions, I feel as if the way I work is too unconventional to be acknowledged as an architectural and urban practice,' she reveals. 'Partly because of the narrow perception of what this profession includes, but also because of the political aspect of it that I emphasise ... in a context where architecture

has structurally been depoliticised.' She feels that the current, male-heavy profession makes it tough for many to progress and that this can be overcome by collectiveness and solidarity. 'Patriarchal patterns of creating hierarchies, individualising success and neglecting unequal power relations dominant in Serbia, but also in architecture and urban planning as a professional field, made my path quite challenging and it took time and energy to be able to confront it', she tells us. 'Thus,' she continues, 'I decided to embrace an approach that challenges the masculine top-down dynamic, to take over the feminist heritage of self-reflection and sensitivity to differences.'

Fig. 3 Street Gallery, Belgrade, Serbia, 2019. Winter opening for the exhibition 'Vrednost' (Value).

NEREA
AMORÓS
ELORDUY

"Challenges became opportunities to create a grounded narrative of what architecture is and can do in Rwanda and around the world."

Fig. 1 Kiziba refugee camp, Rwanda, 2017. The first application of cow dung and ashes mixed together can be seen here, drying, on two *imigongo* murals.

For over a decade, Catalan architect, urbanist and researcher Nerea Amorós Elorduy has worked on projects that aim to improve living conditions for vulnerable populations in East Africa. She was shortlisted for the Women in Architecture Award's Moira Gemmill Prize for Emerging Architecture in 2021.

In 2011, after completing her architectural studies at the Universitat Politècnica de Catalunya and Universitat Internacional de Catalunya, Elorduy established the Active Social Architecture (ASA) studio in Rwanda with Tomà Berlanda. The studio went on to design more than 20 Early Childhood Development (ECD) centres across the country over two years.

'There was lack of architectural materials, skills and know-how,' Elorduy tells us. 'Rwanda was growing fast, coming from a humble situation, and there weren't enough architects – not to mention female ones. I was the first registered woman and there wasn't yet a clear understanding of what architecture, and its social, cultural and historical values, could do for society – and not enough good contractors and access to building materials.' She continues, 'All of these challenges became opportunities to create a grounded narrative of what architecture is and can do in Rwanda and around the world. It allowed us to investigate, recover pre-existing, and explore new, construction

techniques and design approaches.' ASA was commissioned by UNICEF and the United Nations High Commissioner for Refugees to develop two ECD centres in the then newly established Kigeme and Mugombwa refugee camps. This introduced Elorduy to the challenges of designing within these often permanent, but uncertain spaces.

Elorduy has continued to work within contested environments developing her doctoral research on them, leading a series of transformative, child-friendly interventions at the Kiziba and Kigeme refugee camps in Rwanda.

'Together with a group of young architecture graduates, artisans and refugees, we developed murals and imagined utopic

Fig. 2 Kiziba refugee camp, Rwanda, 2017. An artisan applies pigment to an *imigongo* mural on a wall in a refugee's home.

interventions to incrementally convert the camps into what social historian Colin Ward called "schools without walls",' explains Elorduy. This project typifies her participatory approach to architecture, where 'the final users of the projects are involved as much as possible in all the phases of research, design and construction.'

Much of Elorduy's learning from working with young children and refugees in East Africa has been compiled in a freely available book called *Architecture as a Way of Seeing and Learning* (2021) that aims to inform young designers and prompt more regional research into the long-term refugee camps.

'I do not expect or hope to suddenly transform refugee camp planning and refugee education policies and practices,' writes Elorduy in the book's introduction. 'I desire to inject a sense of urgency into the topics concerning the built environment, the refugees' voice, the development of young children and the need to decolonise the study and practice of refugee assistance in these East African camps.'

While in Rwanda, Elorduy contributed to the establishment of the country's first architecture school at the University of Rwanda and taught at the institution for four years. In 2019 she moved to Kampala, Uganda, and established a new studio, Creative Assemblages. Projects include a pre-primary school largely built from upcycled components sourced from a demolished coffee factory.

Looking to the future, Elorduy hopes that architecture will continue to adapt to meet the challenges of climate change and growing levels of inequality. 'I believe participation and collaborative approaches to design and construction, as well as a focus on the process with a feminist and decolonising intent, will gain even more traction in the next decade,' she says. 'This will influence the way we design and understand urban environments and architectural interventions. These approaches are powerful innovation and creation tools.'

Fig. 3 Kiziba refugee camp, Rwanda, 2017. A group of young children, caregivers, parents and NGO staff discuss child-friendly spaces using a 3D-printed model of the settlement.

MARIA CHARNECO AND ANNA PUIGJANER

Fig. 1 Conceptual Collage of 110 rooms for 22 Apartment Building, Barcelona, Spain, 2016.

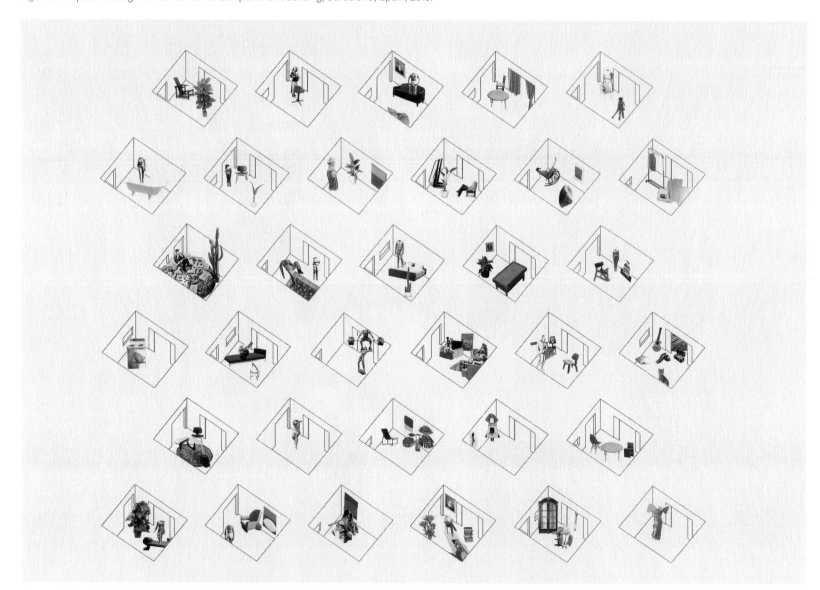

Working out of Barcelona and New York, MAIO is an architectural collective that combines research and practice, confronting the 'complexity of everyday life'.

Practising together for over 10 years, Maria Charneco, Anna Puigjaner, Alfredo Lérida and Guillermo López have established a partnership that has evolved from shared experiences and values. They are all graduates of Escola Tècnica Superior d'Arquitectura de Barcelona. Their work is representative of an emerging approach to practice that is consciously collaborative.

'We design together so we are not like offices where each partner works on one project.' Charneco and Puigjaner emphasise the importance of communication within this set-up: 'We always have a strong concept – the backbone of the project – that we maintain through to the end. We also communicate through collages and models, which allows us to work well together.' The women cite 2011 as a pivotal year for the collective, when social movements such as Occupy Wall Street in Spain and the USA operated as a catalyst for architectural activism. 'We started that year to think about opening a space to gather with friends and colleagues that we admire from the creative world – not only architecture, but also other disciplines that operate around architecture – in order to help us to understand what we were living through.' From this the office now known as MAIO emerged. For Charneco and Puigjaner the space they work in choreographs their practice, allowing what they describe as 'natural interactions' and informing processes and outcomes.

MAIO's interdisciplinary and emergent

Fig. 2 22 Apartment Building, Barcelona, Spain, 2016. (left) Ground-floor stair. (right) Ground-floor volumes.

approach is perhaps best expressed through their work on the 22 Apartment Building on Calle Provença in Barcelona, Spain. As a project, it is characterised by its incomplete nature. It is 'in a permanent state of unfinished business, or in a permanent state of willing-to-be-changed,' they tell us. 'We collaborated with the construction engineer, the landscaper and graphic designers and all of those conversations started right at the beginning. It is difficult to distinguish the work of each because, at the end, the whole is cohesive.' The apartments are designed to be open to adaptation. Although there are core, fixed elements, the domestic arrangement of the space is unfixed and can be changed over time. 'Any room can be the bedroom or living room, even the kitchen can be installed in any of the rooms.'

The project was built as a critique of the contemporary housing market in Spain that addresses only one social structure – that of the traditional family unit. It is intended to reflect a reality where less than 30% of Spanish society is prototypical. The adaptability of the apartments enables residents to remain in their homes over a lifetime, in turn facilitating social cohesion and community stability. We see here how architecture can create solutions that address complex, connected problems of everyday life – while remaining open to as-yet-unimagined possibilities.

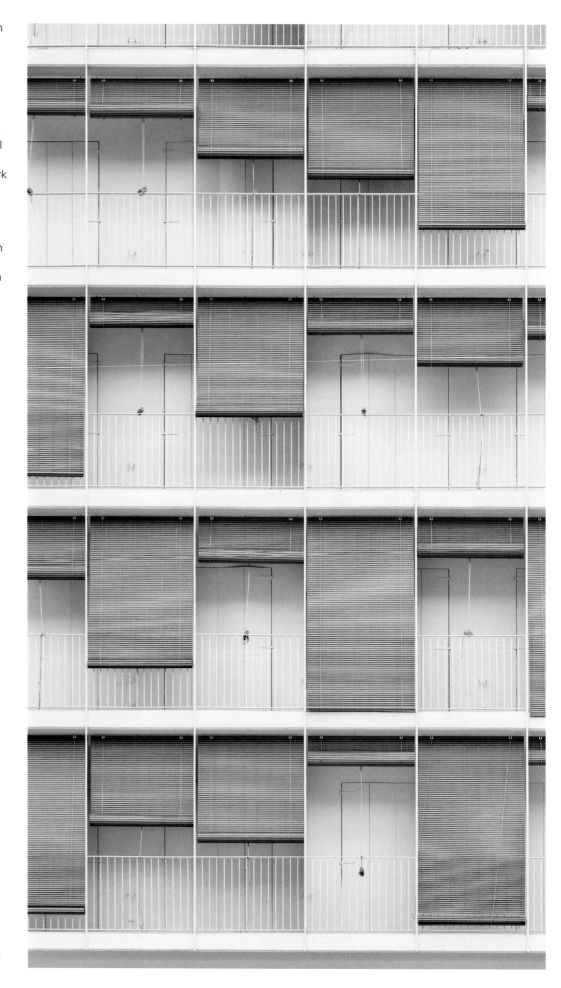

Fig. 3 22 Apartment Building, Barcelona, Spain, 2016. Rear facade with traditional blinds.

MIA
ROTH-ČERINA

"Creating places that trigger togetherness is embedded in every aspect of my work across design, research and teaching."

Fig. 1 Zorka Sever Elementary School, Popovača, Croatia, 2018. Designed with XYZ Architecture, the building includes skylit voids of inner streets, stairs and galleries flanking communal spaces, with colour accents suggesting gathering – yellow mobile benches, recycled rubber outer islands and colour-coded classrooms.

Mia Roth-Čerina is an architect and Associate Professor in the faculty of Architecture at the University of Zagreb, Croatia. One half of Roth & Čerina, a small practice, run with her professional and private partner, Tonči Čerina, Roth-Čerina's architectural upbringing offered what she describes as 'a solid foundation' in the 'modernist tradition'. Yet, she tells us, the 'agility needed to read and operate in the current condition was self-taught'.

As with many architects, the relationship between teaching and practice is fundamental to Roth-Čerina's approach to making architecture. What's refreshing is how she acknowledges the two-way flow of ideas. 'My spatial preoccupations inspire my pedagogies and conversely, my practice is nurtured by the free platforms of thought that architecture school provides. Creating conditions for mutual learning is essential to an agile, evolving curriculum.'

Roth-Čerina's multicultural background (her father is American, her mother Croatian) is reflected in what she describes as her 'Slavic pathos' and her feeling for Mediterranean colour, as well as the 'foggy expanses' of the USA Pacific Northwest. What really shaped her practice, she tells us, was growing up in post-war Croatia. 'My influences are drawn from personal formative experiences, contemporary art, film and everyday observations. The architectural scene my generation entered after graduation allowed a strong connection to these personal positions and idealisms.' Roth-Čerina remembers this time in the early 2000s as a period of opportunity facilitated by 'a wave of open architectural competitions for public buildings. Many practices were launched then, though at the same time, waiting for the next competition perhaps hindered other modes of action one needed to develop. Resilience and agency were certainly not a given skill upon graduating.'

Fig. 2 Visitor Centre, Lonjsko Polji Nature Park, Croatia, 2021. The centre samples rural morphologies (such as neighbouring homesteads) to create a new social focus, and tells the stories of the flora, fauna and cultural heritage of the region.

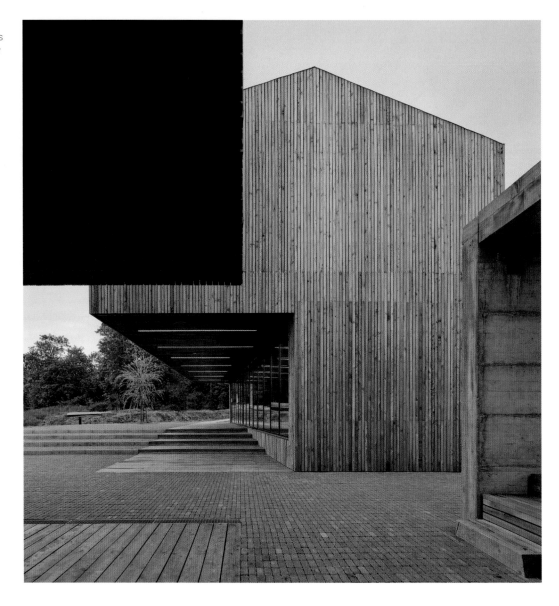

The architecture that Roth & Čerina produce is most often located within the public realm. Their design for an elementary school in Popovača, Croatia, intertwines school, community, public space and sports facilities in a 'binuclear' relationship to one another. The volumes that seem to rest upon the ground plane are connected to the first floor by a common gallery of classrooms and hallways overlooking voids intended for sports and multipurpose halls. The building is covered with slanted roofs.

Roth-Čerina describes her design process as 'discovering and sampling existing patterns' within a landscape. This can be seen in the design of the Lonjsko Polje Nature Park visitor centre. She points out how this project echoes 'the morphology of neighbouring homesteads' – where two wood-clad buildings, with large, blackened wood trapezoid cantilevers, are placed so as to frame a new square. One of the volumes houses an information desk and administration. The other houses a communal hall and interpretative exhibition of analogue and digital interactive displays, sculpture, film and illustration.

The 'accentuation of the communal' is a driving thematic device for the practice, even when they are working for private clients.

The summer house in Palit on the island of Rab, designed for a family of five gathering from different parts of the world to spend summers together, comprises an internal neighbourhood articulated around a void. Roth-Čerina observes that this 'resonates with the energy of a previous summer kitchen, which used to be in the same spot'. All of these projects reflect Roth-Čerina's affinity with architecture that is responsive to context and need. As she says, 'Aiming for a society of care requires a shift towards a more empathic, responsible and inclusive architectural practice.'

Fig. 3 Visitor Centre, Lonjsko Polji Nature Park, Croatia, 2021. The swarm sculptures by Borna Demel hover over the exhibition entrance hall, resonating with the shoals, flocks and herds inhabiting this protected environment.

"Architecture can be part of a process of taking care."

FRANCESCA TORZO

Fig. 1 Z33, House for Contemporary Art, Design and Architecture, Hasselt, Belgium, 2019. Exhibition Room.

Since architect and academic Francesca Torzo established her studio in Genova in 2008, she has worked tirelessly to bring 'dignity and belonging' to people through her work. Rather than exploiting architecture as a tool in service to the logic of capitalism, Torzo passionately believes in its role as empathetic device for connecting people back to the places and spaces they inhabit. 'I think we are in a time where the relationship between individuals and society is very frail,' she tells us, 'but it is innate, the need in

human beings, to belong to something bigger than just yourself.'

Torzo's approach begins with the close observation and analysis of context – including that which has 'survived' over time – before contemplating how to build. Although her working process is fundamentally participatory, she is critical of the language around participatory practices, especially where these absolve those in power from taking responsibility for how our cities look and are made – and

in particular who has agency within this process.

Torzo's proposals for the Z33, House for Contemporary Art, Design and Architecture in Hasselt, Belgium, reflect these core beliefs. Responding to an open call, her winning entry to the competition is a superb example of architecture that is continually in dialogue with its context and users. The building offers a 'continuous flow' of indoor and outdoor spaces, creating a 'scenography of light and shade'. It also highlights Torzo's concern for

architectural detailing. She explains that in designing details, 'there is a beautiful chance to reflect upon our practice and the question of what it means to make a building.'
For Torzo, architecture can be part of a process of taking 'care'. For instance, Bamboo Pavilion, a library pavilion in Yangshuo, Guilin, China functions as both a gathering place for children to listen to stories and a place to 'welcome social gatherings'. The project is also an example of positive collaboration – obligating the local

municipality to repair a walk along the river as part of the outcome for the community.
The attraction of architecture for Torzo is that it opens up 'a vast observatory on humanity'. Within this contexted understanding, she describes architecture as a process of translation, translating ideas into reality. Moreover, she believes that architects have 'a duty and privilege to offer the kind of beauty that is right for our society'. For Torzo that requires 'observing and understanding' people and the spaces they inhabit.

As her portfolio continues to diversify, perhaps the role of Torzo's architecture moving forward is to enable people to enact better versions of themselves. Having reached a lacuna in her career as an architect and academic, she is reflective on the meaning of architecture and her place within it. 'I like to work with people. Collaborating enriches me, challenges me, makes me learn and grow. All this gives me joy.'

Fig. 3 Yangshuo Bamboo Library Pavilion, Guilin, China, 2019. Model of the tower.

ODILE DECQ

"My work is a complete universe, in which architecture, design, art and urbanism come together, challenge each other, respond to each other."

Fig. 1 Le Twiste, Paris, France, 2019. The two lower blocks are limited to six levels to accentuate the third – a tower topped by a square volume that slightly twists itself and thus the tower underneath.

Odile Decq is a French architect, urban planner and academic. Since setting up practice in 1978, she has become known for a unique and inventive style of architecture. She founded the architecture school Confluence Institute in Lyon in 2014 and in 2019 she moved it to Paris to provide a radical training for architects fit for the 21st century. Decq's signature works include the Museum of Contemporary Art (MACRO) in Rome, the Archaeological Museum of Tangshan in China, Le Twiste office building in Paris, through private houses to a residential tower in Barcelona, Spain. Her international awards are numerous.

Decq trained in France in the mid-1970s, in the aftermath of the Paris student and worker protests of 1968. 'My chaotic studies provided me with a very strong determination, a good ability to find my own way in the system and taught me not to fight a wall in front of me but to turn around and find how to go further in the other direction.' It's perhaps not such a surprise then, that she opened her own studio right after her diploma without going to work for an architect first. Sexism proved one of her greater challenges. Coming second in an early competition, Decq was told 'this is very good for a young woman'.

'My approach is intuitive, never ideological,' she tells us. Her way of working is both pragmatic, in response to a brief and site, and inventive; 'to go beyond the limits of the client's expectation and create uniqueness' is her objective. A good example is the striking residential tower in Barcelona, comprising of 88 apartments with two penthouses at the top. The undulating facade was designed

Fig. 2 Tour Antares, Barcelona, Spain, 2022. The residential tower's undulating facade is designed to challenge the typical straight, vertical typology of the high-rise.

to challenge the typical straight, vertical typology of the high-rise. Le Twiste, an office space in Paris, was built in three sections, two parallelepipeds and a head, which are all fully visible from a distance. Here, the tower was designed to be transparent and reveal its interior, which Decq 'designed like a landscape, an idea of nature at the scale of its inhabitants'.

Decq increasingly takes a holistic approach – involved in the design from the architecture of the building to the interiors, landscape, lighting and product design. 'My architectural philosophy is to envision each project as a global oeuvre where all scales are in coherence,' she tells us. Her design involvement also goes from large to small-scale – down to details such as the chairs. It also includes engagement with all technical aspects of a project, from structure and new technologies to climate. Decq credits this approach to her 1970s education, which drummed into her that a building 'needs to be thought of in relation to the environment of the place' as well as to 'perform for people'. Through the Confluence Institute, Decq supports the generational evolution of architects. To navigate increasingly complex situations, she advocates for an agile approach, open to diverse forms of knowledge and transdisciplinary practice. 'My students will never practise architecture as I do,' she tells us. 'I train them to be autonomous and adapt. Some will become artists, scenographers, dancers, architects and more – to create and invent the 21st century.'

Fig. 3 Tour Antares, Barcelona, Spain, 2022. Lobby area.

"There are a lot of materials given by nature for free and all we need is our sensitivity to see them and our creativity to use them."

ANNA HERINGER

Fig. 1 Elevation drawing for Anandaloy, Dinajpur district, Bangladesh, 2020. A centre for people with disabilities and Dipdii Textiles studio.

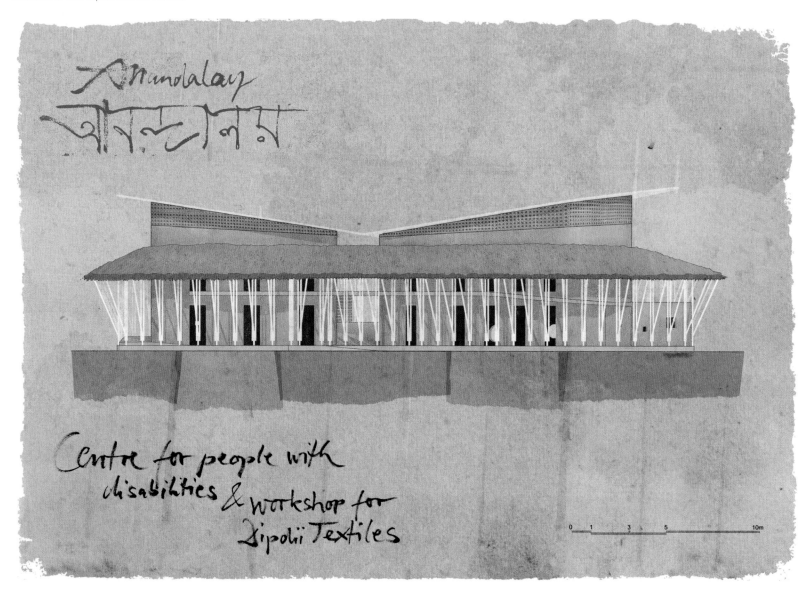

German architect Anna Heringer believes that 'architecture is a tool to improve lives'. She puts this into practice through her eponymous studio that is known for a series of innovative, sustainable buildings in Asia, Africa and Europe that combine local materials, resources and know-how with global knowledge. 'We don't believe in a sustainability that can only be afforded by a part of the world's population,' she tells us. 'We build the same way in Bangladesh as we do in Germany, making the best out of locally existing, natural materials.'

Harnessing what already exists to create buildings that are appropriate to their context, Heringer's first project, begun shortly after graduating from the University of Arts and Industrial Design in Linz, was the physical manifestation of her thesis project, 'School: Handmade in Bangladesh'. Officially it is known as the METI Handmade School and was realised with Eike Roswag in Rudrapur, a northern part of Bangladesh. The mud and bamboo building epitomises many of Heringer's ideals, using the traditional building materials and construction methods of the region. In 2007, the school won the prestigious Aga Khan Award for Architecture, with Heringer going on to be recognised with a Global Award for Sustainable Architecture, the Loeb Fellowship at Harvard's Graduate School of Design and a RIBA International Fellowship. The potential of earth as a building material is showcased in her co-authored book *Upscaling Earth: Material, Process, Catalyst* (2019).

A more recent example of Heringer's approach to making architecture is the Anandaloy community centre, which won the OBEL Award for architecture that contributes to human development. Located in a small village in northern Bangladesh, the building is constructed using cob technology from locally sourced mud, straw and bamboo. Anandaloy, which means place of deep joy, contains therapy spaces for people with disabilities and a studio for Dipdii Textiles, a women-led textile workshop that promotes fair-trade fashion. It has an elegant form, built around a curving ramp that makes each room accessible to all, something that

Fig. 2 Anandaloy, Dinajpur district, Bangladesh, 2020.

has prompted numerous discussions about accessibility in a community not used to such provision. Although the building and its purpose are admirable, it is the construction knowledge transfer to and from locals that Heringer is most proud of. 'Because the Anandaloy project is mainly built out of mud and bamboo from local farmers, the biggest part of the budget was invested in local crafts(wo)men,' she says. 'Thus, the building is much more than just a structure, it became a real catalyst for local development.'

Looking to the future, Heringer hopes that architects shift their focus away from aesthetically pleasing edifices towards more meaningful, context-appropriate architecture. 'There are plenty of functional and good-looking buildings around, but what is needed now is a meaningful architecture,' she says. Nevertheless, she continues, 'Beauty is a formal expression of love, and if we create things out of love towards the people and the planet, towards every being, it means we also do it sustainably. So, to us the new mantra for future architecture is "Form follows love".'

Fig. 3 Anandaloy, Dinajpur district, Bangladesh, 2020. Veranda.

"I'm an architect, not a female architect, but if I can give inspiration to other women then that is not a bad thing."

FRANCINE HOUBEN

Fig. 1 Library of Birmingham, UK, 2013. The LoB is designed to be a people's palace, a centre for learning, information and culture that unites people of all ages and backgrounds.

As founding partner and Creative Director of Mecannoo, Francine Houben is one of the world's best known architects. Through all of her work, no matter the scale, she aims to create spaces that respond to the users' needs. 'My last book was called *People, Place, Purpose*, and that is a redline through my whole work,' she tells us, 'and in that order. My work is driven by the human senses. So it is about acoustics, about seeing, it's about your experience, how you move through space.'

This focus on process and purpose, over form, has led her to create a visually diverse collection of buildings that do not have a unifying aesthetic. 'When I was studying architecture you had to find your own aesthetics – all glass buildings or all fluid buildings, or whatever – and then you put it everywhere in the world,' recalls Houben. 'You can see in the work of Mecannoo, everywhere it's different – and I love that. Often, we design public buildings and I want

people to feel that it's made for them.' Houben established her studio in 1984 while still studying at Delft University of Technology. Now 130-people strong, the studio has created high-profile buildings all over the world including numerous housing schemes and skyscrapers in the Netherlands, the world's largest performing arts centre in Taiwan, the Library of Birmingham in the UK and the renovation of Mies van der Rohe's Martin Luther King Jr Memorial Library in Washington DC, USA.

Fig. 2 National Kaohsiung Centre for the Arts, Kaohsiung, Taiwan, 2018. The centre symbolises the transformation of Kaohsiung, once a major international harbour, into a modern, diverse city with a rich cultural climate.

However, it is one of the studio's smaller projects – the St Mary of the Angels Chapel in Rotterdam – that Houben feels best embodies her ethos. 'It's based on the senses, the flow of people, the experience,' she explains. Set within the footprint of a 19th-century ruin, the funeral chapel consists of a 'blue continuous wall' topped with a golden roof and broken by two doors to allow the coffin to take a processional journey through the building.

'The coffin goes in one door and out another – it's symbolic that life continues,' she tells us. 'For me the building is very special as we had funerals there for both my parents and it is really beautiful how it works.'
Although Houben has had a 40-year career she still looks towards the future and has a flexible, adaptable attitude towards ideology. 'I want to be visionary, I'm also serving the society,' she says. 'I'm opposed to the old-fashioned philosophy that you take one line

and you have to defend it for 100 years.' Houben won the Woman Architect of the Year Award at the Women in Architecture Awards in 2014 and although she does not define herself as a female architect, she acknowledges that her position makes her a role model for other women. 'I'm an architect, not a female architect,' she says, 'but if I can give inspiration to other women then that is not a bad thing.'

Fig. 3 National Kaohsiung Centre for the Arts, Kaohsiung, Taiwan, 2018. Inside, curving walls expand and contract like the branches of a banyan tree, creating organic spaces for multiples uses.

"I am interested in how culture affects the way that we understand space."

JEANNETTE KUO

Fig. 1 International Sports Sciences Institute, University of Lausanne, Switzerland, 2013. The compact form unites four public and private institutions in a park-like landscape at the edge of Lake Geneva.

Jeannette Kuo is one half of Swiss-based Karamuk Kuo Architects and, with her partner Ünal Karamuk, advocates for architecture as a collaborative practice. To this end, their office is deliberately small: 'We always imagined ourselves to be a size where we could somehow fit around a table,' she explains. This enables team members to collectively work through ideas before they are realised in built form. 'Even for interns, one of the requirements is that they're unafraid to be vocal.'

Karamuk Kuo's approach addresses the performative aspects of architecture, which emerge at the intersection of structures, space and culture. 'I am interested in how culture affects the way that we understand space.'

However, this wasn't what drew Kuo to architecture in the first instance. Instead, she notes, 'What spiked my interest was how it is artistic on the one hand, and scientific on the other.' Later, 'what became apparent, and I think what kept me in it, was the cultural end of things. I grew up in an Asian setting, where you're taught to respect the establishment and tradition.' Kuo moved from Indonesia to train in the USA before moving to start her practice in Switzerland. 'I was living in dramatically different conditions. It showed me how we can affect our built environment and how that, in turn, affects the way that we understand society and how we live together.' Kuo cites Lina Bo Bardi as a key influence – an architect whose output defied disciplinary boundaries. 'From jewellery design to theatre design to props and sets, what really struck me was how broad her reach was.' Certainly, Bo Bardi's playfulness is evident in Kuo's approach.

For over a decade, Karamuk Kuo have worked across scales and typologies from ephemeral

Fig. 2 Concept model for the International Sports Sciences Institute, University of Lausanne, Switzerland, 2013. Karamuk Kuo use models as tools of communication and collaboration.

installations to large, complex and permanent projects involving multiple clients. 'For us, it's really about the balance between the spatial experience and constructive performance. There's a certain rationality to our projects, but we're also trying to find a moment of surprise.' This ethos can be seen in the Sports Institute at the University of Lausanne, which reimagines the conventions of the office as dynamic and collaborative.

The building houses different organisations with the aim to create 'a space that allows them to share a collective identity, promoting the synergy between the different entities'. The building consists of a 'ring' of workspaces around a sculptural atrium such that 'when you're moving through you're conscious of spaces opening up beyond'. Kuo notes, 'This internal mass is infrastructural – it is the structural bracing for the building, housing the labs and back-of-house facilities – but at the same time becoming a shared internal landscape.'

Kuo brings her social understanding of architecture to the building process too. 'The fact that you have to communicate, and that it is more about the coordination of processes than it is just about sitting down and drawing through something, that is what is exciting.'

In 2022, Kuo became Professor of Architecture and Construction at TU Munich – a professorship that in Central Europe very rarely goes to a woman, let alone one who is of non-European descent. For Kuo, education is core to professional development. She tells us, 'To remain relevant, we have to keep questioning ourselves.'

Fig. 3 International Sports Sciences Institute, University of Lausanne, Switzerland, 2013. Collective space/study area. The lightweight and repetitive ring of offices is braced by a central core offering informal meeting areas.

"My heart is in public projects rather than private – they offer opportunities for innovative, sustainable design solutions."

VERONIQUE TAVERNIER

Fig. 1 Sketch of Brunfaut 35, Brussels, 2022. This shows the north facade, which is completely closed off today. The design opens up the ground floor on all sides to activate the public space around it.

Veronique Tavernier is Director of Belgium-based VELD, one of the most pre-eminent architecture practices in Belgium. Their work shows how creative renovation and multiple-use approaches can solve the urgent issues of dense urban living.

Tavernier initially hoped to pursue a career as a baker but, preferring late nights to early mornings, she entered KU Leuven to study Civil Engineering with a specialisation in Architecture and a Master's in Urbanism. She worked in Sao Paulo, Brazil and then in Paris at uapS, a studio working on urban renewal, where she met her future co-directors of VELD (meaning 'field' in Dutch).

VELD, Tavernier tells us, likes clients with 'high ambitions' and a willingness to leverage latent opportunities and add value to the original brief. She says, 'The signature component of our methodology is really about how we respond to the context. We like to push the designs to the edge or beyond the brief.' This approach ensures VELD's projects are visionary from the start.

Tavernier points to VELD's public housing projects. The CityDox complex in Anderlecht includes homes, a school and retail space, but it's the new, proposed work in Brussels – Brunfaut 35 and Abricotier – which exemplifies the value that her practice can bring to a brief. Brunfaut 35 involved renovating 93 existing social housing units into 91 units with the ground floor transformed into bike parking and common space, while private balconies were extended to increase access to outdoor space. The aim was an energy-efficient building and an increase in residents' well-being. Taking what Tavernier calls a 'skin in' approach – renovating the apartments from the exterior rather than the interior – allowed residents to remain in their homes throughout, which Tavernier highlights as a successful test-case for the viability of inhabited construction projects in future.

Abricotier – a mixed-use building in Brussels' inner-city neighbourhood, les Marbles – combines 14 social housing units with a kindergarten, office space and shop, and also functions as an entry point to the emergency service department at the Hospital of Saint-Pierre. With its multiple functions, the building

Fig. 2 Render of Brunfaut 35, Brussels, 2022. For the facade, the existing metal cladding is reused and complemented by the wooden structure of the terraces and ground-floor arcade.

is an example of the densification that, in Tavernier's view, all urbanisation projects need to adopt if they are to cope with the demand for social housing and childcare facilities in cities. Integrating emergency access demanded creative solutions, including inserting parking facilities on the first floor. Sensitive to the political pressures that densification can add to contrasting resident typologies, VELD worked with various stakeholders – end users, planning departments and public organisations – to facilitate a consensus-driven approach. Architects working creatively with planning departments or clients is not typical of the traditional Belgian approach to affordable housing design, but opening up this space for dialogue has allowed VELD to offer innovative and sustainable design solutions in public housing.

During her training, Tavernier's entry from classic engineering meant that, initially, she felt 'too practical' to thrive in the creative environment of the design studio. Yet, while the theoretical emphasis of university has proved less relevant, her training in 'problem-solving' and ability to speak three languages on the construction site has served her well. Looking forward, her attention to 'lived experience' leads Tavernier to worry about the creep of automation in architecture and the position of women. Tavernier suggests that 'Architecture education has an important role to play in teaching young architects to not let aspects of their work unknowingly slip to automation and risk losing the core skills needed in good architecture practice.' Moreover, while there were more women than men on her degree course, 'a decade having passed, the majority of those colleagues remaining in architecture practice are men.' Echoing others in this book, she argues that more work needs to be done to provide the conditions for women to flourish in practice.

Fig. 3 CityDox Lot 7, Anderlecht, Belgium, 2023. Construction of the project includes 78 homes, a secondary school for 500 students and retail spaces on the ground floor.

OCEA

NIA

SOPHIE DYRING

"Good design should be available to everyone, regardless of their background."

Fig. 1 Coburg Townhouses, Melbourne, Australia, 2016. Women's Property Initiatives (a community housing provider) engaged the studio to design seven townhouses with landscaping for female-headed households.

Australian architect Sophie Dyring, who leads Melbourne-based studio Schored Projects, believes that access to good design is everyone's right. Her aim is to create more equitable built environments, creating social housing for some of the city's most vulnerable people.

After studying at RMIT University in Melbourne, Dyring worked as a sole practitioner before setting up a studio with Australian Institute of Architects Gold-Medal-winning architect Graeme Gunn in 2009. After six years she left to establish her own studio so she could focus entirely on housing for resilient communities.

'We did mainly private housing, and I wanted to diversify into social housing and I think that decision was born out of being raised by a single mum, who was a nurse, and just having that sort of life education to think about others,' she tells us. 'I get really bored with the idea of working for very rich clients

Fig. 2 (top and bottom) Drawings showing flexible use for Coburg Townhouses, Melbourne, Australia, 2016. The interior and exterior spaces were designed to accommodate future residents' personalising their home.

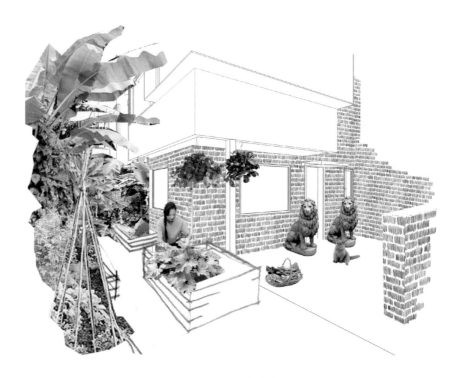

who can select tiles that are A\$2,500 per m² and I haven't done that for a very long, long time.'

The studio has created numerous social housing schemes across the state of Victoria. The Coburg Townhouses scheme provided seven secure homes for women and their children, and Harris Transportable Housing created 57 transportable homes for people at risk of homelessness.

'It's a bit selfish,' says Dyring, who enjoys working on schemes that have a direct impact on improving individual's lives. 'I can't tell you how much reward there is. I've never met a resident who isn't more grateful for the home that they've been given,' she explains. 'To be a part of someone's journey, where they've finally got a secure home that they know will be theirs for as long as they need it. It's life-changing. And I'm a part of that.'

The Coburg Townhouses scheme demonstrates how Dyring aims to go beyond delivering the robust, functional spaces required by housing associations to create architecture that stretches the tight budgets and that residents can be proud of. Often this means creating homes that are more visually impactful and less obvious than the majority of social housing schemes.

'We make very critical decisions about where money can get spent. An objective of ours is to get spaces to work in multiple ways so they really work hard for the budgets that we have and we add little moments of luxury or joy that elevate the design for little to no extra cost. It's really important to avoid any stigmatism for residents, so it's an objective of ours that we don't design a building that you can point your finger at and say "that's social housing".'

Beyond her studio's work, Dyring aims to be an advocate for creating more equitable, well-designed housing across Australia – for instance, her part in a research project that culminated in the publication *The Design Guide for Older Women's Housing*. Dyring believes that more architects need to be vocal about engaging communities and fighting for their beliefs. 'I really pride myself on my architectural practice being a vehicle for advocacy,' she explains. 'More architects need to become advocates for something that they're passionate about.' She adds, 'We need to move away from this idea that we're in our little bubble, that we are elitist and precious in some way. Just get your hands dirty and get a bit real. It would benefit our profession if we started being voices for change.'

Fig. 3 Harris transportable housing, Melbourne, Australia, 2019. The studio designed a 20m² tiny home called 'Freddie' and 57 were constructed for people who were homeless or at risk of homelessness.

ELISAPETA HETA

"States have differing and complex relationships to indigeneity but, particularly in colonised lands, there is an uprising of Indigenous voices and agency beginning to take hold again."

Fig. 1 New Zealand Pavilion, World Expo 2020, Dubai. The theme reflects the Maori value of *kaitiakitanga*, which emphasises the deep kinship between people and the environment.

Elisapeta Heta is a principal and Kaihautū Whaihanga (Māori Design Leader) at Jasmax, a multidisciplinary architecture and design practice based in Aotearoa New Zealand. A founding member of Jasmax's Waka Māia team, she is primarily responsible for engaging in dialogue with iwi Māori (the Indigenous people of Aotearoa New Zealand) and embedding *kaupapa* Māori thinking within the practice's approach to architecture and design.
A graduate of the University of Auckland and member of the Te Kāhui Whaihanga New Zealand Institute of Architects, Heta's architectural journey has been framed by her educational experience. 'As a student there were very few Māori or Pasifika academics, tutors, designers or thinkers to reference, read about or learn from,' states Heta. 'The voices, experiences, architectural history and relevance of Indigenous design in Aotearoa New Zealand was not prioritised, which was (and still is) a constant source of tension.'
Two Jasmax projects that illustrate Heta's current practice include the New Zealand Pavilion at Expo 2020 in Dubai, themed 'Care for People and Place', and Tāmaki Makaurau Auckland's City Rail Link (CRL), the largest infrastructure project in Aotearoa New Zealand's history. Both projects are underpinned by a belief in the interconnectedness of people and environments.
The Pavilion focused on the Whanganui River – recognised as a living entity in 2017 through the Te Awa Tupua (Whanganui River Claims Settlement) Act – as a storytelling device, 'highlighting how an Indigenous culture can redefine not only architecture but how we

Fig. 2 Film room in the New Zealand Pavilion, World Expo 2020, Dubai.

see the world'. Utilising the principles of *kaitiakitanga* or 'guardianship', this project highlights the need for multiple agencies to work together in order to look after the places and spaces that we live in.

The CRL rail network project, located in Aotearoa's largest city, Tāmaki Makaurau Auckland, also acknowledges the need to express Indigenous cultural identities through architecture. Due to open mid-decade, and with construction impacted by the Coronavirus pandemic, each station on the network will intersect narratives of people and place, which Heta suggests 'will provide a powerful expression of Māori identity, creating an authentic and globally recognisable image of the city for the future'. Her ambition is for an architecture that 'reflects the Te Ao Māori world view that people and the land are one'. Looking ahead, Heta speaks eloquently of the opportunities that her new role as principal and Kaihautū Whaihanga enables. 'I am excited to see and experience industry, and the built environment, evolving to become more reflective of Indigenous peoples' relationship to site, place and land, both locally and internationally. What I am seeing is that projects, environments and buildings that intrinsically weave through the stories of place from an Indigenous perspective result in all peoples (Indigenous and not) having a deeper connection and relationship to that site. If I could impact anything it would be to see this flourish and thrive and for our industry to enable this through authentic relationships with Indigenous peoples.'

Fig. 3 Render of City Rail Link, Aotea Station, Auckland, New Zealand (under construction). Designed with Grimshaw Architects in partnership with *mana whenua*.

LOATA HO

"Women practice directors can build more solid foundations for our daughters coming after us."

Fig. 1 Community consultation with Na I Soqosoqo Vakamarama iTaukei, Cakaudrove SVTC executives and members in Savusavu, Fiji, 2007. First design briefing using photo elicitation of historical images of women crafting.

Loata Ho is a feminist, Indigenous architectural researcher and the Founding Director of WomenBuild Australia. Born in Fiji, from mixed iTaukei and Chinese heritage (iTaukei meaning 'owner', in this case of the land and resources in Fiji), she set up the Sydney-based WomenBuild community development and research practice to collaborate with women's groups and organisations on building resilient homes for Fijian villages. The practice's 'Build to Nurture' mandate draws from Indigenous Fijian knowledge systems to help Fijian women create civic and domestic environments tailored to their identities and needs. The practice also seeks to increase the number of Pacific women entering architecture and private practice.
Loata Ho graduated with a joint degree in Architecture and the Built Environment from the Queensland University of Technology in 2008, going on to work for award-winning practices in Fiji, Brisbane and Sydney. While still a student, she initiated the project ITatadra: Cakaudrove Women's Resource Centre – now known as the Ra Marama Village (Ra Marama meaning 'many groups of women' in the Cakaudrove dialect). The project involved collaborating with a group of village women from her maternal community to design and develop a great hall, office, temporary accommodation, commercial kitchen and landscape design featuring indigenous Fijian plants. In 2008, the project was adopted by Architects Without Frontiers, Australia; in 2020, it won an International Good Design Award; and in 2021 it was included in the Australian Pavilion for the Venice Architecture Biennale. The architect's unique approach to community-engaged architectural research is rooted in 'understanding Indigenous Fijian culture, with its own social structure, that I am an equal part of, and finding my position – objective, expert professional or otherwise – within this.' Striving to ensure women are a priority in any community development process – from initiation to design, development to procurement – her methods involve indigenising traditional design processes as a means to decolonise spatial outcomes. Initially, she had to gain the trust of her community, 'because I had been removed from this context for such a long time, after years spent studying and working in Australia'.
Loata Ho sees complexity as a means through which each project can reflect its context, using local resources, Indigenous, vernacular, traditional design and existing

Fig. 2 Concept for Lewa's house, WomenBuild research, Emma Healy, 2022.

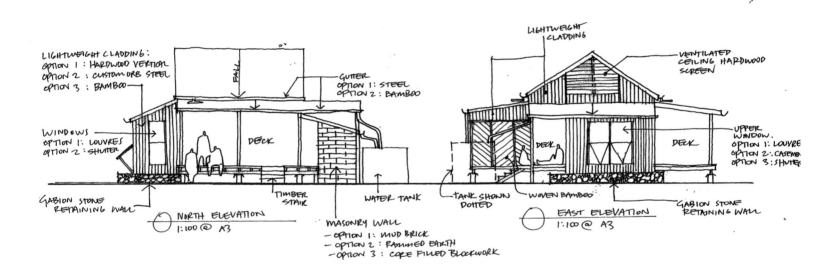

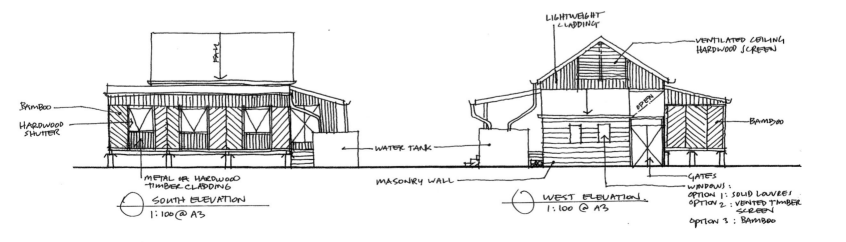

social structures. She says, 'Cultural and contextual factors are often complex, and the processes I was taught in architecture school were mismatched somehow. In usual circumstances, architects can choose to detach, get the job done and move on. But this was my community, so that option wasn't really one I could contemplate taking.' While forms of community participation and co-design have proved effective in fostering strong stakeholder engagement, there is no methodological consensus – or constraint – on what approach works best, offering architects an opportunity to define

a 'signature style'. Perhaps one reason why there is no consensus is the lack of women role models or mentors. When asked whom her role models were, rather than identify another architect, Loata Ho tells us she is most inspired by the rural women of Cakaudrove and Macuata 'for their faith-based humility that is the foundation for their resilience', her Grand Auntie 'for her soft-spoken approach to adapting to the challenges of life in Australia while still holding on to her Fijian culture and values', and her mother 'for her stubbornness and ability to set boundaries'.

One of a growing number of women architects who sees building female role models as a professional responsibility, Loata Ho is committed to encouraging more women to have their own practices and 'stop working for somebody else'. Drawing on her own experience of starting WomenBuild with few resources and operating outside of established practice paradigms, she urges women to design the practice models that 'don't exist yet' – to provide a 'solution' to the kinds of clashes and conflicts that continue to limit women's access to and advancement in the profession.

Fig. 3 Visualising the three dimensions that are typical Fijian spaces in a Fijian home. Loata Ho's Master's research, 2019.

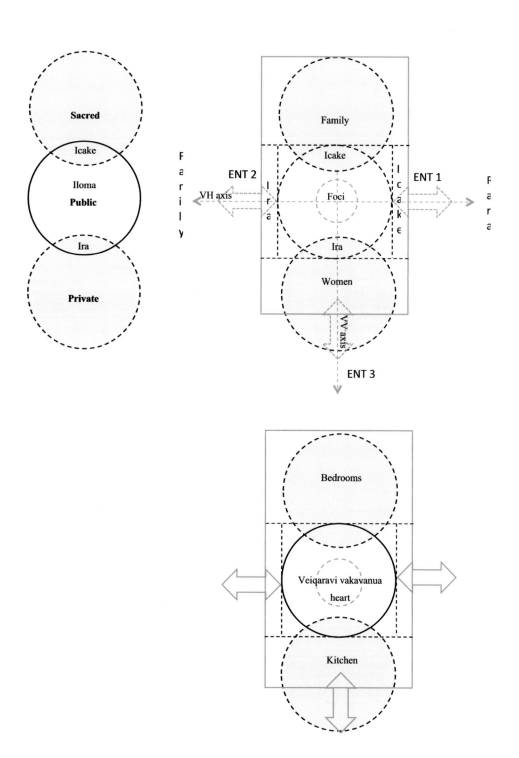

SARAH LYNN REES

"Architecture has the power to give identity and health back, that architectures of the past have typically taken away."

Fig. 1 Installation view of 'Gathering Space: Ngargee Djeembana', for the 'Who's Afraid of Public space?' exhibition, Australian Centre for Contemporary Art, Melbourne, Australia, 2021. The installation includes seating made with materials indigenous to the geographical region now called Victoria and readily available as built environment materials.

Sarah Lynn Rees is a Palawa woman descending from the Trawlwoolway people in Tasmania. A prominent advocate for indigenising the built environment, her practice incorporates a range of roles across First Nations peoples, social and cultural organisations and government bodies. Rees works as an Associate at Jackson Clements Burrows Architects (JCB) and in a practice-based research and teaching capacity at Monash University. She also finds time to do cultural programming for the commissioning organisation MPavilion, and for advocacy work – as Director of Parlour, a platform for gender equity in architecture and as Co-Chair of the Australian Institute for Architects' First

Nations Advisory Working Group.
Rees' focus is on Indigenous-led, systemic change. 'Every project in Australia is within an Indigenous Country and architecture can often be destructive,' she tells us. 'The systems in which architects work often reflect the ongoing structures of settler colonialism. They become so deep-seated they're now our "normal".' Until 2021, there has been no formal recognition of the responsibility of architects (as visitors) to First Nations peoples and 'Country' – the term that recognises the way that culture, nature and land are all interlinked.
Change is on the horizon. The National Competency Standards for Architects

have included eight First Nations-specific performance criteria for architects to comply with and – crucially – they have recommended integration into the training process from year one. In Australia, most graduates haven't experienced First Nations content in their architectural degrees, and so the impact over the next decade will be closely watched. Rees tells us, 'My position is that we must start from a baseline position of "do no more harm" while aiming to repair and heal Country – and celebrate it.'
One of Rees' signature projects for JCB Architects is the Hub for the Atlantic Fellows for Social Equity (AFSE). This is an Indigenous-led social change fellowship programme

Figs. 2 and 3 AFSE Hub, Doug McDonell Building, Parkville Campus, University of Melbourne, Australia, 2021.
(left) Illustration of the key 'Welcome' concept designed to facilitate induction into the fellowship programme, connecting individuals back to the country they have come from and map ongoing relationships.
(right) Render of entry space, AFSE Hub, Doug McDonell Building, Parkville Campus, University of Melbourne, Australia, 2021. The entry space illustrates the key 'Welcome' concept.

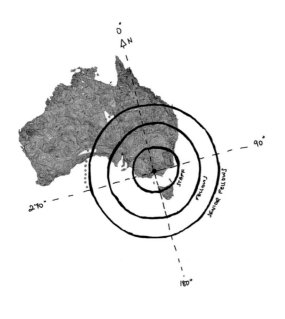

located at the University of Melbourne, where the teams worked in collaboration with Traditional Owner Groups. Located in an existing building, the design was based on a 'Welcome' concept that reflects Country and connects with other nations representing the people who work there. The project provides a blueprint for practice: led by Indigenous voices, grounded in their own knowledge-system, developing relational bonds and showing how Indigenous experience and practice can inform spatial planning. The process included research to explore 'how the design could materially embody the tangible elements of Country and the cultural practices that connect them'.

In Rees' work, visualisation provides an important tool of communication. She re-deploys diagrams, detailing and cross-sections to show the values on which Indigenous architecture is grounded. For instance: how functional spaces and cultural connections come together to facilitate change and revealing the ecological, geological and geographical elements of the site.

For Rees, empathy is important: 'the ability to listen, be introspective, to act without egotism'. She emphasises that indigenising the built environment demands new kinds of professional empathy – both with humans and nature.

A renewed attention to the materials employed by built-environment practices became the subject of a 2021 commission for the exhibition 'Who's Afraid of Public Space?' at the Australian Centre for Contemporary Art in Melbourne. The keynote exhibition, 'Gathering Space: Ngargee Djeembana' – one of four commissioned – displayed seating elements for public spaces that use local, Indigenous materials. The process included mapping local geology, ecology, mining and extraction, and engaging with fabricators/suppliers. Rees and collaborator Senior Boonwurrung Elder Dr N'arweet Carolyn Briggs AM won a commendation for the show at the 2022 AIA awards.

Fig. 4 Installation view of 'Gathering Space: Ngargee Djeembana' for the 'Who's Afraid of Public space?' exhibition, Australian Centre for Contemporary Art, Melbourne, Australia, 2021, by Rees in collaboration with N'arweet Carolyn Briggs AM. The project was commissioned by the Australian Centre for Contemporary Art, Melbourne.

"Design is always advocacy – for a better way. We leverage off the official project brief to benefit and care for others including the environment."

KERSTIN THOMPSON

Fig. 1 Bundanon Art Museum and Bridge, Illaroo, New South Wales, Australia, 2022. The 65m-long bridge – which contains 34 bedrooms, dining spaces and a café – takes its cue from trestle bridges that are common in Australia's flood landscapes.

Set up in 1994, Melbourne-based Kerstin Thompson Architects (KTA) combine expertise in architecture, landscape and urban design to create projects with transformative and restorative potential. KTA's philosophy is to foreground strong ethical relations. This centres on the value of mutual benefit; 'in meeting the aspirations of the client, the design also contributes something positive for the neighbourhood'. Their work encompasses schools, museums, university buildings, commercial and green spaces at a range of scales.

The value that Thompson places on the everyday, rather than high-profile, projects can be traced back to her training at the Royal Melbourne Institute of Technology University (RMIT) in the 1980s. There, tutors like Peter Corrigan emphasised 'the need to seek a local answer, be both parochial and global in outlook and influences for a dialect that is *of this place*'.

KTA's early reputation was built on housing but once established, they made a strategic shift to building in the public realm. 'As a woman-led practice,' says Thompson, 'I was always cautious about how I could be pigeonholed. So it was important to maintain an acute awareness of how I positioned the practice.' She reminds us that 'Unambiguously, "public" space is under threat. We as architects must advocate for and defend it. We are its guardians and protectors.'

KTA's place-making approach can be seen in the renovation of Broadmeadows Town Hall, in Melbourne. The design created more useable and accessible space by transforming the car park and opening up the building's facade. Inside, they created a north-south street through the building and, on the northern face, they cut a circular portal to allow for views of activities over three floors. The building's once-singular programme became a hybrid of civic, cultural and commercial functions – a community business incubator, gallery, office space and, of course, town hall and event space. Reflecting on the bigger lessons, Thompsons tells us, 'The project heralds a shift in what we value in architecture: that the reuse of existing buildings can enrich a community in a way that far exceeds the resources used.' For KTA it's important that the value of

Fig. 2 Broadmeadows Town Hall, Melbourne, Australia, 2019. A large round cut reveals the inner programme and activities over three floors of the commercial hub.

mutual benefit extends to ecological repair. Set in a 1,100ha site, a project for the Bundanon Trust provided the opportunity to integrate architecture and landscape within the broader continuum of the site's ecology. Their design for the Bundanon Art Museum and Bridge includes a learning space for students, contemporary visitor hub, accommodation and art gallery – all partially buried into the landscape. The project 'addresses how buildings and landscapes can be both resilient and resistant. The Art Museum has to be resistant to fire. The Bridge has to be resilient and let the flood waters flow unimpeded. The architecture is a celebration of these forces on the site.'
An interesting distinction of KTA is their aim to create exemplar projects, which can contribute to the discipline of architecture as 'a body of shared knowledge with replicable lessons through teaching, research and advocacy'. In 1990 Thompson returned to RMIT as a self-described 'pracademic', combining teaching with practice. 'The idealism, clarity of intent of the design studio, the pragmatism, ability to effectively negotiate the contingency of building and day-to-day practice: good architecture demands both.'

Thompson remembers that it wasn't always easy to advocate for better architectural and public outcomes when starting out. Confidence comes as buildings prove their impact. 'Now,' she tells us, 'the challenge is to continue to speak out as a critic while you are also doing the work – there are very few people who can do that.

'These times call for precise and strategic thinking; a resourceful architecture that deploys an economy of means yet is transformative; that finds an ease of fit between old forms and new uses; that prioritises strategy over material change and that confounds opposites – strength with gentleness, subtly with drama, creation with repair.'
As with so many architects who are facilitating dialogue between client and community, KTA's practice of 'mutual benefit' models a different kind of design leadership. 'True design leadership', Thompson argues, 'is to accommodate with intent.'

Fig. 3 Bundanon Art Museum and Bridge, Illaroo, New South Wales, Australia, 2022. The subterranean Art Museum is resistant to fire with precious artworks housed and exhibited in an underground building, buried within the reinstated hill.

REFERENCES

Preface

i.   The authors also discuss this point in Harriss, H. and House, N., Greta Magnusson Grossman: Modern Design from Sweden to California (Lund Humphries, 2021).

ii.   'Survey Shows Best and Worst Countries for Female Architects', Arch2o, 2016, https://www.arch2o.com/survey-shows-best-and-worst-countries-for-female-architects/ [accessed 9 March 2023].

iii.   Ibid. Male architects outnumber women architects by three to one.

iv.   France Gross Domestic Product is US$2.958 trillion per year, compared to Vietnam's at US$366.1 billion, making it precisely 8.07975962852 times higher.

v.   Rory Stott, 'The Best (and Worst) Countries to Be a Female Architect', ArchDaily, 16 December 2013, https://www.archdaily.com/458792/the-best-and-worst-countries-to-be-a-female-architect [accessed 4 April 2023].

vi.   Kyodo, staff report, 'Law amendment aims to make paternity leave more accessible in Japan', Japan Times, 4 April 2022, https://www.japantimes.co.jp/news/2022/04/04/national/social-issues/child-care-leave-law-amendment/ [accessed 5 April 2023].

vii.   In the words of Angela Davis, 'In a racist society, it is not enough to be non-racist, we must be anti-racist.' Women, Race and Class (Random House, 1981).

viii.   Anna McKie, 'Casualised staff "dehumanised" in UK universities', Times Higher Education, 20 April 2020, https://www.timeshighereducation.com/news/casualised-staff-dehumanised-uk-universities [accessed 8 July 2020].

ix.   Sarah Repucci, 'Media Freedom: A Downward Spiral', Freedom House Report, 2019, https://freedomhouse.org/report/freedom-and-media/2019/media-freedom-downward-spiral [accessed 8 July 2020].

x.   S. Surface, 'Smash the Patriarchy: How the "Shitty Architecture Men" list can address abuse in architecture', Architect's Newspaper, 30 March 2018, [accessed 9 March 2023].

xi.   A summary of the #Metoo movement and trajectory can be found here: 'Gender Justice Movement: "Me Too", Global Movement', Global Fund for Women, Atlanta, US, 2023, https://www.globalfundforwomen.org/movements/me-too [accessed 5 April 2023].

xii.   United Nations, Department of Economic and Social Affairs, Statistics Division, Methodology, https://unstats.un.org/unsd/methodology/m49 [accessed 9 July 2020]. The latest version of country codes can be found here: https://www.iso.org/iso-3166-country-codes.html. The listing of countries or areas in the six official languages of the United Nations can be found on the UNTERM website here https://unterm.un.org/unterm2/en.

xiii.   Fairs, M., 'Survey of top architecture firms reveals "quite shocking" lack of gender diversity at senior levels', Dezeen, 16 November 2017.

xiv.   Nat Barker, 'Gender pay gap widens at almost half of UK's largest architecture studios', Dezeen, 5 April 2022, https://www.architectmagazine.com/practice/market-intel/female-architects-earn-14-877-less-than-male-architects_o [accessed 4 April 2023].

xv.   Allison Arieff, 'Where Are All the Female Architects?', New York Times, 15 December 2018, https://www.nytimes.com/2018/12/15/opinion/sunday/women-architects.html [accessed 4 April 2023].

xvi.   'Why Is Diversity and Inclusion Important? Diversity in the workplace statistics', LinkedIn Learning, https://learning.linkedin.com/resources/learning-culture/diversity-workplace-statistics-dei-importance#:~:text=Diverse%20companies%20earn%202.5x,decisions%2087%25%20of%20the%20time [accessed 4 April 2023].

xvii.   Karsten Strauss, 'More Evidence That Company Diversity Leads To Better Profits', Forbes, 25 January 2018, https://www.forbes.com/sites/karstenstrauss/2018/01/25/more-evidence-that-company-diversity-leads-to-better-profits/#2eca9ec61bc7 [accessed 4 April 2023].

xviii. Schwartz, S. H., 'Individualism–Collectivism: Critique and Proposed Refinements, Journal of Cross-Cultural Psychology, 21, 2, June 1990, pp.139–157, doi:10.1177/0022022190212001.

xix.   For a good definition of co-operative practices, and some interesting references and visualisations of British connections see 'Co-operative Practices', Spatial Agency, https://www.spatialagency.net/database/cooperative.practices [accessed 4 April 2023].

IMAGE CREDITS

p2 *portrait* Tatu Gatere/Buildher;
pp2-4 *all* Buildher;
pp5-7 *all* Victoria Marwa Heilman;
pp8-10 *all* Irene Masiyanise;
pp11-13 *all* Design Source;
p13 *portrait* Rahel Shawl;
p13 *below* RAAS Architects. Photo credit: Bemnet Teklemariam;
p14 Rahel Shawl (Architect of Record), Dick Van Gamren and Bjarne Mastenbroek. Photo credit: Iwan Baan;
p15 RAAS Architects. Photo by Bemnet Teklemariam;
p16 *portrait* Caroline Barla;
p16 *below* Barla Barla Architectes;
pp17-18 *all* Barla Barla Architectes;
p19 *portrait* Valérie Mavoungou;
p19 *below* Valérie Mavoungou, Atelier Tropical;
pp20-21 *all* Valérie Mavoungou, Atelier Tropical;
p22 *portrait* Paula Nascimento. Photo by Raul Betti;
p22 *below* Paula Nascimento;
pp23-24 *all* Paula Nascimento;
pp25-27 *all* Hayatte Ndiaye;
pp28-29 *all* Caroline Pindi Norah;
pp30-32 *all* Nada Elfeituri;
p33 *portrait* Shahira Fahmy. Photo by Misan Harriman;
p33 *below* Shahira Fahmy Architects;
p34 © Tarek Zaki;
p35 Shahira Fahmy Architects;
p36 *portrait* Samia Henni © Argenis Apolinario;
p36 *below* © Photo by Martin Stollenwerk, gat Exhibitions, ETH Zurich; a
p37 © Photo by Martin Stollenwerk, gat Exhibitions, ETH Zurich;
p38 Samia Henni;
p39 *all* Salima Naji;
p40 © Mehdi Benssid;
p41 © Salima Naji;
pp42-44 *all* Sarah Calburn Architects;
p45 *portrait* Nina Maritz;
p45 *below* Nina Maritz Architects;
pp46-47 *all* Nina Maritz Architects;
p48 *portrait* Sithabile Mathe;
p48 *below* Sithabile Mathe;
pp49-50 *all* Sithabile Mathe, Moralo Designs;
p51 *portrait* Sumayya Vally / Counterspace. Photo by Lou Jasmine;
p51 *below* Counterspace. Photo by Iwan Baan;
p52 Counterspace. Photo by George Darrell;
p53 Counterspace;
pp54-56 *all* Wolff Architects;
p57 *portrait* Olajumoke Adenowo;
p57 *below* Olajumoke Adenowo, AD Consulting;
pp58-59 *all* Olajumoke Adenowo, AD Consulting;
p60 *portrait* Patti Anahory;
p60 *below* Patti Anahory. Photo by César Schofield Cardoso;

pp61-62 *all* Patti Anahory;
p63 *portrait* Olayinka Dosekun-Adjei;
p63 *below* Olayinka Dosekun-Adjei, Studio Contra;
pp64-65 *all* Olayinka Dosekun-Adjei, Studio Contra;
p66 *portrait* Mariam Issoufou © Mariam Issoufou Architects;
p66 *below* ©Mariam Issoufou Architectsi. Photo by Maurice Ascani;
pp67-68 *all* ©Mariam Issoufou Architects. Photo by Maurice Ascani;
p69 portrait Mélissa Kacoutié;
p69 *below* © Bain de Foule studio;
p70 © Tora San Traoré;
p71 © Joe Penney;
p72 *portrait* Tosin Oshinowo. Photo by Spark Ng / Spark Creative;
p72 *below* Tosin Oshinowo;
p73 Tosin Oshinowo;
p74 Tosin Oshinowo, cmDesign Atelier. Photo by Tolu Sanusi;
pp78-80 *all* Celia García Acosta;
p81 *all* Patricia Green;
p82 Bob Marley Museum;
p83 *portrait* Lavina Liburd;
p83 *below* © Stefan Radtke and Lavina Liburd;
p84 Lavina Liburd, TigerQi architecture. Photo by Alton Bertie;
p85 Lavina Liburd, TigerQi architecture. Render by PixelArt Studio;
p86 *all* Laura Narayansingh;
p87 © Chad Lue Choy;
p88 © Bliss Carnival;
pp89-90 *all* Vicki Telford;
p91 *portrait* Tatiana Bilbao. Photo by Ana Hop;
p91 *below* Photo by Iwan Baan;
pp92-93 *all* Photo by Iwan Baan;
p94 *portrait* Fernanda Canales. Photo by Carlos Jurica;
p94 *below* Fernanda Canales and Claudia Rodriguez;
pp95-96 *all* Fernanda Canales. Photo by Rafael Gamo;
p97 *portrait* Frida Escobedo, Frida Escobedo Studio;
p97 *below* Frida Escobedo Studio. Photo by Rafael Gamo;
pp98-99 *all* Frida Escobedo Studio. Photo by Rafael Gamo;
p100 *portrait* Gabriela Etchegaray. Photo by Victor Deschamps;
p100 *below* Ambrosi Etchegaray. Photo by Arlette del Hoyo;
p101 Ambrosi Etchegaray;
p102 Ambrosi Etchegaray. Photo by Sergio Lopez;
p103 *portrait* Rozana Montiel;
p103 *below* Rozana Montiel, Estudio de Arquitectura. Photo by Sandra Pereznieto;

pp104-105 *all* Rozana Montiel, Estudio de Arquitectura;
p106 *portrait* Dorel Ramirez. Photo by Jorge Mejia;
p106 *below* Dorel Ramirez. Photo by Eva Bendana;
p107 Dorel Ramirez. Photo by Jorge Mejia;
p108 Dorel Ramirez. Photo by Eva Bendana;
p109 *portrait* Katherine Darnstadt;
p109 *below* Katherine Darnstadt, Latent Design;
pp110-111 *all* Katherine Darnstadt, Latent Design;
p112 *portrait* Liz Diller, Diller Scofidio + Renfro. Photo by Geordie Wood;
p112 *below* Diller Scofidio + Renfro. Photo by Iwan Baan;
p113 Courtesy of Diller Scofidio + Renfro;
p114 Diller Scofidio + Renfro. Photo by Iwan Baan;
p115 *portraits* Catherine Johnson and Rebecca Rudolph, Design, Bitches;
p115 *below* © Bruce Damonte Photography;
p116 © Laure Joliet;
p117 Design, Bitches;
p118 *portrait* Eladia Smoke;
p118 *below* Smoke Architecture;
pp119-120 *all* Smoke Architecture;
p121 *portrait* Deanna Van Buren. Photo by Alexa Trevino;
p121 *below* Deanna Van Buren. Photo by Emily Hagopian;
p122 Deanna Van Buren. Photo by Ellyce Morgan;
p123 Deanna Van Buren. Photo by Emily Hagopian;
p124 *portrait* Sandra Barclay;
p124 *below* © Christobal Palma;
pp125-126 *all* © Christobal Palma;
p127 *portraits* Micaela Casoy and Paula de Falco, OCTAVA ARQUITECTURA;
p127 *below* OCTAVA ARQUITECTURA. Photo by Gonzalo Viramonte;
p128 OCTAVA ARQUITECTURA. Photo by Gonzalo Viramonte;
p129 OCTAVA ARQUITECTURA;
p130 *portrait* Carla Juaçaba. Photo by CJ Alta;
p130 *below* Carla Juaçaba. Photo by Leonardo Finotti;
p131 Carla Juaçaba. Photo by Leonardo Finotti;
p132 Carla Juaçaba. Photo by Federico Cairoli;
p133 *portrait left* Catalina Patiño © Catalina Patiño;
p133 *portrait right* Viviana Peña © Viviana Peña;
p133 *below* © Viviana Peña, CtrlG;
p134 © Catalina Patiño;
p135 Photo © Federico Cairoli;
p136 *portrait* Verónica Villate;
p136 *below* Verónica Villate, Minimo Comun Arquitectura;
pp137-138 *all* Verónica Villate, Minimo Comun Arquitectura;
p139 *portrait* Sofia von Ellrichshausen. Photo by Ana Crovetto;
p139 *below* Photo by Pezo von Ellrichshausen;

INDEX

Page numbers in **bold** indicate figures.